T0319938

# DATA MONEY

DATA MONEY

# DATA MONEY

## INSIDE CRYPTOCURRENCIES, THEIR COMMUNITIES, MARKETS, AND BLOCKCHAINS

## KORAY CALISKAN

Columbia University Press    *New York*

Columbia University Press
*Publishers Since 1893*
New York    Chichester, West Sussex
cup.columbia.edu

Library of Congress Cataloging-in-Publication Data
Names: Çalışkan, Koray, 1972– author.
Title: Data money : inside cryptocurrencies, their communities,
markets, and blockchains / Koray Caliskan.
Description: New York : Columbia University Press, [2023] |
Includes bibliographical references and index.
Identifiers: LCCN 2022051408 (print) | LCCN 2022051409 (ebook) |
ISBN 9780231209588 (hardback) | ISBN 9780231209595
(trade paperback) | ISBN 9780231558013 (ebook)
Subjects: LCSH: Cryptocurrencies. | Digital currency. |
Blockchains (Databases) | Currency question.
Classification: LCC HG1710.3 .C45 2023 (print) |
LCC HG1710.3 (ebook) | DDC 332.4—dc23/eng/20230306
LC record available at https://lccn.loc.gov/2022051408
LC ebook record available at https://lccn.loc.gov/2022051409

Printed and bound by CPI Group (UK) Ltd, Croydon, CR0 4YY

Cover design: Noah Arlow
Cover image: Shutterstock

*To Elif and Cem,*
*for everything they taught me*

# CONTENTS

# CONTENTS

# TABLES AND FIGURES

# ACKNOWLEDGMENTS

**M**y first long-term research project examined a global market and the people who made it. From villages in western Turkey to hamlets in Lower Egypt, from the pits of Izmir to the giant fields of Tennessee, and from futures markets in New York City to trading locations in Alexandria, I followed a single commodity, cotton, and learned about how commodity markets are made on the ground. I used my computer to type my notes, check a few emails, and organize my data. All interviews, observations, and engagements were in person.

That was twenty years ago. Amazon was minuscule; Google was not yet dedicated to making its money from advertisements; Bitcoin did not exist. Now, carrying out global fieldwork entails keeping a mouse in hand almost all the time. Interviews over Zoom, fieldwork on Discord, six weeks of big data downloading from Twitter, and computational text analysis on R required me to draw on an army of people. As we move to platforms from in-person geographies, it seems we need more people supporting us.

I thank the wonderful community of Electra and then Electra Protocol for inviting me into their lives. I want to acknowledge the help of two individuals, Electra01 and Aykut Baybaş, for meeting me many times, answering all my questions, educating me on the intricacies of cryptocurrencies and their communities, and being ready to pick up the phone to help me understand their new economic world, of which they are masters. Furthermore, Electraoı became my best critic, reading every chapter and even engaging in a close reading of chapter 5. I would also love to thank the following individuals for supporting me during my in-person fieldwork: Burak Arıkan, Engin Erdoğan, Asmoth, Aykut Baybaş, Robert Bakker, Ruanne Lloyd, Jamie Chapman, Eileen Vogl, Bob van Egeraat, Antoine Aimé, and Greg Cherry.

I first tested many of the arguments of this book on the people I trusted the most in terms of creativity and theoretical rigor: Michel Callon, Gözde Güran, Don MacKenzie, Tim Mitchell, Janet Roitman, and Sevde Ünal. Without their timely interventions, support, ideas, and corrections, this book would have been a weaker one. Furthermore, Quinn Dupont, Lana Swartz, and Simone Polillo have become friends and collaborators, and I have learned much from them during the course of research and writing. I thank them wholeheartedly.

I would like to thank Shalini Randeria, Will Milberg, David Stark, Nigel Dodd, Paul Langley, Paraskevi Katsiampa, and Fran Tonkiss for supporting my research and helping me reach out to readers and social scientists. I also acknowledge the support of the following colleagues and friends during the years I tried to understand cryptocurrencies and their universe: Diane-Laure Arjaliès, Claire Ingram Bogusz, Taylan Cemgil, Raphaële Chappe, Jillian Crandall, Nejat Dinç, Paul Dourish, Roger Friedland, Clement Gasull, Hanna Halaburda, Victoria Hattam, Benjamin Kodres-O'Brien, Ekin Kurtiç, Vincent Lépinay, Daniel Levy, Leila Lin, Michael Lounsbury, Chase Madar, Emre Mermer, Andrew Moon, Lydia Nobbs, Emma Park,

Vassily Pigounides, Paolo Quattrone, Ludovico Rella, Ted Schatzki, Michael Smets, Anna Thieser, Marc Ventrasca, and Matt Wade.

I would especially thank Platform Economies Research Network, whose meetings helped me imagine and develop a few central ideas that I discuss in this book. I would also like to thank the Heilbroner Center for Capitalism Studies for awarding me a fellowship that made it possible to pursue research in 2018 and 2019, as well as for providing me a wonderful academic setting at the New School of Social Research. Falling Walls Foundation selected the research on which this book draws as a winner of the Scientific Breakthrough of the Year in Social Sciences and Humanities Awards in 2021. I am grateful for such a prestigious acknowledgment.

I want to thank my good friend Janet Roitman for being a comrade and sister in times of difficulty, with her intellectual brilliance, sweetness, and power. Joining Parsons School of Design as a professor turned out to be a second graduate training for me. I learned from many designers and design scholars who helped me understand the potential of design not only in making things but also in creating knowledge. I thought I knew how to think, but learning to make to think was a challenge for me. Tim Marshall has been a great adviser in helping me understand design scholarship. Rhea Alexander, John Bruce, Anthony Dunne, Aaron Fry, Fernanda Flores, Raz Godelnik, Adam Hayes, Jamer Hunt, Michele Kahane, Matt Robbs, Jane Pirone, Fiona Raby, Christian Madsjberg, Elliot Montgomery, Mariana Amatullo, Sam Mejias, Daniel Sauter, Evren Uzer, Otto van Busch, and Jen van der Meer helped me in various ways in making sense of and teaching design. Cynthia Lawson Jaramillo's friendship and support will always be a source of inspiration for me.

As I carried out research and writing, I relied on the help and support of many collaborators. Ilker Birbil has been a great friend and research collaborator who helped me understand the small details of big data. Enis Simsar, thanks to the timely introduction by Taylan Cemgil, has been a collaborator in downloading and analyzing vast Twitter data. Graduate and undergraduate students who have taken my cryptocurrencies and blockchains classes at the New School have provided wonderful critiques of my writing and thinking. I first tested with them all my strange ideas, some of which became the main arguments of this book.

My design collaborations with Nishant Wazir, Lauren Stobierski, and Stephen Johnson not only represented cryptocurrency markets and communities but also contributed to our better understanding of this complex universe. Sevde Ünal, Collin McClain, Hasine Güler, Sıla Eser, and Onur Koçan have been very helpful research assistants. Without their support and guidance, this book would be incomplete. Nina Macaraig edited everything I published in English. Without her touch, even this sentence would be more difficult to understand. Two anonymous reviewers made the arguments tighter and stronger. Finally, I would like to thank my editor at Columbia University Press, Eric Schwartz, who supported this book since I first conceived it in 2019.

My family—Ruhsar Abut, Süleyman Çalışkan, Sezer Çalışkan, Sezin Okkan, and Ekrem and Nedret Çatay—have been amazing sources of support and wisdom. Without my wonderful wife, Zeynep Çatay, neither this life nor this book would be complete. Finally, I would like to thank my brilliant children, Elif Nare Çalışkan and Ömer Cem Çalışkan, for everything they taught me; for this, I dedicate this book to them.

Parts of this book have been published in earlier versions as "The Elephant in the Dark: A New Framework for Cryptocurrency Taxation and Exchange Platform Regulation in the US,"

*Journal of Risk and Financial Management* 15, no. 3 (2022): 118; "The Rise and Fall of Electra: A Cryptocurrency Community in Perspective," *Review of Social Economy* 79, no. 4 (2022): 1–25; "Data Money Makers: An Ethnographic Analysis of a Global Cryptocurrency Community," *British Journal of Sociology* 73 (2021): 168–87; "Platform Works as Stack Economization: Cryptocurrency Markets and Exchanges in Perspective," *Sociologica* 14, no. 3 (2021): 115–42; and "Data Money: The Socio-technical Infrastructure of Cryptocurrency Blockchains," *Economy and Society* 49, no. 4 (2020): 540–61. I would like to thank the editors and these journals for permitting me to use the material they published for this book.

# DATA MONEY

DATA MONEY

# 1

# THE HISTORICAL NOVELTY OF DATA MONEY AND ITS MAKERS, MARKETS, AND REGULATION

Thinking about money is the shortest way to make sense of our economies. This book looks at cryptocurrency as a historically new money form in order to make sense of how it is made and exchanged. Instead of calling it digital money, currency, or cash, I propose the concept of *data money* as a way to identify the specific materiality of cryptocurrency, thus allowing us to understand more accurately the economic and sociological universe of these new monies, their markets, and their communities.

Monies emerge in multiple forms and materials; they are created, re-created, valued, and devalued by a variety of human individuals (such as homemakers) and collectives (such as social classes), as well as nonhuman actors (such as banks). From clay tablets to cigarettes, the materials used for monies are limited only by the boundary of human imagination. Despite such a well-documented, rich universe of money forms, however, there have been only three hegemonic materialities of fiat currency used within and across politically defined boundaries: metal, paper, and data.

Monies as units of account first emerged in Mesopotamia and Egypt as early as 3000 BCE. They were followed by metal fiat money, a creation of the Lydians around 550 BCE in today's Anatolia. This first metal money was minted with electrum, a natural alloy of silver and gold found in the River Sart (formerly Pactolus).[1] It was heavy and difficult to mint, imitate, spend, and steal. Today's metal monies still are. Minted to weigh 2.5 grams, a U.S. cent is a copper-plated zinc coin.[2] The metal money with the largest circulation value in the United States is the quarter. Being also the heaviest U.S. coin, with 11.34 grams of cupronickel alloy, buying the computer on which I write this book would require carrying a sack of coins as heavy as my body. One million dollars would be more than eleven tons of quarters. If minted as quarters, the U.S. fiat currencies currently in use would weigh around one thousand times more than the Empire State Building. As a result of such material limits that metal imposes on monies, all metal fiat currencies have since their emergence been represented by other things, such as paper or a promise, eventually giving birth to the second materiality of money: paper.

About a millennium after the Lydians' pioneering monetary experiments, the first paper monies emerged in China. By the thirteenth century, Kublai Khan was printing them for use as fiat currency.[3] The most common, valuable, and popular materiality of money in the contemporary world—paper money—is, in fact, made from a variety of fibers: it contains a small amount of wood pulp, mashed with a lot of cotton and linen and washed with gelatin or alcohol. Compared to metal money, it is more difficult to counterfeit, but it is relatively cheaper to reproduce because it represents a greater value with a smaller material expenditure. Made of three parts cotton and one part linen, and 60 percent lighter but a thousand times more valuable than a dime, one U.S. hundred-dollar bill weighs only 1 gram. With 10 kilograms of hundred-dollar bills, one can carry a million dollars in a backpack. To transport a billion dollars, however, one needs a truck.

Since the 1970s, paper and metal monies have been mostly represented not physically, by metal alloys or fibers, but digitally. As the use of paper money has declined, we can observe more and more fiat currencies being digitally represented, transferred, and exchanged. Yet whether cash or a number on a screen, digital money is still a computational representation of originally metal and paper fiat currencies, or their representation imagined as debt.

The appearance of Bitcoin in 2009 marked the emergence of the third hegemonic materiality of money: data. When one owns a quarter or a hundred-dollar bill, one owns the material that carries its imagined value. Yet Bitcoin is not a data entry in one's computer or cell phone. It is the exclusive *right* to send data. When one transfers a Bitcoin to someone else, one sends the right to transfer data from one location to another. This is new.

Cryptocurrencies are not merely digital money or cash, for this would make them categorically the same as other fiat currencies, such as the U.S. dollar or the euro. They are not digitally *represented* but rather computationally *made*. They are as material as metal and paper monies but intangible when compared to other money types. They are not passive memory entries in a memory device. Computers are essential for them to exist, but computers alone are not sufficient. What makes these data monies new is not that they are made with data but that they are imagined *as the right to send data*, with a new accounting mechanism called blockchain.

Materialities used to imagine value create certain limits on how we can transfer monies, envision them as assets, and account for them. The weight of tangible materials used to make money creates a double advantage: it is difficult to imitate them, and it is impossible to double-spend them because, once given away, they are gone. These two simple advantages, however, require complex accounting systems—in face, scholars identify accounting as one of the institutional practices that made fiat currencies possible in the first place.[4] Furthermore, it has been shown that modern monies were reinvented by new representational and accounting practices of modern governance, which allowed hard-to-carry materialities to disappear as monies moved from premodern commodity forms to modern fiat currencies.[5] Beginning at the end of the seventeenth century, this transformation entailed everyday political struggles, colossal legal and organizational investments, and complex accounting practices. Creating such modern monies also required a level of exclusion of the general public from the practices of accounting and minting. Housed in castle-like buildings, mints and banks communicated such exclusivity through their architectural designs.

The beginning of the twenty-first century saw the emergence of Bitcoin, the first data money, with new accounting, minting, and transaction practices. Before Satoshi Nakamoto created Bitcoin, it was possible to digitally represent currencies and transfer them via cables. Thanks to the services of banks, the guarantees of the state, and the accounting practices documenting these transactions, transfer records could be kept, to be checked by the sender, the receiver, the state, and the bank. Unless a legal problem arose, these records stayed private among these actors.

The emergence of the blockchain accounting system changed this division of labor, distributing accounting responsibility to an unlimited number of actors. Nakamoto's Bitcoin blockchain offered a new way to transfer monies, much like the system explained previously but without banks and states. Instead of banks and states serving as guarantors, it is now the miners who carry out daily bookkeeping tasks with their computers, writing down all transactions on Bitcoin's digital ledger, which can be seen and used by everybody. The blockchain mechanism may look complicated, but it rests on a very simple logic.

Imagine Alice wants to send 1 Bitcoin (BTC) to Bob. She first posts it in the network as a proposal. She cannot send it without accountants writing the transaction on the books, for without being written on the books, transactions are not realized in data monies. (For paper and metal money, a transaction is realized when the materiality of money changes hands.) This transaction proposal is encrypted by cryptographic programs to add a *unique* digital representation that cannot be re-represented without a series of passwords. Then this proposal to transact 1 BTC appears on an internet network, where the community of accountants sees this digital proposal, among hundreds of others around it. These accountants then choose to write the proposed transaction down on a digital page called a block. If they manage to add this new page or block to the Bitcoin ledger and chain of blocks, the proposed transaction between Bob and Alice is *realized*. Once it is written down in the Bitcoin digital ledger, it is almost impossible to modify or cancel this transaction, thanks to the infrastructural protocol that runs the accounting system. In reality, it is not data representing 1 BTC that is being transferred; it is the right to send it privately in a public ledger. Everyone sees that 1 BTC has changed hands, but no one knows who sent it unless the sender or the receiver wants the transaction to be public.

It takes a great deal of computing power, time, and energy to carry out cryptocurrency accounting. It would not be rational to carry it out if one did not earn something in the process. Nakamoto addressed this problem by giving what he saw a digital thing that may be found valuable to any accountant who manages to add one more page to the ledger. And this digital thing is called a Bitcoin. What makes it valuable is not only an abstract and subjective belief but also Bitcoin's material utility in providing an actual *service* of value creation and transfer, without the necessity of a central accounting institution or intermediary.

Yet a new materiality of money and a new accounting system to keep track of that money's movements among actors are not enough to make data monies. Nakamoto's success drew not only on his technical preparations and enhancement of cryptology but also on one of the oldest notions we have about monies: that monies are also social things.[6] Without people valuing monies— whether they consist of stones or clay tablets, paper or metal, cigarettes or data—they are worth no more than the materials of which they are made. People make money. Cryptocurrencies are not an exception but just another articulation of money making in a social and political context.[7]

Therefore, Nakamoto knew that for his Bitcoin to pick up, he first had to build a community. Without a forum, communities could not gather, for people make organizations as they talk about organizations. Nakamoto began to talk about Bitcoin with those on a mailing list; then, knowing he needed a place for people to gather, he built a forum for discussion on Bitcoin.org. As the forum became more active, Nakamoto built Bitcointalk.org and posted its first message as administrator in 2009. He had designed the money, the forum, and the accounting system to work as a sociotechnical infrastructure that would give birth to other monies, forums, and blockchains.

It is a telling fact that the first Bitcoin transaction deal took place not in an organized market but in this discussion forum. A year after Bitcoin's emergence, Laszlo Hanyecz bought pizza with 10,000 BTC, and the transaction was registered in the blockchain. A few months later, with the opening of the first digital currency exchange market, Bitcoinmarket.com (a now defunct intermediary institution designed for Bitcoin exchange), the value of Bitcoin began to pick up. It had an intangible material to exchange, a community to value it, and accountants to record its transactions. In April 2011, Bitcoin's value surpassed that of the effective currency of the world, the U.S. dollar, and by June, it was thirty-two times more valuable.

Ten years later, as I write this book, 9,671 data monies are being exchanged in more than 30,000 markets, organized in 376 exchanges that are open around the clock. Exceeding $2.5 trillion[8] in market capitalization, the data money economy is larger than 96 percent of the world's national economies. This book tells the story of these data monies, their markets, and their communities.

## THE RESEARCH

I developed an interest in cryptocurrencies as I listened to a podcast while running alongside the Bosporus in Istanbul. Having spent some time in a detention center and more time under house arrest with a digital cuff around my left ankle as a result of criticizing the authoritarianism of President Recep Tayyip Erdogan, I had developed an interest in both being outside and learning about digital things. As I listened, I found myself running faster as my gut told me that the host was wrong about almost everything as she announced a revolution I had never heard of and insisted that the dollar would be replaced by Bitcoin and that the world would be turned upside-down in terms of people's finance power. I had to look at it for myself and began to buy cryptocurrencies, follow their communities, and study the computing industries that support them.

Seeing many interesting new developments, I decided to pursue long-term research about them and sold almost every cryptocurrency I had bought. For ethical reasons, I did not own any data money as I carried out research between March 15, 2018, and March 15, 2021, except for a portfolio that I traded for research purposes. This portfolio's collective worth never exceeded $100. Following an unprecedented surge in cryptocurrency prices, the relatively small positions I closed in March 2018 were worth around $6 million in May 2021.

The first question I had to address was how to approach the vast and multilayered socioeconomic universe of data monies, with thousands of cryptocurrencies and their markets and hundreds of new projects emerging every month. Focusing on a small part would prevent me from seeing the larger whole, whereas scanning only the larger universe would prevent me from focusing my research on the everyday lives of people and their monies. I used two strategies to approach this complex and dynamic universe, deploying micro and macro perspectives simultaneously.

First, drawing on anthropological research methods, I carried out ethnographical research at two fieldwork sites: the X Exchange (a pseudonym) and the Electra community. On one hand, I wanted to understand a community of economic actors that made a cryptocurrency; on the other, I wanted to examine a platform of market actors that served as one of the world's top ten cryptocurrency exchanges in terms of transaction volume.

In 2018, I started to observe Electra, a cryptocurrency and its blockchain developed in 2017 by an unknown young man, Electra01. After its emergence in the cryptocurrency markets in 2018, its market capitalization reached $136 billion as result of its original supply mechanism, briefly exceeding Bitcoin in value and making its founder a theoretical billionaire. With an emergent community, an unknown founder, and an international network of enthusiasts, Electra was a perfect fieldwork site where I could study a successful project. Yet the number of unsuccessful crypto projects far exceeds that of successful ones, much like in other walks of economic life. Aiming to understand failed projects, I had to study a failure. I had no idea Electra was going to afford me such an unexpected and surprising opportunity to do that.

As I studied the project, I suspected that a fundamental controversy was surfacing quickly between the founder and the community. In November 2020, the project failed as the founder began selling off his hundreds of millions of Electras in a variety of markets, thereby effectively killing the project. This happened while I had access to Electra's core team, administrative decision-making processes, and forum discussions. Thus, I had a front-row seat and an unprecedented chance to study how, over several unfortunate days, dreams can be destroyed by political economic realities on the ground. Yet in a surprisingly short period of time, the entire community left the founder behind and moved to another platform in order to bring about the rebirth of its money, this time calling it Electra Protocol. This novel migration process entailed disassembling Electra's every device, network, and architecture and building them anew, with almost the same community minus the founder. Such an exciting fieldwork site provided me with the opportunity to observe and analyze an empirical case of the emergence, success, collapse, and sociodigital migration of a cryptocurrency project.

Furthermore, during this process I had access to both the founder and the community's leading actors and core team. The latter term is used by many other data money communities to refer to a handful of active members who maintain community relations, develop and repair tangible and intangible infrastructures and networks, and represent the community in forums— in short, members who are responsible for the management of the community. By allowing me to conduct surveys among all its active members, the community helped me better understand the making of data money from within. I also shared most of my findings with a few of the leading community members and asked them to read drafts of these chapters. Rewriting and revising the chapters that tell the story of the rise and fall of Electra took three months because of the controversies that led to the collapse of the money project; however, this process helped me comprehend what the community was and how it wanted to represent itself with the help of competing narratives. I have made sure that the readers of this book can see these narratives, and I have also shown that some of the central actors of Electra did not agree with my interpretation of the history and workings of their community.

While the Electra price was collapsing in the markets, I was also carrying out fieldwork at a global cryptocurrency exchange that I call X Exchange. Because these intangible platforms are enmeshed in various legal and compliance requirements and are the targets of frequent hacks, these "uber-transparent" exchanges—as one employee of X Exchange put it—require excessively secretive arrangements. Obtaining access to the exchange required a long networking and approval period, and I am not allowed to use the exchange's real name or refer to its employees by their real names.

Although I walked through the corridors and sat in the offices of X Exchange, mingling with around two hundred mostly young employees scattered over multiple floors, I found myself interacting with them more through digital means: many of my interviews and chats *within* the exchange took place over audiovisual conversation software, such as Zoom. In-person and short conversations were taking place *on site*, but formal interviews and discussions were *online*. Soon I was to realize that *online* was also *on site*. One informant told me that it was easier to talk to me over Zoom than climbing up to the second floor of the office building to meet me in one of the "cold" and "intimidating meeting rooms" dominated by large tables.

I had to discontinue my in-person research in March 2020 as COVID-19 brought human bodies to a standstill and redistributed this already globally scattered business operation. During the pandemic, I continued to interact with the people I had met at the exchange as they worked even harder, responding to the ebbs and flows of buy and sell orders. Interestingly, the pandemic took all of us out of X Exchange's offices, but it gave me the opportunity to interact with the employees of the exchange more often. We were all "in the exchange" while being at home, adding a new dimension to the distributed nature of late modern economic agencies and geographies. Strangely enough, during the pandemic I found more occasions to talk to people from the exchange, even seeing them in their homes and meeting their significant others, children, and pets for the first time without the human relations officer who had to follow me around at the exchange. Market capitalizations were skyrocketing, making platform workers very happy. They were distracted from the daily events, smiling, and working very hard, leaving me *alone* in X Exchange more often.

To support these two fieldwork projects, I visited a variety of other exchanges around the world, observed the conferences of several cryptocurrency communities, and conducted unrecorded and recorded interviews with a total of 112 people. With two exceptions, no one gave me permission to record these interviews. In my previous work with working-class and poor farmer communities, I had come to realize, as have many other researchers, that a recorder changes the voice and perspective of the recorded. Yet I had expected a more liberal and relaxed attitude about sound recording among these young, university-educated informants, many of whom hold a graduate degree.

In the end, I used my high-end transcription software only twice. I took all my notes in my fieldwork notebook and then typed these field notes into my computer, anonymizing the names of the interviewees. Nowhere in my computer will anyone be able to find data that will allow them to match anonymized names and real persons. In 2017, when I was detained for five days and had to spend part of the summer under house arrest in Istanbul because of my critical commentary about Erdogan's government, I once again realized the importance of such precautions. While raiding my home and my office at Bogazici University, the police seized all my computers and copied the hard disks. One can never be sure who may read the files.

The second strategy I used to approach this expanding universe of cryptocurrencies entailed moving far enough away from them to see their larger socioeconomic geography. Most cryptocurrencies are offered together with a white paper,[9] and I focused on the white papers of almost all cryptocurrencies with significant value. These position papers are written by anonymous, pseudonymous, or known individuals or groups of individuals, making data money the first money form that is created, in part and to varying degrees, by scientists or people who use scientific and designer competencies without the support of a bank or state. These more than two thousand white papers comprise more than fifty thousand pages. Most of these documents, however, introduce cryptocurrencies of only negligible economic value. As of June 1, 2018, the ten most valuable cryptocurrencies represented 75.01 percent of all cryptocurrency value in the world while the one hundred most valuable cryptocurrencies represented 90.06 percent.[10] In this book, I draw on an interpretive and computational text analysis of the white papers of the one hundred most valuable cryptocurrencies as of June 1, 2018,[11] the terms-of-service texts of all the cryptocurrency exchanges in the world,[12] and all Bitcointalk forum discussion pages of the Electra community[13] and also on a network interaction analysis of all followers of Electra (around 18,600 addresses) and their 358,000 followers, a vast data set that Twitter Inc. authorized me to download in January 2021.[14]

During the first months of my research, I received a fellowship at the Heilbroner Center for Capitalism Studies at the New School and began working with new colleagues, who generously offered new and exciting intellectual stimulation and collaboration. In 2019, I joined the faculty of the New School's design school, Parsons. This intellectual migration added a whole new dimension to my social-scientific practice. With our seemingly unsurmountable methodological and epistemological differences, we social scientists basically look through our own windows and write about what we see. Sometimes this window is game theory; at other times, it is ethnography. In either case—regardless of whether one interacts with informants at fieldwork sites or remains in an office and describes the world from there—social-scientific inquiry rarely entails studio time during which scientists and designers work together to make tangible or intangible material things.

At Parsons, I found the opportunity to pursue a scientific design practice based on making to think and thinking to make. In my studios and seminars, my colleagues, my graduate students, and I constructed public open-accounting blockchains, created speculative and actual monies to better make sense of them, designed and distributed banking systems, and imagined speculative economic futures and presents. One of my students actually paid off all his student loans with the money he made and still managed to save much for later. Another design team invented a process to describe platform economic interactions more accurately than most social-scientific descriptions.

Two designers founded a barter economization platform with its own money.

Bringing together making and thinking allowed me to use the power of design in social research in a new way. In various collaborative initiatives, I worked with strategic and transdisciplinary designers on how to imagine organizations, platforms, relations, networks, and economic agencies and devices while being critical of social engineering or design solutionism. These activities, which complemented advanced approaches already employed in anthropology and sociology, helped me understand socioeconomic processes through a new lens while giving me and my collaborators a forum in which to make intangible material processes visible through novel tools, as one can see in the analyses, visualizations, and research findings in this book.

## FINDINGS AND SUMMARY OF DISCUSSION

Chapter 2 of this book approaches cryptocurrencies from a philosophical vantage point and backs its analysis with empirical research and evidence. Drawing on my training and research in cryptocurrency trade and design and supported by a computational and interpretive text analysis of the white papers of the one hundred most valuable data monies, the chapter describes three fundamental qualities of cryptocurrencies and their blockchains: (1) the materiality of cryptocurrencies as data money; (2) the evolution of blockchain architecture, with reference to the economic services it supplies in accounting for data money transfers; and (3) the socioeconomic consequences of these technically diverse blockchain architectures and their monies.

The chapter defines cryptocurrency as data money and describes its ownership as the possession of an exclusive *right to move data* privately in a public or private space. Describing a blockchain as a digital actor-network platform that facilitates the definition and distribution of these data-transfer rights, the chapter then focuses on the three specific phases in the evolution of blockchain architectures. First-generation blockchains, like that of Bitcoin, are *value-exchange blockchains*, making it possible to transfer the rights to send data. Although it is possible to embed simple conditions and programs in these first-generation blockchains, it is only after the emergence of the second generation—*contract-exchange blockchains*, such as that of Ethereum—that users have been able to exchange computer programs that can operate as contracts. This development has made it possible to build new value- or contract-exchange platforms within or on one blockchain. It seems that in the long term, third-generation blockchains, which may be called *interchains*, will be hegemonic, since they allow a variety of separate blockchains to be connected on an interoperable platform, such as the platforms of the Cardano, Avalanche, and Polkadot blockchains.

Understanding this evolution is essential for making sense of blockchains, and understanding blockchains and their typology is essential for rethinking regulation, taxation, and central bank digital currencies, as we will see later. However, the chapter shows that we also need to consider an actor-based taxonomy of blockchains—one that references the two groups of actors that maintain them, transactioners and accountants—to appreciate their functions and political economic consequences. Transactioners send data monies over blockchains, whereas accountants carry out the bookkeeping functions for these transactions through a variety of mining services such as proof of work or stake.

Looking at the perspectives of actors, the chapter identifies four types of blockchains. *Open-accounting blockchains* allow every accountant to perform mining at will as long as they have the necessary computing power, whereas *closed-accounting blockchains* can choose which actors can perform accounting and to what degree. This option introduces a more centralized blockchain operation by increasing the speed of transaction registration in the chain. The chapter then approaches blockchains from the vantage point of transactioners. *Public blockchains* are open to anyone to securely transfer private data, the movement of which represents a kind of value. One does not have to be registered, accepted, recognized, or permitted to become a transactioner in such a sociotechnical architecture. *Private blockchains* require one to obtain permission or acceptance to become a transactioner in their architecture.

Moving away from the nature of data monies and their accounting practices to the universe of cryptocurrency exchanges, chapter 3 then presents several findings, some of which may be surprising. Contrary to expectations, my research shows that the proliferation of cryptocurrencies is, in fact, supporting the dollarization and euroization of world trade, not posing a threat to sovereign fiat currencies. Furthermore, and even more counterintuitive, my research proves that centralized cryptocurrency markets, which are regulated by states and draw on nonblockchain accounting systems such as double-entry bookkeeping, have been replacing public open-accounting blockchains, such as those of Bitcoin and Ethereum, in registering transactions. More than 90 percent of Bitcoin owned globally is not registered in personal accounts but instead is kept as custodial assets in centralized exchanges. It seems that much like in the first decade of data money, organized conventional markets have remained hegemonic over blockchains. Yet I believe that in the long run, decentralized and blockchain-based data money markets like Uniswap will be able to catch up with and even exceed nonblockchain and centralized data money markets, such as Binance and Coinbase.

The third chapter's main empirical question is this: How do data money markets work? Drawing on an analysis of global data-money exchanges based on social-scientific research among exchange actors, as well as a computational text analysis of cryptocurrency markets' terms of service, the chapter shows that it is inadequate to view these exchanges as mere markets. It argues that these exchange platforms go beyond marketization relations in that they provide a multiplicity of products and services such as banking, exchange infrastructure, minting, payment-system maintenance, software development, security, and centralized extrablockchain accounting. Proposing *stack* as a theoretical construct to qualify a new sociodigital economization process taking place in these data money exchanges, this chapter argues that these exchange platforms can best be understood as economization stacks of multiple interactive layers with an ancillary relationship, in that they deliver an empirically observable range of economic functions. *Stack economization* refers to the mutually supported and enabled platform-based exchange, production, barter, and representation processes that are identified by their makers and observers as economic. Unlike underdigitalized economic relations that draw on infrastructures such as railroads or waterworks, hyperdigitalized platforms work in digital sociotechnical spaces where users and makers simultaneously imagine, enact, build, operate, and invert stack economization.

Chapter 3 also includes a descriptive account of how a data money exchange works, based on my fieldwork in the offices and on the communications platforms of X Exchange. As one of the top data money exchanges in the world, it provides us with a unique internal vantage point from which to better understand these new market platforms. By including a computational and interpretive text analysis of the terms-of-service agreements of all of the data money exchanges in the world, the chapter is also able to describe the priorities and preferences of the exchange architects and owners. Contrary to many mainstream approaches that see a rupture between material and digital economies, the chapter shows us that market actors and designers do not operate along a digital/material divide. For them, data have a materiality that is distributed among tangible and intangible properties. Their job is to build new architectures by using or drawing on these materialities.

The chapter also introduces a visualization of the stacked economization processes in a cryptocurrency exchange platform, helping regulators and researchers "see" intangible relations and networks with tangible analogies and constructs. Together with colleagues at the Parsons School of Design, I organized a design challenge, and this illustration is the result of a collaboration between two of the winners, Steven Johnson and Lauren Stobierski. They managed to describe complex economic relations with creative simplicity, presenting a rare example of a visualization of what some economists call two- or multisided markets.

Following this more general analysis of cryptocurrencies, their blockchains, and their markets, in the next two chapters of the book I present a specific analysis of the rise, fall, and rebirth of a cryptocurrency project and its community—that is, Electra. Taking his inspiration from the electrum alloy, which the Lydians used to mint the first metal fiat money, an unknown man, Electra01, developed Electra in 2017. Following its emergence in the cryptocurrency markets in 2018, its market capitalization reached $136 billion, exceeding Bitcoin in value. The project's community of approximately twenty thousand individuals wrote its white papers, updated its blockchain, established a foundation, and introduced a payment system, and in 2020, Electra was named the world's best crypto project in a global vote organized by Binance, the world's largest exchange by volume in 2021. Following a fundamental controversy within its community, Electra collapsed when its founder sold his hundreds of millions of Electras in November 2020, effectively killing the project. Within a short period of time, the community left the founder behind and moved on to a new project, enabling the rebirth of its own community money, this time called Electra Protocol.

Chapter 4 focuses on the sociological universe of Electra's community, whose members live in various time zones all across the world and work around the clock to make data money. It presents the demographic characteristics of this community and the members' general take on cryptocurrency economies, based on a member survey. Employing a computational text analysis of Bitcointalk's Electra forum, the chapter sets out a variety of concerns that mark the main contours of discussion and contestation in the community. In order to complement this analysis, it utilizes a network analysis of all Twitter interaction data among the 18,600 followers of the handle @ElectraProtocol, as well as their 358,000 followers, be they groups, persons, or bots. This analysis enables us to identify and visualize the community's relatively more powerful actors and clusters.

The chapter presents three clusters of findings. First, it presents a visual representation, created in collaboration with the designer Nishant Wazir, of all actors within the Electra community, underlining the concentration of power, in line with the actors' own descriptions of these relations. In this introduction to the demographics of the people who make up the supposedly "open" Electra community, we see the unprecedented dominance of well-educated white men who live in the West. We observe that there exist clearly identifiable centers of power in this "decentralized" financial infrastructure, marked by race, education, gender, and geographic location. Yet this community is also open and quick to address such asymmetries. After seeing the survey results, which I made available to participants, the Electra community decided to take concrete steps toward inclusivity, equity, and diversity by deploying what may be termed *everyday performativity*. Such a development calls for a rethinking of questions of economic performativity, which takes place between scientific practices and economization processes on the ground.

Second, drawing on a computational text analysis of forum discussion content, the chapter identifies the most frequently used words. It then interprets the results with a second derivative analysis that plots the most frequently used social-scientific terms in these discussions. This analysis moves beyond a descriptive account of the distribution of actors' intentional choices of concepts; with the help of a big data analysis of Twitter interactions, it renders observable which actors' intentional utterances carry more power. Offering a second visualization of the same community, this time by analyzing Twitter data, the findings present a more nuanced understanding of relations of power. We see that it is not those who post most frequently or those who are followed by the largest group that carry more weight; instead, those who help build clusters and then bridge them to others are more influential.

Third, and rather surprisingly, the findings show that it is not the most influential actors on the Bitcointalk forum or Twitter that have the greatest influence on Electra community affairs; rather, it is the agents who manage to control and shape "the parliament of the community affairs," those community members on Discord, another communication platform. We see that the agency of these actors is so powerful they can even induce a vast digital/material migration of the Electra community. This entire move was planned by a handful of individuals in the core team and administered by the 369 members of Electra's Discord platform.

Chapter 5 moves in from the general bird's-eye view of this data money community to take a closer look at the dynamics of continuity and change. The unfortunate collapse of Electra and the spectacular emergence of Electra Protocol afforded me a unique opportunity to study both success and failure in a crypto-economization process. Drawing on fieldwork among the members of the Electra community, I provide an empirical case study in which I analyze the distributed interaction among actors, representations, networks, and organizational frameworks and devices that contributed to the making, maintenance, and death of a data money project.

I was fortunate to find a way to meet Electra01 in person. He is a young British man with a degree from a Scottish university. A major in economics and a minor in computing had greatly helped him as he figured out the future economic potential of Bitcoin when it had been worth only $13. In part inspired by Bitcoin's legendary founder, Satoshi Nakamoto, he decided on the pseudonym Electra01 and began working on a cryptocurrency. I contacted him through a common acquaintance. After reading my CV, previous publications, and research proposal, he contacted me using his private email and then decided to meet with me in person in 2018.

From then until March 2021, when I concluded my research, I spent numerous hours with him on conference and telephone calls, in person, and over email, discussing Electra and other issues related to cryptocurrencies. Knowing the real identity of "the Satoshi of Electra" was both a privilege and a source of stress, especially when the core team and Electraoi faced a conundrum and parted ways. Because of the sensitive content of my writing, I sent my final drafts to both Electraoi and a core team member with whom he disagreed fiercely. After reading many revised drafts and a few times accusing me of doing him and his motivations an injustice, Electraoi finally approved the current fifth chapter and its direct quotations from him, giving readers an unprecedented chance to learn more about these anonymous economic actors and their world.

Chapter 5 makes three general points. First, it maps the organizational devices, innovations, and strategies that data money communities use—among them, gifts, sprints, conferences, prizes, and a variety of architectural, infrastructural, and platform formations. The proliferation of digital devices that data money communities use seems not to support the thesis that they embody an organizational revolution by moving from institutions of trust to trustless systems of blockchains. We have seen how a collapse of trust between the founder and the community leadership led to the phenomenal collapse of the very data money itself.

Second, the chapter shows the importance of agency and institutions in data money communities. Electra resorted to one of the oldest human organizations to communicate an identity of trust in the world of data monies. The Electra Foundation, established in the Netherlands, had more functions than merely legitimation. The community decided to use it as an economization device to increase the power of its own agency vis-à-vis the founder. While testifying to the continuing importance of conventional organizations (such as foundations) in the world of data money communities, the chapter also discusses the institutional and organizational terrain that data money communities create and populate.

Finally, chapter 5 analyzes what happens when all devices and organizations of trust and cooperation collapse. We saw how the community decided to move on and use its platform's economic tool kit and possessions to build an entirely new money. By examining the power relations in this data money community and the way in which it responded when it was faced with an extreme challenge, the complete collapse of Electra's monetary value, the chapter demonstrates that economic actors can be quite innovative in solving their problems. Instead of accepting the collapsing market price of their data money, the community members moved beyond the solutions that markets impose on them, such as buy or sell, and embraced a new economization strategy: starting up a new infrastructure following a historically new digital migration.

The last chapter of the book can be read as a stand-alone essay that aims to achieve three objectives. First, it summarizes the philosophical foundations of the crypto-economic universe. After illustrating the material political economy and foundations of cryptocurrencies and their blockchains, it argues for increased awareness of the historical novelty of data monies: namely, that they draw on monetizing the right to send data for the first time in history.

Second, the chapter shows that transformations associated with data monies, their trading, and their communities do *not* entail a revolutionary parting from the past. Cryptocurrencies have not been replacing fiat currencies, and blockchains have not been replacing markets as places of transactions. The empirical findings show that centralized exchanges such as Binance have been replacing blockchains' transactional functions, pushing the proliferation of decentralized exchanges, such as Uniswap, which have narrower channels to connect their monies to fiat money universes. Data monies are contributing to the dollarization of trading in the world, since people buy more data monies as assets and they move dollars more frequently. Moreover, the volatility of cryptocurrency values pushes economic actors to "park" their money in dollars, thus creating another dynamic for the dollar's use.

These two major conclusions of this book lead to a third one, this time concerning the following question: What is to be done with cryptocurrencies? Regulators have been facing difficulties in making sense of data monies' nature and the workings of their exchange platforms. One cannot regulate something that one fails to comprehend. Many people imagine data monies as mere digital currencies, while many regulators think that economic actors are pushing for an alternative currency and looking for ways to avoid regulation and taxation in pursuit of illegitimate financial gain. My research showed that many data money actors, exchange leaders, blockchain enthusiasts, and institutional investors seek regulation and are not motivated by unacceptable or illegitimate objectives. They seek regulation by agencies that understand what they do.

Data monies are neither metal/paper monies nor their digital representations. They are made by monetizing the right to send data. This material quality of data monies makes it possible for economic actors to build new exchange platforms that mobilize an assortment of economic functions and services whose rich world confuses regulators. These exchange platforms go beyond being mere marketization relations. That is why one cannot regulate them by imagining them as two- or multisided markets. Trying to understand cryptocurrency as either an asset or a digital version of fiat currency fails to capture its historical novelty and flattens the ways in which it is used in the multifunctional crypto exchanges.

This book suggests an innovative strategy for regulatory approaches. First, regulators should imagine tax not just in terms of fiat currency. Because regulators currently register income only in terms of fiat currency, they need economic actors to sell their assets and return to fiat currency to identify taxable income. Such an insistence narrows regulatory options to a spectrum with banning all use of crypto assets at one end and closing certain economization functions of exchange platforms at the other.

Yet there is an alternative. If regulators also imagine tax collection in terms of data monies, they can still register income without a necessary conversion to fiat currency. In this way, they tax economic value creation in the new money forms. It is not wise or economical to tax data money with fiat money. One can tax each monetary income with its own material form. This idea is new in the sense that it draws on taxation in a new money form, but it is also old in the sense that in 2018, Ohio's state treasury became the first state entity to accept a data money (Bitcoin) as tax by converting it to a sovereign fiat currency (dollars). John Mandel, then state treasurer of Ohio, had launched OhioCrypto.com, making it possible to imagine taxation with data monies—although still by converting them into fiat currency. The payment system was discontinued in 2019 after the new state treasurer found it too risky.

Second, regulators can approach platforms not as mere markets but as stack economization processes. This strategy change has two advantages. It moves away from the flattening effect of seeing platforms as markets and opens up the regulatory imagination to a series of new contributions that are keyed to the nature of platform economic relations. Also, stack economization allows regulators to empirically map numerous functions of cryptocurrency exchanges and clearly mark areas of regulation, such as the minting of new data monies. Currently, one can buy billions of dollars' worth of Ethereum from an under-regulated market in the United States and send it to anywhere in the world. Not understanding the stacked nature of data money markets, China decided to ban them. This led to an increase of the use of Bitcoin, pushing the data money's value up. Another possibility is to incorporate data monies into our current regulatory framework, with the introduction of a state-registered electronic metawallet. Such an acceptance entails imagining economic agency with regard to not only individuals or legal entities but also digital wallet constellations. Hence, income can also be identified in terms of data money, and financial transactions can be regulated and controlled without necessarily banning data money movements.

Third, this book's approach helps us analyze and think about central bank digital currencies (CBDCs) in a new way. By and large, there is a tendency to confuse CBDCs with cryptocurrencies that operate on public open-accounting blockchains. As of December 2021, no central bank had issued such a cryptocurrency. This book shows that by minting data money that operates on a public open-accounting blockchain, a central bank becomes a decentral bank because both the right to mint new money and its transaction accounting would be transferred to actors that cannot be controlled by the central bank. The current experiments with CBDCs all rely on digitalizing fiat currencies and building a central bank–controlled transfer system for them. Without raising awareness about the difference between data monies and digital currencies, it is not possible to analyze CBDCs and imagine ways of discussing, regulating, and improving them. Without raising awareness about the types of blockchains, it is infinitely difficult to make sense of CBDCs. One has to address this question to start a meaningful discussion: What type of blockchain would a central bank need to issue a cryptocurrency?

# 2

# THE MATERIALITY OF DATA MONEY
# AND THE INFRASTRUCTURE AND
# TAXONOMY OF BLOCKCHAINS

Contemporary economic relations revolve around 180 fiat currencies issued by states and marketed by banks. Since 2008, and for the first time in history, cryptocurrencies and their blockchains have been forging a parallel economic universe that needs neither states nor banks for printing and transferring monies. By 2021, the market capitalization of this economic universe reached $2.5 trillion, exceeding 96 percent of the world's national economies in terms of GDP.[1] In the same year, more than ten thousand cryptocurrencies were being exchanged in more than twenty thousand cryptocurrency markets all over the world, making them both the most varied money and the most rapidly emerging market form in history.

Despite the existence of such a rich universe of economic interaction, populated by thousands of cryptocurrencies and markets, no extended empirical social-scientific study with detailed fieldwork has been conducted on (1) this new global economic universe, (2) the sociotechnical architectures on which such a universe is based, (3) the way in which cryptocurrency exchanges work, and (4) the international communities that make and exchange these monies. Popular and journalistic accounts of these currencies tend to revolve around clashing reactions. Those who are under the influence of Bitcoin schaden-freude have described them as a bubble that is doomed to van-ish. An influential editorial has called them "a greater fool's gold."[2] Those who see cryptocurrencies as launching a revolution say they have the potential to facilitate autonomous economic action in an extrapolitical world without state intervention.[3] Such a stance took a new turn when crypto evangelicals declared "Bitcoin's Independence" in 2014.[4]

Academic literature disagrees. Empirical research has shown that money, whether represented digitally or physically by paper, is not a thing but a process; it is produced and maintained by social relations, political institutions, and symbolic valuations.[5] Its very existence implies an a priori political and social realm.[6] We also know that the bursting of the dot-com bubble did not prevent Silicon Valley from giving birth to the world's first trillion-dollar companies, such as Amazon and Google. Therefore, many academics are not convinced that Bitcoin's volatility or "bubble" will bring about the end of blockchains and cryptocur-rencies.[7] Furthermore, it has been shown that these new curren-cies are "multi-faceted, politically contested and sociologically rich in [their] functions and meanings. There is not one Bitcoin, but several."[8]

Scholars have not eschewed political considerations in the form of right-wing motivations for Bitcoin's proliferation.[9] Furthermore, almost 80 percent of Bitcoin mining in 2017 was carried out by only five mining pools, thus implying power asymmetries.[10] The assumption that states and banks cannot control cryptocurrencies creates the illusion that a blockchain operates without the institutional mediation undergirding social and political relations.[11] Yet banks and states have devoted unprecedented resources to the production and use of block-chains and cryptocurrencies at a time when blockchains are presented as *the* historical instrument to undermine their power. This detracts from the credibility of evangelicals who argue that blockchains are antisystem, anticapitalist, and antistate.

However, there is one gap in the emerging literature. The scholarly literature addresses this unquestionably new development in two ways, neither of which is adequate for analyzing and explaining the working of blockchains and cryptocurrencies. First, those doing microeconomic research on crypto-asset pricing and blockchain architecture have built models that draw on problematic neoclassical assumptions about how actual markets work.[12] They assume that the specific nature of the commodity and the sociopolitical nature of its universe, whether pork belly or Bitcoin, have no significant effect on the ways in which its price is determined. Those who take macroeconomic approaches, usually drawing on these microeconomic frameworks, do not rely on a conceptual distinction. They treat cryptocurrency and digital money as if they are the same and do not consider the political-economic differences between blockchains in their analysis.[13] Furthermore, they do not draw on contemporary economic sociological research on the political, economic, and social universe of cryptocurrencies and instead operate in a conceptual vacuum, created by their monodisciplinary silo. As empirically demonstrated in the literature, both the nature of the object of exchange and the infrastructure of the market itself have a formative effect on data money prices. This infrastructural dimension among markets has to be studied, not edited out.[14]

Yet digital infrastructures and platforms are different from material infrastructures such as roads, electricity networks, dams, irrigation canals, and mines. To Brian Larkin, "infrastructures are matter that enable the movement of other matter."[15] However, computer programs are *not* just matter; they are also protocols that operate through matter, such as the hardware that consumes electric power, all made possible by labor power. Blockchains are accounting infrastructures that enable the movement of data as value. Digital infrastructures, like blockchains, require social researchers to adopt a critical and empirical approach to determining how they build sociotechnical universes based on invisible, intangible, and observable protocols that nevertheless elicit heterogenous materialities and how they operate, given matter and labor considerations.[16] Like constitutions, protocols constitute relationships by imagining rights, subjects, objects, and trajectories of actions and inaction. But unlike constitutions, one cannot disobey them, for they make action impossible if one does not follow the trajectories of movement that they define. They display a syntax error unless they are hacked.[17]

Second, many analysts work on showing either what cryptocurrencies are *not* or how they are, in essence, *not new*. With few exceptions,[18] the existing social science literature rarely draws on empirical social analysis; it puts forward interpretations about the emergence and working of blockchains and cryptocurrencies by drawing either on anecdotal experience or on the theoretical premises of the very empirical developments they are seeking to understand in the first place. It is this gap in the literature that this chapter addresses by offering an actor-based taxonomy of blockchains via analyzing cryptocurrency white papers.

Theoretically, the discussion draws on contemporary social studies of economization, as I proposed with Michel Callon.[19] The study of sociotechnical infrastructures and architectures plays a crucial role in making sense of economic action and agency because they structure possible fields of actions in a given setting and in specific and identifiable ways.[20]

In that sense, a distinction should be made between infrastructures and architectures. Infrastructures shape the ways in which networks of relations connect and bypass each other. They are metastructures that make possible the building of architectural designs that harbor and form possible trajectories of action. Organizational architectures are built on infrastructural platforms. A sociotechnical architecture refers to a structural formation that distributes devices and agencies built and/ or imagined in an infrastructural network, such as the internet or a blockchain. Depending on one's strategic vantage point, structures may function like infrastructures. The internet is infrastructural to blockchains, and a specific blockchain can be infrastructural to the architecture of a cryptocurrency exchange platform. In that context, the term *sociotechnical* refers to an arrangement of material devices and human agencies whose interactions produce empirically observable consequences. These technical platforms define instruments and devices of action that are shaping and shaped by human intentions, interests, mistakes, and plans.[21]

Almost all cryptocurrencies are offered with scientific-looking digital publications called white papers.[22] These are position papers written by anonymous or known individuals or groups of individuals, historically making cryptocurrency, or data money, the first money form created, in part and in varying degrees, by scientists or people who use scientific tools and competencies without the necessary contribution of banks and states. These more than two thousand white papers now make up a text corpus of more than fifty thousand pages. Most of these documents, however, introduce cryptocurrencies of only negligible economic value. As of June 1, 2018, the ten most valuable cryptocurrencies represented 75.01 percent of all cryptocurrency value in the world, and the one hundred most valuable cryptocurrencies represented 90.06 percent.[23] This chapter draws on an analysis of the white papers of these one hundred cryptocurrencies.[24]

Because white papers develop, describe, and present major forms of blockchains and their respective cryptocurrencies, they provide social science researchers with an invaluable opportunity to study the historical evolution of blockchain architectures.[25] The first part of the chapter presents the historical evolution of blockchain architectural forms from the value-exchange-distributed ledger of Bitcoin and smart-contract-exchange platform of Ethereum to market-making blockchains like that of CyberMiles. Without developing a critical awareness of the sociotechnical evolution of these digital ledgers, one cannot grasp the specificity, nature, and consequences of their architecture, which shapes possible fields of action (and also dormancy) for economic agents.

Blockchain and cryptocurrency communities deploy nouns that refer to tangible things, like *blocks*, *chains*, *clouds*, and *mining*, to describe intangible economic devices and computational industrial practices. Such an analogical framework provides blockchain projects, especially during their early phases, with a number of tools of intervention in actual economic universes. But this same false naming makes it difficult to understand blockchains if one uses these analogies, which blockchain architects themselves use to understand what they do. The term *Bitcoin mining* is a good example of this elusive nature of blockchain architecture. One does not dig out or extract data to find Bitcoins in a digital mineshaft or pool.[26] Mining, an analogy Satoshi Nakamoto used for the first time in his Bitcoin white paper, is a form of computational accounting, in which the underlying protocol rewards the miners, or accountants, with crypto coins.[27] Furthermore, crypto coins are not metal like coins per se; rather, they are digitally represented exclusive *rights* to send data privately in a public economic space. Market actors exchange these specific rights and trade these data coins as rights for services and goods.

Analogical conceptualization not only prevents us from seeing the material universe of blockchains but also makes it difficult to appreciate the historically novel materiality of cryptocurrencies. There has been a tendency to see cryptocurrencies as digital cash or digital currency. This chapter shows that a cryptocurrency is *not* a mere digital money. All fiat currencies in the world are also made digitally, either by representing their value, which itself is represented by their metal and paper materials, with computers or by producing debt and digitally monetizing it. What one sees on a computer screen is already the digital representation of fiat currencies. Calling Bitcoin a digital money at a time when all fiat monies are digitalized is not a good idea. Cryptocurrencies are not digitally represented but are computationally made. They are as material as metal and paper monies; yet they are intangible compared to other money types. They are not passive data entries in a memory device. Computers are essential for these monies to exist, but computation is not enough. What makes these data monies new is not that they are made with data but that they are imagined as the right to send data with new accounting mechanisms called blockchains. By identifying the historical material specificity of data money, this chapter presents a preliminary framework for analyzing it.

The second part of the chapter describes the content of data money white papers, their writers, their arguments' scientific and quasi-scientific qualities, and their social imaginaries. Drawing on a computational text analysis of these white papers, we see that seemingly revolutionary blockchains do not even mention revolutions but busily theorize about the maintenance of reintermediations, markets, and economies in a social context.[28] Furthermore, these white papers, all written in English by male authors, propose a specific social world that draws on a bifurcation between digital and nondigital things. Imagining their separation is an intervention tool in economization relations.

The third part of the chapter presents an actor-based taxonomy of blockchains in terms of their control mechanisms, which structure identifiable courses of action for the economic agents, as defined by the white papers. It is important to understand and analyze blockchains' heterogeneity so as to better grasp what types of sociotechnical assemblages they are and what consequences those different types entail in relation to economic agency. Assuming the homogeneity of blockchains and not controlling for their actor-network heterogeneity may lead to erroneous theoretical generalizations or empirically incomplete observations. The chapter shows that blockchain digital infrastructure contemplates two major types of actors: transactioners and accountants.[29] Furthermore, it argues that blockchains can be categorized based on how their architectures define who can be active and in what capacity, transactioner or accountant.

Drawing on this distinction, this chapter demonstrates that there are two types of blockchain architectures—public and private blockchains—based on who may be a transactioner within them. Furthermore, these blockchains are of two types: open-accounting blockchains and closed-accounting blockchains based on who could be an accountant in them. The first type is open to anyone who would like to be an accountant in its system. This is the case with Bitcoin's blockchain. The second is closed to people who do not qualify as an accountant. For example, Avalanche is a closed-accounting blockchain that is open only to those who own more than 2,000 AVAX, its cryptocurrency, and accept to be a validator by proving that they will be working as an accountant. In discussing the consequences of these four blockchain categories, I show that without developing a nuanced understanding of the heterogeneity of blockchain architecture, it is not possible to make sense of whether and how blockchains work. We should not be asking questions about *what a blockchain does* without specifying *what type of blockchain we are talking about.*

## THE EVOLUTION OF BLOCKCHAINS

When the Bitcoin blockchain was developed by Nakamoto more than a decade ago, its cryptocurrency was referred to as electronic cash, and the platform for its production and exchange was presented as a peer-to-peer network without calling it a blockchain.[30] The terms *block* and *chain* never came together as one word in that paper. Yet this nine-page white paper introduced an economy whose market worth would surpass that of Visa, the world's largest credit card company, by $50 billion in only eight years and whose capitalization would reach $2.5 trillion in its first decade.

Before Bitcoin, it was possible to digitally represent currencies and transfer them via the internet. Yet such transfers over the internet required the services of a bank, the guarantee of a state in case the bank fails, and private accounting of this transaction, the records of which can be seen only by the sender, the receiver, the state, and the bank. Unless a legal matter arises, these records stay private among these actors.

The first blockchain in the world managed to imagine, produce, and transfer value in a publicly visible manner without an intermediary such as a central bank or a state. The mechanism looks complex, but it draws on a simple principle of accounting. Imagine that Alice sends $1 to Bob. Alice's bank withdraws $1 from her account, and Bob's bank adds $1 to his. The transaction appears in the double-entry bookkeeping system of the bank and can be reported as part of aggregate accounting data to the state. Alice cannot spend the same $1 again, for it is physically gone from her account, and if she goes to the bank to withdraw all her money, she will end up having $1 less in cash.

Nakamoto proposed a way to transfer value that was much like this system, minus banks and states. Alice sends 1 Bitcoin (BTC) to Bob without going through a financial institution;

an attendant problem is how to prevent Alice from spending that 1 BTC again. This is a challenging problem to address because, unlike difficult-to-forge *physical* papers that represent value, it is very easy to copy and paste a *digital* representation, whether it is digital money, an article, or a photograph. Digital currencies are categorically different from cryptocurrencies in two ways. First, they are not data monies. Neither their circulation nor their exchange involves the transfer of exclusive rights to send data. Second, digital fiat currencies, although lacking the physical representations, are still minted and supplied by banks and states. Hence, what makes data money unique is its novel treatment, which prevents it from being forged, copied, or spent again while at the same time ensuring that its transfer is not reversible at will. Bitcoin's blockchain developed a system to address this difficulty, generally called the double-spend problem.

Here is how it works. Let's say Alice wants to send 1 BTC to Bob. This transaction proposal is encrypted by sophisticated programs to make it a *unique* digital representation that cannot be re-represented digitally without a series of passwords. Then this proposal to transact 1 BTC appears on an internet network, where the community of accountants sees this digital proposal among hundreds of others around it. These accountants then choose to write the proposed transaction down on a digital page called a block. If they manage to add this new page to the Bitcoin digital ledger, the proposed transaction between Bob and Alice is *realized*. Once recorded in the digital ledger, it is almost impossible to modify or cancel this transaction, thanks to the infrastructural protocol that runs the system.

Why would someone volunteer to be the accountant of such a system unless they earn something from it? Nakamoto addressed this problem by giving a digital thing that may be found valuable to any accountant who managed to add one more page to the ledger. And this thing is called a Bitcoin. What makes it valuable is not an abstract and subjective belief but its material utility in providing an actual *service* of value creation and transfer without the necessary presence of a central institution.

In the beginning, "the digital thing" was 50 BTC, which represented some value to the accountants, whom Nakamoto called miners; yet until March 2010, Bitcoin did not have any significant monetary value. There was no Bitcoin market—only scattered auctions here and there, with no market price to quote. However, with the opening of the first digital currency exchange market in 2010—that is, bitcoinmarket.com, an intermediary institution designed for the first data money in history—the value of Bitcoin began to pick up. An innovation with the stated aim of disintermediation began to be valued only after it contributed to the creation of a new intermediary institution, such as a Bitcoin exchange market. Such an unprecedented valuation of Bitcoin was most probably also due to the 2008 crisis that eroded much trust in conventional financial institutions. Ten months after the emergence of the first Bitcoin exchange market, 1 BTC was traded for $1, changing the entire landscape of its accounting because more and more miners now could earn more by contributing to the Bitcoin accounting process. A currency issued and backed by no state had reached the value of a currency issued and backed by the United States.

The Bitcoin protocol was programmed to take on the challenge of Bitcoin creation by means of four mechanisms: First, the amount of Bitcoin per each mined block would be halved after every 210,000 blocks. In 2009, it was 50 BTC, while in 2012 this number decreased to 25 BTC, in 2016 it became 12.5 BTC, and in May 2020 it went down to 6.25 BTC, where it stands at the time of writing. The more miners the accounting system attracts, the faster its rewards shrink. Second, one receives an automatic reward as soon as one mines a block—in other words, adds one's own page to the pages of a ledger. Many miners compete for this; therefore, a chance event also controls the number of miners who can receive the reward. The miner who guesses a number that the protocol uses once, called the nonce, is given the right to close that block, and only after this correct guess, that miner's block is added to the ledger. The difficulty of guessing this number is also controlled by the protocol: it becomes more difficult as the active miner population increases. Third, the value of the cryptocurrency itself is in part controlled by the protocol in a deflationary context by fixing the number of Bitcoins to be mined at 21 million. Finally, the protocol defines a transaction fee that can be set as zero or more by the transactioner. This fee once exceeded $20 million on December 21, 2017, when 1,496 BTC were paid to miners.[31] Thus, after the twenty-one-millionth Bitcoin is mined, transactions would be carried out only upon receiving this fee. The person who wants a transaction to be realized faster is free to increase the fee; in other circumstances, they may decrease it all the way to zero.

For example, Alice, after attaching an attractive transaction fee to her proposal, has her transaction included in a block. As soon as the block is added to the ledger, thanks to a successful miner, that 1 BTC (minus the fee) becomes Bob's property. What if Alice wants to re-spend the Bitcoin she sent to Bob? She cannot because *spending* means transferring the right to send it to someone else and because Bitcoin is the *right* to *send* fixed and nonreplicable data privately to someone else in a public ledger; once sent and registered, that right has been transferred to Bob for good. When one transfers data money, what one sends is *not* data but the *right* to send it. To be able to reach your right to send a specific amount of data money, you have to reach it in the blockchain ledger. After you send it, the ledger registers it to someone else.

Double-spending and irreversibility are enhanced by making every transaction public but without giving Alice's and Bob's real names. Imagine a magical notebook: You write something in it, and this note pops up on everyone's notebook and can no longer be altered as soon as the majority of the other notebook owners accept its validity. Even if you erase the note in your own notebook, it will remain on record in others' notebooks. The attempt to change the ledger and thus to spend the same Bitcoin again or send it to someone else is so costly that anyone who uses the Bitcoin blockchain avoids it.

Despite the strength, security, and durability of Bitcoin's value transaction system, it still has drawbacks. While making it possible to imagine and transfer value without a physical representation and the intermediation of banks and states, it nevertheless does not allow the transfer of computations, only the value that is computationally represented. Accounting or mining then checks this value to determine whether it matches a certain algorithm or not.

Following Bitcoin, various other blockchains were designed and constructed either independently or as a derivative of the Bitcoin algorithm. With the emergence of the Ethereum blockchain, it became possible to send digital assets only if certain conditions were met, thus embedding value in the computation itself. Vitalik Buterin published the Ethereum blockchain white paper, giving birth to second-generation blockchains.

First-generation blockchains facilitated sending data, whereas second-generation blockchains made it possible to send data if certain conditions were met. In other words, Ethereum allows one to embed contracts into digital value and transfer a short computer program, thus changing the nature of accounting from checking for a value to checking for a working contract or a program. Let's say Alice decides to send Bob 1 BTC—but only if Carol sends Bob 2 BTC. This is a conditional transaction: the transfer of value from Alice to Bob happens only if a certain condition is met on Bob's end, which is the successful transaction between Carol and Bob.

The outcome was revolutionary in the sense that the advanced computer language of the Ethereum blockchain rendered it possible to imagine value as a contract, and with minor and relatively easy alterations; thus, others began to use Ethereum as a framework for imagining new cryptocurrencies without building new blockchains. Without changing the main logic of imagining value as a right to send data, Ethereum gave birth to the big bang of the cryptocurrency universe—as of December 2018, 43 percent of the one hundred most valuable 100 cryptocurrencies were Ethereum-based tokens.

These second-generation blockchains continued to develop in terms of their infrastructural capabilities—so much so that the Truthcoin blockchain managed to include out-of-chain conditions in smart contracts. Let's say Alice sends 1 BTC to Bob only if the temperature in New York City is 35 degrees Celsius or above. Obviously, the weather is not a blockchain event; it is what coders call an off-chain event. However, the data generated by meteorological sources can be coded into smart contracts to create off-chain events that trigger the realization of in-chain contracts—coders refer to this as making "oracles." This new development facilitates the transfer of almost any financial off-chain instruments, such as stop-loss orders on derivative contracts, into blockchains.

The opening of such a wide spectrum of options in blockchains led developers to imagine more complex transactional relations and infrastructure making, giving birth to the third-generation blockchains that are now building two new platforms of interaction: First, since the publication of Casey Detrio's paper on market making by blockchains,[32] it has become possible

TABLE 2.1 EVOLUTION OF BLOCKCHAIN INFRASTRUCTURE

| Evolutionary type of blockchain | Example | Function |
|---|---|---|
| Value-exchange blockchain | Bitcoin | Value transfer |
| Program-exchange blockchain | Ethereum | Program transfer |
| Interchain | Avalanche | Interchain operability |

to build an entire market as an in-chain field of action. Second, blockchain architects have developed systems that create an interchain network of layers, such as Avalanche, by enabling a number of blockchains to have contact and engage in transactional relations with each other.

As such an evolution took place (table 2.1), corporations and states also started to develop their own blockchains, for there is nothing fundamentally public about blockchain technology. Depending on one's intentions, one can create specific keys to lock or unlock relations in a blockchain, as this chapter demonstrates in the next section. However, paying attention to the evolution of blockchain platforms into more complex and structurally rich infrastructures over the last decade assists in a more nuanced analysis of these infrastructures and the specific ways they affect economic agency in their sociotechnical universe. To address this issue, one needs to study the specificity of these architectures by looking at the white papers that construct them in the first place.

## CRYPTOCURRENCY BLOCKCHAIN WHITE PAPERS AT A GLANCE

A white paper is a curious thing, stuck between science and investment. Emerging at the beginning of the twentieth century in Great Britain, white papers originally presented a government's position on a matter of controversy. The most famous white paper of the period was the Churchill White Paper of 1922, representing his government's position on the Jaffa Riots of 1921, the demonstrations that took place in response to the Zionist colonization of Palestine. Its cover was white—hence the name. Many governmental and nongovernmental institutions then began to write white papers—if shorter, called blue papers—that were scientific or popular presentations of their official stance on and investment in a certain problem. Almost one century after their emergence, however, a new type of white paper emerged, this time digitally.

With the publication of Nakamoto's Bitcoin white paper on the internet, it became customary to write one to propose a new cryptocurrency or blockchain system. These white papers have three functions: (1) They have to persuade. A blockchain used by no one is a chain with no valuable cryptocurrency. All individuals or groups that develop a blockchain system should convince as many agents as possible that its services are useful.[33] (2) They have to prove. A blockchain architecture can look useful on paper, whether or not it works in real life. Thus, the white paper has to present in detail, usually by mathematical modeling, the proof that it works. (3) They have to educate. These white papers also teach the reader how to use their models, programming technique, and framework of exchange. As a result, white papers not only understand and describe a world of interaction but also design and produce the very world that they are depicting, thus forging unique and radical forms of performativity in late modern relations of economization that have never been seen before.

Cryptocurrency white papers usually open with a historical discussion of blockchains and, without exception, with a reference to Nakamoto. Then they move on to describe the shortcomings of the state of the art, define a gap in practice, and present a service that they can supply with their specific blockchain or cryptocurrency, after which they describe how the underlying algorithm and protocol work. The majority end with a list of the authors, teams, or advisers—at times supplemented by photographs and biographies, in part showing how they have been recognized as entrepreneurs, business administrators, or academics. Much like a scientific article, almost all end with a conclusion and bibliography.

Their length is reminiscent of articles in the world of the social sciences. The average length of a white paper is 25.74 pages, with an average of 8,060 words. The shortest paper is a single page, whereas the longest runs 62 pages, excluding appendices.[34] The writers of 56 percent of these papers have chosen to remain anonymous, and these anonymous papers present cryptocurrencies that carry more than 70 percent of all cryptocurrency value. It is a telling irony that these white papers' authors claim to address questions of trust but keep their identity secret.

The remaining 44 percent of the white papers display the names of actual people, all with working email addresses, LinkedIn entries, and Twitter handles. On average, a white paper is authored by 2.59 writers, and yet none of the writers of the white papers for the one hundred most valuable cryptocurrencies are women.[35] Of these papers, 59 percent start with an abstract, and, on average, they cite 14.60 publications in their bibliographies. Academic publications make up 24.31 percent of these references. Wikipedia is the most commonly cited source in the bibliographies, appearing at least once in 26 percent of the white papers. Nakamoto is the most cited writer, referred to at least once in 40 percent.

Of all these papers, 14 percent display the place of publication by mentioning either a company address or the place itself, and 21 percent make their publication year visible. It is possible to learn the publication date of the rest with a simple internet search, but the authors have chosen not to include this date. The majority of these white papers (88 percent) came out between 2015 and 2018, following the publication of the Ethereum white paper. This supports the validity of this chapter's observation that the emergence of the Ethereum blockchain marked a big bang for cryptocurrencies.

It is possible to learn more about these white papers if we plot the relative frequency of the words used by their writers in the white papers' corpus. A computational text analysis of the white papers shows that the most regularly used words fall into three frequency categories (figure 2.1). The first category incorporates words used more than 2,500 times—*transaction, node, blockchain, user, network, token,* and *data*—making this set the center of intellectual attention in white papers that propose a new money form materialized in the right to transfer data among users, with the accounting function assigned to nodes on the blockchain network. The second set—words that appear between 1,250 and 2,500 times—reflects the urgency of the writers' task of making visible the blockchain's new, novel, and/or original service and its main building blocks (literally). The third group—words that appear between 500 and 1,250 times—focuses mostly on the technical and social aspects of these platforms that operate as markets or transaction infrastructures in a decentralized and orderly manner.

Looking at the simple frequency of the words that appear in white papers is of limited help in making sense of the nature of the social-scientific attention on which these white papers draw, for it should not be a surprise to see that the terms *transaction, node,* and *blockchain* appear very frequently in white papers that propose transactions over a blockchain. Such a

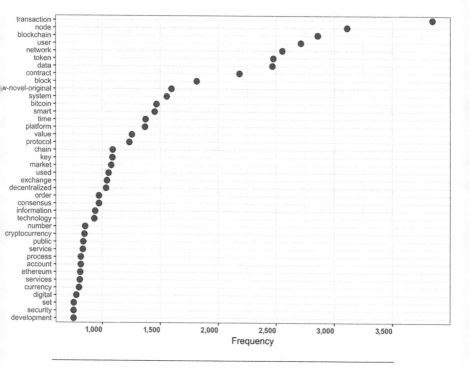

**FIGURE 2.1** Frequency of words used in blockchain white papers.

challenge can be addressed by supporting the analysis with a social-scientific filter. Constructed on a calculation of the supervised frequency distribution, this new analysis can check for the appearance of social-scientific concepts that appear in a social sciences dictionary. Craig Calhoun's *Dictionary of the Social Sciences* is the most useful dictionary, with 1,800 entries supported by an extensive bibliography.[36] The rationale for my choice of this dictionary as a filter draws not only on its popularity and social-scientific care but also on the transdisciplinary focus it deploys in the social sciences, allowing for a robust sociotechnical attendance.[37]

Such a filter makes visible a different picture of these white papers, where *value* is the most frequently used concept, followed by *market*, *exchange*, *technology*, and *currency*, alluding to their focus on a market phenomenon that is surrounded by the development of a technology for a currency exchange ecosystem. Furthermore, these five most frequently used social-scientific terms, as plotted in figure 2.2, are the only ones that also appear in figure 2.1. *Money*, *rights*, and *credit* also reoccur frequently, usually in making visible the function of cryptocurrency as medium of exchange, store of value, and unit of account. *Infrastructure* is among the most frequently used space-related social-scientific

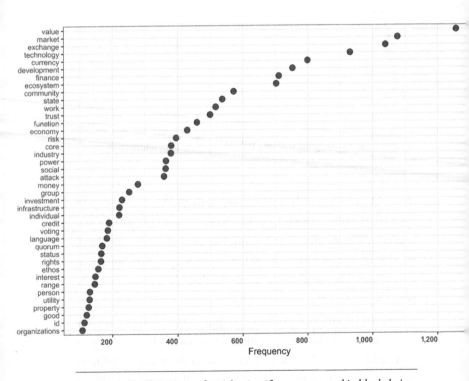

**FIGURE 2.2** Frequency of social-scientific concepts used in blockchain white papers.

terms, referring to the digital geography in which *nodes, actors, persons, consumers,* and *individuals* relate to each other.

In terms of the core concepts of the social sciences, white papers refer to finance-related concepts such as *financial* more than 700 times, economy-related concepts such as *economy* and *economical* more than 400 times, and *social* and derived concepts more than 350 times. Culture-related and politics-related concepts did not occur often in the white papers, appearing 30 and 29 times, respectively.[38]

Absences say much regarding priorities one can observe in the corpus of the white papers. For a sociotechnical development that is presented by many of its evangelicals as "revolutionary," white papers do not frequently refer to any kind of revolution: the term appears in only 1.3 percent of the papers. Furthermore, other rarely appearing terms include *freedom* (thirty-five times), *equality* (nine times), and *liberty* (one time). In terms of economic actors, the white papers refer to the *individual* as an economic agent more frequently than any other. *Class* is used frequently—but to mean a cluster of variables or factors; *social class* is never used. One paper refers twice to *gender* in its disclaimer-of-liability section, and another refers to it once, to mean "male." *Trust* is used very often, always referring to the absence of the need for a third party or intermediary to validate or make possible transactions. *Attack* refers to an attempt by anonymous or known economic agents to rewrite, erase, or damage any data (and thus trust) in the ledger.

Drawing on a lexicon populated by the concepts and qualifiers mentioned previously, the white papers imagine a world divided in two (table 2.2). They define the place where blockchains operate as a *digital* or *virtual world,* sometimes referred to as a *crypto-world* and *new world.* The other is called the *real world* (in forty-seven papers) and *physical world* (in four), referring to

## TABLE 2.2 THE IMAGINATION OF TWO WORLDS
## IN WHITE PAPERS

|  | Physical world | Digital world |
| --- | --- | --- |
| **Age** | Industrial age | Information age |
| **Infrastructure** | Material | Digital |
| **Representation of value** | Gold (metal) | Cryptocurrency (data) |
| **Symbol** | Engine | Computer |

anything that is located outside the blockchain. The same bifurcation is at times constructed as *off-chain* and *on-chain worlds*.[39]

When it comes to describing "their world," the white papers see it as an *architecture, infrastructure*, or *platform*, very frequently using these concepts to mean more or less the same thing: a sociotechnical arrangement that makes possible a certain field of action in a given system. *System* refers to a larger universe that incorporates "everything," physical or digital, yet nevertheless requires a specific architecture, infrastructure, or platform to work.[40] A quarter of the white papers also identify a fundamental change, characterizing "the previous" age as traditional, old, or industrial, while invariably defining the current time as the information age. Three white papers mention gold as the currency of the industrial age and Bitcoin as the gold of this age.

One should not expect scientific diligence and social theoretical discipline from these white papers, for they do not claim to be scientific in the first place, but they draw on scientific research and argumentation to propose an economic service. Their sole aim is successful performativity, as they are forging a technical world with the intention of building a social interaction. The next section describes the various types of sociotechnical infrastructure constructed in these white papers and used on the ground today.

## A TAXONOMY OF BLOCKCHAINS

It is a myth to think blockchains are *public* ledgers that create *disintermediation* via distributed bookkeeping that can be carried out by *anyone*. Blockchains are not necessarily public digital ledgers. There are many private blockchains and even hybrid blockchains that allow private domain accounting in a public setting.[41] Blockchains are not necessarily free either. A transaction fee accompanies almost all Bitcoin transfers, even when the person who proposes the transaction does *not* attach a transaction fee to their proposal: if they are performing a transaction on a cryptocurrency exchange, the exchange automatically adds a fee to its pool of transactions to ensure that its "customers" get their transactions approved faster.

Blockchains do not create disintermediation in economic relations, as they may or may not need conventional intermediary institutions, such as states or banks; however, they do create new intermediations.[42] That is, they do not disintermediate; they reintermediate. This is true even for the Bitcoin blockchain, which is presented as the ultimate force of disintermediation.[43] In 2018, 87.2 percent of Bitcoin transactions took place in tens of thousands of cryptocurrency markets, the number of which has exploded since Bitcoin emerged.[44] One immediate consequence of this process of reintermediation is the possibility that anonymity will disappear. A great majority of exchanges now require their clients to register with formal identification and credit cards, thus subjecting cryptocurrency owners to the visibility of conventional accounting systems and networks that banks and states use.

Thus, cryptocurrencies are one of the driving forces creating new intermediaries in economization relations, not a force erasing them. Finally, their accounting or mining can be open to everyone; yet in reality, much like in conventional accounting practice, only specialized accounting systems and experts can operate mining operations for Bitcoin, after mobilizing important financial investments. There is no free bookkeeping even in the cryptocurrency universe. Thus, it would be erroneous to treat blockchain architectures as monolithic entities that structure economic relations in only one way. One needs to be attentive to their types.

Since the emergence of the third-generation blockchains, which allow the building of in-chain markets and interchains that can trade contracts with off-chain conditions attached to them, it has become possible to move any conventional economic sector to blockchains. Hence, it would not be practical to categorize blockchains with reference to their services or products, since this would be an exercise in categorizing all economies and economic processes in their entirety, only this time based on blockchains. Such attempts in popular representations of blockchains have given birth to tens of different types of blockchain categories that confuse rather than help an observer in making sense of the blockchain universe.[45] There are also technical classifications of blockchains according to their various consensus mechanisms, such as proof of work, stake, velocity, asset, activity, access, capacity, devotion, importance, elapsed time, alienation, spending, and reserve. One can also propose categories based on the nature of digital block-making. While very useful and legitimate for understanding the purely technical operation of chains, however, these technical taxonomies are less helpful in understanding how economic agencies are imagined, mobilized, and equipped in blockchains.

This chapter proposes a categorization that accounts for the mutually exclusive configurations of actor-network interactions in terms of transaction and accounting practices in crypto infrastructures. White papers propose two groups of actors in all blockchains: *Transactioners* are those who use the digital ledgers to realize their transactions—as do Alice and Bob, whose transaction involved the exchange of 1 BTC. *Accountants* are those who account for these transactions by mining. These two are mutually dependent groups of actors. Without accountants, no transaction is registered in the ledger. Without transactions, accountants cannot account for anything. Transactioners receive accounting services from the accountants via the blockchain, and accountants receive cryptocurrencies as their fees for mining the data and permitting blockchains to use their computer hardware. A transactioner and an accountant can be the same person, but from the perspective of their economic activity, they play categorically different roles.

Blockchains vary according to the extent to which transactioners and accountants are excluded from or included in the blockchain infrastructure, regardless of the nature of the transaction (such as a value transaction or a smart-contract transaction) or the nature of the accounting (such as proof of stake or proof of work). There are two forms of transactioner participation in blockchains: (1) private blockchains, such as that of Ripple, can block who may participate in a certain blockchain; and (2) public blockchains, such as those of Bitcoin and Ethereum, are required by their protocols to allow any actor that wants to use that particular blockchain to be a transactioner. There can also be hybrid blockchains that provide their users with rooms for private or consortium activity in their infrastructures. Third-generation blockchains are generally equipped with these hybrid characteristics.

Blockchains can also block those who want to participate as accountants. A closed-accounting blockchain selects who can be active in its accounting system. An open-accounting blockchain permits any actor with the necessary technical devices to serve as an accountant for its operations; for example, Bitcoin mining is open to anyone who has the skills and devices to join. This does not mean that anyone can be an accountant in an open-accounting blockchain such as Bitcoin, although Nakamoto thought he wrote that option into the Bitcoin code. One cannot be a Bitcoin miner without investing in expensive and superfast processors called application-specific integrated circuits (ASICs). However, this is not an infrastructural impediment in the design but an economic cost that many actors cannot bear even if they wanted to.

Each of these blockchain types draws on mutually exclusive infrastructural qualities and implies varying sociotechnical configurations of actor-network relations (table 2.3). Public open-accounting blockchains cannot prevent any actor from joining their transactional or accounting practices. These human actors use material devices that are both tangible (like a computer) and intangible (such as a program) to interact with the blockchain. Let's say Alice wants to send 1 BTC to Bob; therefore, she is a transactioner who cannot be prevented from using the Bitcoin blockchain because it is a public blockchain. Alice turns on her computing device, starts an application (usually called a digital

TABLE 2.3 AN ACTOR-BASED TAXONOMY OF
BLOCKCHAINS

|  | Public | Private |
|---|---|---|
| **Open accounting** | Anyone can transact | Protocol decides |
|  | Anyone can account | Anyone can account |
| **Closed accounting** | Anyone can transact | Protocol decides |
|  | Chosen accountants | Chosen accountants |

wallet), and writes down the amount she wants to send to Bob; then, with a click, she sends a transaction request from her wallet to the blockchain network. Alice's wallet is represented by an encrypted password made up of sixty-four digits, and each digit can be composed of hexadecimal characters. These passwords are very difficult to guess and, in reality, consist of hashes of an even longer binary representation. Such a password may look like the following:

02646711598afe981a6018a6299d9803a4dc04f328f22041bedff
886bbc2962e

One has to remember that all these accounting practices are performed by computers with enormous hash power. They are owned by companies, and these companies hire workers to plug in those computers, turn on the fans and air-conditioning units to cool their processors, clean around them, and fix and maintain them for smooth operation. Thus, in reality we can argue that at least Bitcoin's public open-accounting blockchain by and large brings together human transactioners and corporate computers in order to build a value-exchange architecture.[46]

Public open-accounting blockchains bring together transactioners and accountants in an open and public digital space. They function like states because they issue currencies, like banks because they approve and account for transactions, and like marketplaces because it is possible to send and receive value on their infrastructures. Yet, because anyone can make a contribution to their operation without needing their permission, they have to play with time. Since they do not have a central authority to approve transactions and write them down, they are slow and have to slow down in order to factor chance events into their accounting system.

The problem of this slow pace is addressed by public closed-accounting blockchains, such as CyberMiles. These blockchains permit anyone to operate as a transactioner in their system but decide who may serve as an accountant for these transactions. They can choose as accountants those who have a stake in holding a particular amount of a particular cryptocurrency for a set time-period, as identified by the protocol. Closed-accounting blockchains do not allow chance and computing power to determine who can close a block, thus preventing the creation of a fully distributed and decentralized mining or accounting system. Yet they gain speed in their operations. Their accounting systems work faster than any open-accounting system, and they need less electricity and thus less hash power to operate.

Private open-accounting blockchains subcontract the mining of their transactions at the protocol level to anyone who would like to pursue mining. One can imagine it as the private blockchain of a union whose members would like to subcontract the accounting practice of their possible interunion member transactions to a distributed system. In this blockchain, only an approved transactioner can initiate a transaction, but they will have to wait until their transaction is accounted for by anonymous and public accountants.

Private closed-accounting blockchains, on the other hand, decide who may be transactioners and accountants in their system. These blockchains are built by corporate entities that use blockchain technology to decrease their bookkeeping and transaction costs. All private and public banks are either operating or developing a private closed-accounting blockchain. There are also hybrid open- or closed-accounting blockchains, which are a type of *public* blockchain that can have a *private* space in their interaction architecture. They can choose to operate on an open-accounting mining system, or they can determine a priori who may account for their transactions, thus choosing to draw on a closed-accounting system.

Public open-accounting blockchains are *not* public in terms of the ownership of their means and devices of production and maintenance. A public open-accounting blockchain, such as that of Ethereum or Bitcoin, can be developed and proposed to the public by a corporation, an individual, a political party, or even a nation-state. There is no point at which one *possesses* a blockchain for they cannot be "owned" like a piece of land or a webpage. In reality, they are *networks* of claims that distribute ownership *rights* among the *actors* that use them; in other words, they are actor-network platforms incorporating agency into digital frameworks. These private or public networks create the possibility of attaching *nondigital* value to the *digital* representations of owning the right to move data. In any blockchain, anyone may hold the right to move data, but in a public blockchain, the protocol cannot block anyone, whereas in a private blockchain, the protocol can prevent anyone from pursuing this right.

Approaching blockchains as actor-network digital platforms that render possible the valuation and transfer of the rights to move data privately provides social researchers with the theoretical capacity to describe and analyze the rich universe of blockchains without imagining them as rigid devices or monolithic infrastructures that do (or do not do) things just because of their mere existence. In this way, it becomes possible to observe under which conditions and how they produce disintermediation and reintermediations, whether and how they can compete with and replace the functions of banks and states, how they both empower and limit individual and collective economic action, and, finally, whether they hold any revolutionary or reformatory potential at all.

## CONCLUSION

Empirically studying the evolution of blockchain infrastructure and the white papers of the one hundred most valuable cryptocurrencies, this chapter has proposed a three-tiered evolution of four types of blockchain architecture, all bringing together the sociotechnical infrastructure of this novel digital ledger technology. We saw that the categorical transformations blockchain infrastructure has undergone in the first decade of its existence require social researchers to attend to its dynamic evolution in studying the social and economic consequences of blockchain technology. Value-exchange blockchains, like that of Bitcoin, are simple, slow, and yet effective platforms that make it possible to imagine and transfer value in novel ways. Contract-exchange blockchains enable users to exchange simple computer programs that can operate as contracts, thus making it possible to build new value- or contract-exchange platforms within one blockchain.

Third-generation blockchains allow for the building of interchain operability with off-chain data flowing in them. This possibility permits blockchain architectures to operate as markets—not only registering individual transactions but also bringing together dynamic encounters of supply and demand, as long as the underlying commodity can be represented digitally. Furthermore, these third-generation blockchains make it possible to construct relational bridges between blockchains that operate on different protocols, opening a way to build interchains. Drawing on this analysis, we can conclude the following: First, it is impossible to make universal and categorical statements about how blockchain technology works, since there is no single architecture that can be located and evaluated. Second, blockchains' dynamic evolution poses a challenge for social scientists, as they have the potential to revise and reform many aspects of contemporary economization relations.

Taking on such a challenge requires critical attention to the types of blockchain architectures that stand on general block-chain infrastructure. Proposing an actor-based taxonomy, this chapter has demonstrated that blockchains are created by two types of actors: transactioners and accountants. Their agency, however, is structured in reference to the specific architecture of the particular blockchain in question. Open-accounting blockchains allow every accountant to perform mining at will as long as they have the necessary devices, such as ASICs. Closed-accounting blockchains can choose which actor can perform accounting and to what degree. This option introduces a more centralized blockchain operation by increasing the speed of transaction registration in the chain.

Approaching blockchains from the vantage point of transactioners, the chapter has observed two types of architecture: First, public blockchains allow anyone to securely transfer private data, the movement of which represents a kind of value. One does not have to be registered, accepted, recognized, or granted permission to become a transactioner in such a sociotechnical architecture. Second, private blockchains require permission or acceptance to become a transactioner in their architecture. These permits can be given to a consortium or an individual—in either case, this renders the blockchain a private one.

This chapter has defined blockchains as actor-network plat-forms that facilitate the imagining and transfer of economic value by digitally representing it as a right to move data securely. In practice, blockchain infrastructure constitutes a *network* of claims that provides actors with the devices and competencies necessary to transfer ownership *rights* among each other. Yet no one can own this platform of rights, like a piece of land or a webpage, for once "owned," the blockchain cannot operate as an infrastructure, even if it is a private blockchain. The various types of blockchain architecture are supported and surrounded by formalized digital exchanges that make it possible to exchange value off-chain and then have it registered on-chain.

This book aims to stimulate more future research concerning the sociotechnical universe and implications of blockchain infrastructure. It presents an actor-based taxonomy of the blockchain architectures that facilitate the exchange of data monies, or rights to send fixed and nonreplicable data, using a public ledger that both addresses the double-spending problem and makes it impossible to reverse transactions. These data monies are different from digitally represented fiat currencies and other payment systems because they minted, accounted for, and controlled without the authority of a bank, state, or corporation. They are made by monetizing the right to send data over the transparent accounting system of blockchains. If we do not recognize this historically novel money-making technology, it becomes impossible to make sense of cryptocurrency markets and economies, let alone regulate them.

This chapter's analysis, however, is limited in the sense that it does not say much about the practical working of the thousands of cryptocurrency exchange markets created in part thanks to the seemingly disintermediating blockchains. We still do not know how these markets relate to and configure blockchain architectures or how they work and interact with each other. We still know very little about the social world of digital economic markets and their prices, power asymmetries, and valuation processes. We address these concerns in the next chapter.

# 3

## UNDERSTANDING CRYPTOCURRENCY EXCHANGE PLATFORMS AND MARKETS

**A** curious double movement marked the first decade of the twenty-first century. As markets collapsed with an extraordinary velocity, we witnessed the simultaneous emergence of the most varied monies and the most rapidly emerging markets in history. In the decade following the 2007–2008 financial breakdown, 30,677 new cryptocurrency markets popped up across the world. As of November 2021, more than ten thousand data monies were exchanged around the clock, under the digital roof of 339 centralized exchange platforms. These platforms have no closing or opening time and enjoy an overall market capitalization that is larger than the GNP of 90 percent of the countries in the world. This marks an unprecedented expansion of markets in recent economic history. There are also hundreds of *decentralized* data money exchanges with thousands of markets working in them, with no central body to coordinate their trades other than their algorithms. According to one industry estimate, the aggregate monthly trading volume of these exchanges reached \$18.7 billion as of August 2020.[1]

These two clusters of exchanges are bridged by anonymous digital wallets. All organized exchanges accept fiat currencies. One buys data money with paper money. Imagine one buys 1

Ethereum (ETH) with their dollars. They can keep it in the centralized exchange or "withdraw" it, putting it in their digital wallet. Then they can send this same amount to a decentralized exchange such as Uniswap because they almost never use fiat currency. Such possibilities complicate regulatory practices and make it very challenging to tax income if one does it only with sovereign fiat currency.

As these new markets and institutions began to dot the global digital landscape, early approaches to cryptocurrencies and their blockchains gravitated toward mobilizing a discourse of revolution, a clear rupture from the past, a fundamentally new and usually better economic future that does not need formal institutions. This discussion of cryptocurrencies was rupture talk, a style of popular and scientific thought in need of imagining a big rupture from the past—as Gabrielle Hecht would call it.[2]

Labeled a "masterpiece" by the free-market radical Hernando de Soto, *Blockchain Revolution*, a popular book on cryptocurrencies by Dan and Alex Tapscott, announced the blockchain revolution to the world. For the authors, blockchains provide "the new digital economy" with optimal solutions that address problems of trust without the need for intermediaries such as formal markets, accounting institutions, and states.[3] Such rupture talk has attempted to mobilize public sentiment about data monies' advantages and necessity. There also exist equally popular negative sentiments about cryptocurrencies. One has called Bitcoin "a greater fool's gold."[4] For Warren Buffet, it is an illusion attracting charlatans.[5]

Academic literature has taken yet another path. Social studies of cryptocurrencies and their blockchains have shown that these currencies display characteristics that align with the previous understanding of money as process, produced and maintained by social relations amid political institutions.[6] Making visible the exaggerated notion of economic rupture, researchers have demonstrated the political qualities of "trustless" blockchains, things designed to be extrapolitical in essence;[7] the oligopolistic tendencies of mining pools;[8] the mushrooming of new institutions around cryptocurrencies;[9] and the ways blockchain communities build social institutions and networks to make them active in the first place.[10]

Researchers drawing on microeconomic assumptions have also seen a continuity and therefore no need to invent original ways of approaching this new type of money. Many of them have studied cryptocurrency trading,[11] financial assetization and pricing,[12] the comparative hedging potential of crypto assets,[13] pricing volatility,[14] trading rules and regulations,[15] derivative cryptocurrency markets,[16] the evolution of crypto markets,[17] and the price discovery of spot crypto assets with reference to their future value.[18]

Such a burgeoning literature, in part made possible by the abundance of data concerning data monies and the ease of finding them, has emerged with an ironic twist. Although it is common knowledge that price manipulations and wash trading are rampant in these markets, many researchers have not shied away from drawing on data collected by a handful of webpages that do not filter out wash trading.[19] A great majority of papers written on data money markets and their prices are based on historical market price data from CoinMarketCap.com, the most popular market information website for data monies. Yet the Blockchain Transparency Institute (BTI) has found that many of these webpages have been hiding the extent of wash trading in data money exchanges. It has shown that, until 2018, "at least 7 of the top 10 exchanges engag[ed] in excessive wash trading."[20]

Even though such manipulative practices are now factored out,[21] there is further evidence that the nature of market prices' realization on the ground should be studied, not taken for granted as mere data. Researchers who draw on posted prices to understand markets operate on the assumption that there is no essential difference between data monies and pork bellies when it comes to studying their markets. Both are things that people want, with their utilities subjectively defined. As a result, their prices can be analyzed to make sense of their markets.

A heterodox literature informed by sociotechnical market research has already demonstrated the problems with approaching markets by simply looking at their prices. Social studies of price, worth, and value have made visible the sociopolitical and cultural context in which monetary value is attached to things.[22] They have shown that pricing is an instrument of market power and that it should not be taken for granted as a mere signal or as neutral data to be used to analyze the very market that it makes.[23] Seemingly neutral formulas for "calculating" prices have always been inversion tools, representing the power of the market actors who write those formulas more than displaying the neutrality of the market price itself.[24] Now an entire strand of research, centered around the journal *Valuation Studies*, focuses on the ways in which things are valued on the ground, moving beyond the one-dimensional framework of price and the limited context of economic markets.

The need to move beyond prices in making sense of markets has been further underlined by a variety of sociotechnical approaches that call for a more dynamic and multivariable study of markets. Not only market prices but also trading infrastructures,[25] the very nature of the commodities,[26] the legal context,[27] metrological systems of measurement,[28] social and political organizations of market actors,[29] and myriad discourses and technoscientific information have been proven to contribute to the creation and arrangement of the constituents that make up marketization processes on the ground.[30] These are not processes that emerge *before* the market, giving it a condition of possibility. On the contrary, they *constitute* concrete market making, and they are *endogenous* to working markets rather than exogenous, as an external scaffold encircling the real thing.

Despite such a glasnost in market research, I argue that cryptocurrency markets present a structural and fundamental challenge to the study of contemporary marketization. These markets operate on digital platforms that go beyond marketization that facilitates exchange as the main activity. It is not only market objects that are supplied and demanded but also their very markets. Furthermore, frequently defining themselves as exchange platforms, these new markets organize their economization infrastructure to function simultaneously as digital *mints* that make data monies, *banks* that lend money for trading and charge various forms of interest, *vaults* and *security institutions* that present their clients with safe deposit locations, *insurance agents* that sell insurance against digital theft, *data centers* that sell and process information, *clearinghouses* that facilitate various transactions, *accounting agencies* that bring together double-entry bookkeeping with blockchain accounting, and, in a few cases, even as *courthouses* that run arbitration cases.[31] Coinbase, one of the largest cryptocurrency exchanges in the world, with 35 million users in more than one hundred countries, describes itself as "a wallet, an exchange, and a set of tools for merchants, all built on the same platform."[32]

It is true that almost all exchanges in the world have an ancillary business structure, such as information marketing, built around their primary objective of facilitating trade. However, for most of the cryptocurrency exchange platforms, nontrading activities are not ancillary; rather, they are primary economic engagements to the extent that their economic universe requires more full-time employees engaged in nontrading than in trading functions. Moreover, these employees' work is conducted in multiple places and in the various economic processes of the exchange platform.

What, then, is an economic platform? How do we describe cryptocurrency exchange platforms that have more functions now than being a mere trading place? Historically speaking, economic platformization started in the commodities themselves, not in the infrastructures or processes of their production or exchange. The earliest work on platforms emerged in the literature on industrial organization, focusing on the qualities of industrial commodities that can be redesigned and remarketed from a new perspective.[33] Describing the "architecture of the product" and not the ground on which its production was carried out, these early studies illustrated the way in which "platform products" drew on a modular manufacturing principle that brought together various core and ancillary components. Sony's Walkman was among those platform products whose parts lent themselves to use in other platform products.[34] They were designed with components that could be used by a variety of actors for a diversity of purposes. It is this literature that first considered computers and network services as platforms—but always from the vantage point of a product.

With the new century came the effort to digitize everything, including products and the networks of their production and exchange. For example, IBM's innovative product-planning strategy was based not on curbing competition but instead on inducing cooperation with other companies by encouraging the use of non-IBM elements on IBM "platforms."[35] Following the public discussion of the unprecedented experiences of IBM, we witnessed the emergence of economic platform research as scholars from management studies, economics, law, and their related disciplines turned their attention from industrial products to digital platforms.

Bernard Caillaud and Bruno Julien were the pioneers who introduced a shift in the use of the term *platform*: instead of a characteristic of the product, it became an architecture that served as an intermediary ground where products and services were exchanged.[36] Seeing economic platforms such as Amazon as "intermediation markets," they identified the network effects of platforms without calling them platforms. Their choice was the term *cybermediaries*. It was not adopted. Julian Wright, however, considered economic platforms that entail exchange relations to be *markets* that "involve two distinct types of users, each of whom obtains value from interacting with users of the opposite type. In these markets, platforms cater to both types of users in a way that allows them to influence the extent to which cross-user externalities are internalized."[37] Jean-Charles Rochet and Jean Tirole also approached exchange platforms as markets and proposed a model of platform competition with two-sided markets.[38] For them, "a market with network externalities is a two-sided market if platforms can effectively cross-subsidize between different categories of end users that are parties to a transaction."[39]

Enlarging the scope of analysis from market exchange to all other platforms, from barter to sharing, researchers and platform designers have also approached platforms as a *technology* of intermediation between different economic actors,[40] as coordination *devices* deployed in network markets with effects,[41] and as multisided digital *frameworks* that shape the terms on which participants interact with one another.[42] Drawing on these approaches, researchers have developed theoretical tests to identify the two-sided nature of markets as economic platforms.[43]

An influential OECD symposium that brought together expert delegations from twenty countries reached a consensus about seeing platforms as *firms* that operate two-sided markets with three elements: (1) two kinds of economic actors who rely on the platform to receive or send whatever they demand or supply, (2) indirect network externalities that arise from this economic relationship, and (3) a nonneutral price structure determined by the platform owner.[44]

Yet such a proliferation of research concerning platforms masks an interesting irony. Instead of identifying the historical specificity and empirical novelty of exchange platforms, this emergent literature has chosen to flatten the rich universe of economic platforms. It does so by seeing them as mere markets and thus giving a second life to an already shallow and empirically unfounded neoclassical notion of the market, this time in the study of economic platforms as two- or multisided markets.

This chapter argues that it is radically limited to see platforms as mere markets, let alone ones that are two- or multisided. The multipurpose and dynamic universe of platforms exceeds marketization relations and mobilizes a series of business opportunities that can best be understood as *stack economization*, which not only entails marketization but also makes it possible to move beyond it in pursuing other modes of economization within a single frame from barter to redistribution, from data valuation to money making. The chapter thus draws on and expands the research program on economization and marketization.[45] *Stack* is a term that computer science has borrowed from the tangible world of kitchens. Referring to the stacking of data layers vertically, like plates resting one on top of the other, it describes how multiple layers of representations—in this instance, data—are arranged in relation to each other. In this way, one layer supplies an ancillary structure for another to stand upon while at the same time building a coherent framework of interoperation.

Economization refers to "the assembly and qualification of actions, devices and analytical/practical descriptions as 'economic' by social scientists and market actors."[46] Calling for a move from a study of "the economy" as a mature, systemic object that claims to be independent of its qualifications, economization adherents have found the imagining of "the economy" itself in the study of economization processes. These processes incorporate various modalities from exchange and production, barter and gift, and their hybrids, all taking place in association with certain socio-technical arrangements.

Marketization as a mode of economization refers to the processes that (1) organize the trading of objects of exchange; (2) arrange constituents that deploy the rules, devices, infrastructures, and representations, as well as the competencies and skills embodied in economic actors; and (3) construct a space of power struggles.[47] Associated with actor-network theory, such a definition, instead of being a theory of markets, presents itself as an approach.[48]

This chapter argues that the marketization approach cannot account for contemporary organized cryptocurrency exchanges. This is because an empirical analysis of these exchanges and their operations and an ethnographic study of one the largest market clusters suggest that only part of economic practices taking place in these markets can be captured by the concept of marketization. These exchanges engage in economic practices that exceed the marketization practices defined earlier. How do we address this perplexing situation of new "markets" that go beyond being markets?

One exciting option is to look at platformization as stacking. Benjamin Bratton's work on the historical specificity of stacked economic relations has made it possible to imagine a way to introduce computer science's technical term *stack* into social theory in an innovative way. For Bratton, a new sociodigital geography is emerging, with new possibilities for economic and political engagement. Calling this new megastructure "The Stack," he has theorized the *place* of interaction instead of the *process* of encounter itself and has argued that this megastructure is also a platform.[49] He defines The Stack as a "planetary-scale computing system" and "a mega-architecture for how we divide up the world into sovereign spaces," "informed by the multilayered structure of software protocol stacks in which network technologies operate within a modular and interdependent vertical order."[50]

This spatial approach is theoretically similar to equating an exchange relationship with its building, the geography where it happens. Social geographical approaches to economic relations have many advantages, and Bratton's sociodigital rendering of the stack has informed both our understanding of the geographies of platformization and our potential to imagine interventions to contain their negative consequences. However, my empirical research on cryptocurrency exchanges suggests that what is being stacked is not a *place or geography* of encounter but a *relationship* of economization. Furthermore, in the platforms I studied, I did not observe any spatial formation in their economization relations that occurs in a unitary place or constitutes a larger reality that one can describe as "The Stack." Much like economists identify "The Economy" as the totality of everything economic and use various performative interventions to design it and make it happen, Bratton objectifies stacked economic relations by approaching fluid and nonsystemic socioeconomic processes as if they had a systemic and objective unitary framework, infrastructure, or place. Such a perspective is misleading from a scientific point of view, even though productive from a performative and political perspective. Bratton aims at doing both—and in an exciting way.

Avoiding objectifying tendencies to see platformization as "The Stack," this book shows that cryptocurrency exchange platforms entail the building of sociodigital spaces, the designing of instruments, and the imagining of new digital materialities that make possible stack economization. Stack economization as a concept is a *research tool* that I propose to use to study the rich universe of stacked relations, not to explain the totality of their practices or the nature of their host geography.

This chapter's research draws on four empirical engagements with cryptocurrency markets. First, I carried out fieldwork in a centralized cryptocurrency exchange I call X Exchange, and I also visited a variety of other exchanges. None of these platforms that claim to build trust via blockchains gave me permission to use their real names.

Second, I carried out unrecorded and recorded interviews with seventy-four persons working in or with those exchanges. Only two gave me permission to record their interviews. (Usually, I do not record interviews with a tape or digital recorder in any case.) Previously working with working-class and poor farmer communities, I had come to realize, along with many other ethnographers, that a recorder changes the voice and perspective of the recorded. Yet I had expected a more liberal and relaxed attitude about sound recording among the young, university-educated informants, many of whom hold a graduate degree. In the end, I used my high-end transcription software only twice. I took all my notes in my fieldwork notebook and typed my field notes into my computer, anonymizing the names of the people I interviewed.

Third, I studied the workings of 339 exchanges that operate more than 22,707 markets. I realized that 88 of these exchanges were small and operated on very limited trading pairs of data monies. The 251 most active exchanges had terms of service that defined their operation and objectives. Yet, as Ori Schwarz has argued in the case of Facebook, these terms-of-use documents not only describe the conditions for using platforms but also replace the contractual terms with "quasi-constitutional governing documents."[51] I closely studied the twenty most valuable exchanges' terms of service and interviewed a few of their writers, and I skimmed through the rest; however, I carried out a computational text analysis of all 251 terms-of-service documents, which cover more than 99.99 percent of the cryptocurrency exchange volume in the world.[52]

Fourth, I carried out participant observation as a user of various exchanges. When I traded, I was usually limited by the minimum tradable amount that each exchange imposed on users. My buying and selling of data monies did not exceed a total of $100 worth of cryptocurrencies at any given time during the research period, and I never owned any data money for more than a week or with a value exceeding $100. I am trained in commodity futures and options trading and needed little time to figure out infrastructures of futures and spots in cryptos; regardless, despite my formal training in trading, I was quite perplexed when trying to make sense of these dynamic platforms.

The chapter opens with a microscopic look at X Exchange, one of the larger and more successful platforms in terms of mobilizing stack economization. Here we see how its employees— from information scientists to security analysts, from marketing specialists to doormen—understand the large world of this singular exchange. I discuss their priorities, the ways in which these exchange platforms understand the work they carry out, the worlds they occupy, and the actors they recognize. Following this microscopic approach, we step back and take a general look at the larger universe of exchange markets in the world, analyzing not only how these exchanges work and relate to each other but also how their actors imagine a future of hyperdigitalized economies.

Centralized data-money markets are the exclusive focus of this chapter. There are many decentralized data money exchanges in the world, enabling only data monies to be traded (no fiat currency can be used in them) without an institution operating as a custodial intermediary. Despite their decentralized nature, however, they also display centralized market consolidation: the top two of these exchanges, Uniswap and Curve Finance, dominated more than 70 percent of the entire decentralized data money landscape in September 2020.

I chose not to include these decentralized exchanges in this book's analysis for two reasons: First, when I started my research in 2018, they were still in the making, displaying a minuscule trading volume when compared to centralized exchanges. Second, although they also call themselves platforms in their white papers, their platform qualities, objectives, and offered services are limited when compared to those of centralized exchanges. Yet I believe that those who study markets and platforms have much to learn from this nascent development, which has already forged new forms of pricing prostheses in data money markets, such as gas auctions and flash lending. These decentralized exchanges also foster hybridity by proposing that their relationships take on centralized forms, a novelty we have yet to discover.

## INSIDE X EXCHANGE

Despite their relentless claim to be transparent, "free markets" deny entrance to those who want to study them from within. Having carried out fieldwork in a variety of spot and futures markets in the United States, Egypt, and Turkey, I knew that it would be difficult to be accepted as an ethnographer in any cryptocurrency market. Any sociologist or anthropologist who studies markets knows that markets prefer to be looked at from outside and only through the data they produce.

Data money markets have been the most difficult markets to study for me. I have developed friendships and acquaintances in various trading circles over the last two decades as I have studied commodity and sustainable energy markets; yet it took nine months of searching and corresponding to be accepted into a cryptocurrency exchange to observe and interview its employees. My trader network did not work. No one knew "those" people among commodity traders, according to an old friend who now serves as the CEO of one of the world's top-ten commodity trading companies. For him, "Bitcoin people were trading things that did not exist." I asked him whether trading cotton that will exist in the future entailed trading things that did not exist. He smiled and changed the topic.

Teaching cryptocurrencies helped. A student had told me that he wanted to take my class because his best friend was "totally into Bitcoin." It turned out that his friend wanted to meet me and audit a lecture. Following his visit, we met over coffee, and I asked him whether I could visit the cryptocurrency exchange for which he worked. He reached out to his supervisor, who then reached out to their manager, who wrote to Compliance, and Compliance sent me an email with a contract attached. I reached for my pen to sign it. After having been denied access by thirteen exchanges, the fourteenth accepted me into its global headquarters following an arduous contractual process that took more than two months. I could not use the exchange name or take photographs, and I had to be accompanied by a human relations (HR) representative during my fieldwork, which had to be "short."

I had already started to learn about these exchanges before being admitted to one of them. I accepted, signed the agreement, and entered—at least in theory and on paper. In order to actually enter the building, my picture was taken twice—first downstairs at the reception desk and then just before entering the offices on the upper floors. As I waited for someone to pick me up at the entrance downstairs, I asked the receptionist why he thought there was such tight security. He had seen my university ID card and told me that he loved the progressive school where I taught and that his daughter had studied there. In part drawing on this newfound affinity, he whispered: "Bitcoin people do not trust anyone, but it's good for our business."

He was talking about a new establishment that was proud to operate "trustless" systems of exchange and accounting, without necessarily trusting the people around them. After being profiled one last time, I was taken to an elevator by an office assistant, and then my host handed me over to the HR representative, who took me to the front door of the exchange. There I had to sign another digital contract on a tablet. The employees I encountered were kind and friendly and agreed to give me a copy of the contracts that I had signed. To my surprise, as I wrote my field notes at night, I figured out that these contracts did *not* have any clause about taking photographs. Needless to say, I had not had time to read them as I entered. They were more liberal than their signatories interpreted. It was the HR representative who had politely asked me to keep my cellular phone in my pocket, not the contract.

There were around two hundred mostly young employees scattered across multiple floors. The exchange looked like an endless train of cubicles and did not have a particular appearance or interior design that could identify it as a cryptocurrency exchange. Perhaps the only detail that could remind someone of the office's identity was tangible: printed photographs of the logo of X-Coin (the pseudonym I use for the data money that X Exchange makes with the help of its private closed-accounting blockchain). Similar to many other technology companies, this one offered free coffee, cookies, and lunch at almost all times. One quiet room was designated for reading and research, with an expensive-looking armchair and a designer lamp next to it. In that room, there was a reproduction of a Monet painting on the wall and no poster or sign of any cryptocurrency. One of my informants referred to it as "the empty room": "No one really goes there. Who would like to read at work?"

Unlike others who study data money communities, I did not come across many people with dreams of utopias involving blockchains. The employees were quite unattached to their job, although a number of informants mentioned "an excitement about Bitcoin" as the first reason for looking for a job in the data money sector. "We are running an exchange platform, just like any other market," a coder with an MBA said. When I questioned his "everything is the same" approach to the historical digitalization of everything and asked him whether there was no change at all, he drew a Venn diagram with two intersecting circles on the yellow legal pad he was carrying. Pointing at their intersection with his index finger, he said, "This is new." I saw many people carrying pads and notebooks, in addition to laptops and tablets, as they walked around the enormous open office space of the exchange.

I had expected the exchange to be filled with computers from floor to ceiling and employees in very casual dress; yet it was visually dominated by windows (tangible ones with glass), desks, and human bodies, dressed mostly in formal business attire. Women, as well as people of color, were a significant minority. Although there were many computers with multiple screens attached to single desktops, they disappeared within this huge blue- and black-dominated hall that smelled of coffee, carpeting, and air-conditioning. As I continued to observe the place and interview its employees, I began to realize that "the place" was a mere car in a train. I was in the locomotive pulling the entire global operation. There were at least five other, smaller offices around the world—data centers in the United States, Europe, and Asia. There were coders working all around the world, in either their offices or their homes, from Mumbai to Sao Paulo; a digital security subcontractor in Switzerland; and designers in London and New York City who attached highly edited pictures and photographs to invisible codes for marketing purposes.

I completed my fieldwork in March 2020, just before COVID-19 brought human bodies to a standstill, redistributing this already globally scattered business operation. I continued to interact with the people I had met in the exchange during the pandemic. (I was not allowed to reach out to them without the HR representative on board, but there was nothing in the agreement to prevent me from replying to them if they contacted me.) I made sure that they had my digital card so that I could also have their contact information. Unlike paper business cards, electronic cards help researchers receive contact information as one passes them to others.

I was in their workplace, but half of the employees I wanted to interview talked to me via a secure conference call in a meeting room with giant screens. Surprisingly enough, their technology did not work for the first fifteen minutes, pixelating the visuals and garbling the audio, so people called each other on cell phones, as usually happens when connections do not work. Finally, things began to run properly as people jiggled cables and pushed buttons. My interviews centered on the nature of money, the workings of data money markets, and the economic practices that the interviewees mobilized.

For many of them, a cryptocurrency was "digital cash," "electronic money," "money that lives in a computer," or "a store of value with no central authority." Yet when I asked them about the nature of the data money their exchange was making, they believed that it was legally centralized and drew on traditional double-entry bookkeeping. One accountant in charge of blockchain accounting defined the money they were offering as a "common language to describe value":

> AUTHOR: What do you mean by language and value? What is in a cryptocurrency?
>
> ACCOUNTANT: It's like all other values. A social agreement. Not very different from other monies. We make this one with data. But blockchain does the accounting.
>
> AUTHOR: But your money is accounted differently, in your own books.
>
> ACCOUNTANT: Yes, if you want to withdraw your Bitcoin, then we register it on Bitcoin blockchain. If you keep it here, it is technically ours.
>
> AUTHOR: So you have a twin accounting system.
>
> ACCOUNTANT: Correct. . . . We are not a money market only. We're a platform. Here we make money to exchange it. In the real world, monies are made to buy things. We make cryptocurrencies to make money.

His point about accounting has been the case with almost all data money exchange platforms. When one buys a Bitcoin and keeps it in the exchange's books, one does not "get" it. To "withdraw" it, as exchanges call it, using a banking term, one needs to pay a fee, another source of income for these platforms. These platforms are not mere marketization places, as the previous informant has summarized. They are places that make monies, offer accounting systems and services, and conduct many other economization practices.

> THE AUTHOR: But fiat monies are bought and sold for making money too. How is yours different?
>
> ACCOUNTANT: Yes. Then we're not very different either, I guess.

They were different and, at the same time, not different. For the vice-president of the company, who had been the second person hired by the exchange, cryptocurrency is the only money that "people can control. Dollars and euros are controlled by states and the rich. Bitcoin does not need a central agency."

> THE AUTHOR: You run a centralized exchange here, don't you?
>
> VICE-PRESIDENT: But we don't make Bitcoin. We operate a platform. It brings sellers and buyers together. We help people trade monies.
>
> THE AUTHOR: But the only way to get a Bitcoin without buying it is mining, now only open to rich investors. Where is the "people" here?
>
> VICE-PRESIDENT: They are here in our platform. They can buy it here. They don't have to mine it if they don't have money to invest in mining.

Such a shift from "people" to "platform" emerged frequently during my interviews. The conversation would start with the terms *trustless, no intermediary, stateless,* and *decentralized* and end with the explosion of new intermediaries, the requirements that exchanges report crypto assets to the states, and the institutional linking of fiat and data monies.

One informant compared oil and Bitcoin to explain what they do at X Exchange:

> Oil is money too. It runs through pipes. When there is an accident, it spills. Our money runs through cables, is stored and secured. In reality, it is a piece of data. You send it, you receive it. It's unique, can't be double-spent or replicated. One may think it's the same gas wherever you buy it from. It's not. I fill my car's tank from, say, Shell, but not from a gas station with a strange name. I trust Shell oil. It's the same. People trust us in buying their Bitcoin, Ether has gas, too, you know. [He laughs.] You buy your Bitcoin from us, you sleep well at night. It's our Bitcoin, not *a* Bitcoin. That's why you pay us money to keep it here.

This self-description draws on two important conclusions. First, unlike many, he was not employing digital/material rupture talk but instead alluding to the digital/material infrastructure that cryptocurrency exchanges build and on which they operate. Second, he made visible the relationship between platforms and markets. In markets, one is more concerned about the quality of the product; by contrast, on a platform, one is more concerned about the quality of the platform from which one buys the product or service. Buyers choose platforms first and then the products. What is different is not data money but the platform that moves, keeps, and trades it.

THE AUTHOR: Why should I choose your platform but not the other?

INFORMANT: If you want to withdraw your Bitcoin or Ether, you get it faster from us because we pay more transaction fees compared to others. We're safe. Providing you with vault services, cold wallets, etc. If you want to trade in volumes larger than you

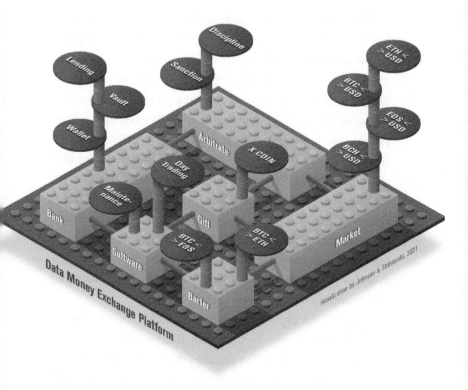

**FIGURE 3.1** The X Exchange platform as a stack and modular
economization process.

have, we lend you crypto money. It is not just a market. It is a
whole world here.

THE AUTHOR: What other things are done in this "whole world"?

INFORMANT: We have teams for everything: product development,
project management, software development, quality insurance,
infrastructure, customer support, compliance, research, admin,
office maintenance, cybersecurity, outside counsels, tens of third-
party vendors, design, HR—you know, like a regular company.

This "whole world" was indeed like a regular company, making and maintaining an exchange platform that brings together buyers and sellers. In all marketization relations, we observe five main practices, all of which can be located on the market side of data money exchanges: (1) pacifying goods, (2) marketizing agencies, (3) designing the exchange encounter, (4) realizing prices, and (5) managing trade politics.[53] In X Exchange, too, the employees control the overflows of the materiality of their exchange objects (pacifying goods); they build institutional agency capacity to facilitate trade (marketizing agencies); they design the modalities of encounter (designing the exchange encounter); they craft various ways to set prices and create pricing prostheses (realizing prices); and, finally, they manage the everyday politics of trade by a variety of instruments (managing trade politics).

However, the expression the "whole world" refers to the fact that X Exchange goes beyond marketization and introduces a new series of economization practices that we do not see in non-platform marketization. Furthermore, these practices were only a part of the general infrastructure on which the exchange was drawing. Since the entire system is data-dependent, it had to be based on a chain of data centers. When I asked where these were located, the HR representative interrupted me: I was not allowed to ask this question due to its sensitive nature. As I apologized and got ready to question its sensitivity, my informant said that the locations of the data centers were common knowledge, as they were posted on the exchange's website.

There is, of course, an entire universe of exchange platforms, many of them with an even higher trading volume and with more markets than X Exchange. To include them in the picture, we need to enlarge the scope of our analysis to take a general look at their operations and the relations they manage.

## GLOBAL DATA-MONEY MARKETS

When it emerged in 2008, Bitcoin was worthless in terms of dollars and remained valueless in terms of fiat currency until March 2010, in part as result of the absence of an intermediary to exchange it. In 2010, the first data money exchange market, the now defunct bitcoinmarket.com, emerged, and the value of Bitcoin began to pick up. It would exceed $20,000 in less than a decade.

The year 2018 marked the second turning point for data money markets in the world. Proving to be a big bang for cryptocurrencies, the emergence of the Ethereum blockchain that year had a structural impact on market emergence. As of 2019, 88 percent of the one hundred most valuable cryptocurrencies in terms of market capitalization were Ethereum-based. Of the 339 exchanges in the world, half emerged after Ethereum. The year 2018 also marked a jump in market expansion, since 36 percent of all data money markets emerged in that year alone (figure 3.2).

Where are these markets located? Singapore (36), the UK (25), South Korea (21), Estonia (17), Hong Kong (17), the United States (15), and Turkey (12) host 57 percent of the data money exchanges in the world, but China's emergent impositions on Hong Kong will most probably move the markets away from that city. The geographical location of these markets is important for legal reasons. Yet the geographical place where the *components* of these platforms operate is an entirely different question. As we have seen earlier, X Exchange drew on a multiplicity of locations around the world to maintain its platform. The legal place is only one of the locations in the sociodigital geography of platform production and maintenance. Furthermore, once one enters the platform, the "place" of interaction is another level in stack economization. This is why it would be problematic to approach these markets from the vantage point of space only;

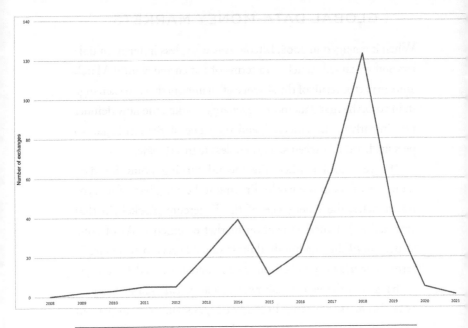

**FIGURE 3.2** Frequency of new exchanges emerging annually.

unlike many conventional exchanges, they show little pride in their physical buildings and even make a conscious effort to hide the offices where they are located.

The heart of any conventional market with pit trading is the pit. Traders often used this material physical space to describe how their markets work, usually by employing a narrative that belongs to Adam Smith rather than their own markets.[54] They would also take visitors or researchers around the building they inhabit, inviting them to associate their trade with the place where it happens. I believe this is in part the reason behind the problematic equating of the marketization process with the material infrastructures that facilitate it. In X Exchange (or any of the other 338 exchanges), there is no pit, no center, no building—in many, not even a headquarters—where one can see the moment of buying and selling. The employees of the exchange call their place a platform.

It is practically impossible to carry out conventional fieldwork in all of these platform exchanges and the larger universe they create because studying derived geographies such as the "global" is possible only by conducting research on their processes of derivation,[55] an approach I have used to study the making of global commodity markets and their prices.[56] With the help of computational text analysis, however, we can get a bird's-eye view of these thousands of markets by focusing on the terms of service that describe and analyze the world they create with their own words.

These cryptocurrency platforms, frequently presenting themselves as trustless systems, require their users to sign these terms-of-service contracts before giving them access. Our age seems to take Durkheim's observation on the noncontractual basis of contracts one step further: platform works stand on the contractual basis of trustless systems.

Referred to as *terms of service, terms of use, terms and conditions*, or simply *terms*, this long contract is required for the users of every exchange with a substantive trading volume. Of the 339 exchanges operating more than 22,707 markets as of July 7, 2020, 251 exchanges, representing 99.99 percent of all world trade in data monies, require users to sign such a contract. I chose to exclude the terms of the remaining 88 exchange platforms, as they represent 0.01 percent of world trade, a negligible trading volume that may also be associated with wash trading.

The 251 exchange platforms operate thousands of markets, based on data–paper money or data–data money exchanges. In other words, if a client buys 1 Bitcoin (BTC) from X Exchange by wiring it euros from their bank account, they are active in one market—that is, the BTC-EURO market—located only in X Exchange. A client can "shop" for other exchanges, for there are at least 250 more exchanges with a BTC-EURO market active around the clock.

As of July 7, 2020, these exchanges traded 5,695 data monies. Bringing together all terms of service for computational analysis produces a single document with almost 1.5 million words, which would fit on 3,232 U.S. legal-size pages. On average, a cryptocurrency exchange contract contains 5,754 words, or around half of the length of this chapter.

A close reading of the terms of use of the twenty exchanges with the largest monthly trading volume[57] and a computational text analysis of all 251 platforms' contracts open a limited yet general window into their workings. The twenty largest exchanges define themselves as a *platform* but also use other terms such as *marketplace, exchange platform, world,* and *ecosystem.* The top exchange in our list states:

> Binance refers to an ecosystem comprising Binance websites (whose domain names include but are not limited to https:// www.binance.com), mobile applications, clients, applets and other applications that are developed to offer Binance Services, and includes independently-operated platforms, websites and clients within the ecosystem (e.g. Binance's Open Platform, Binance Launchpad, Binance Labs, Binance Charity, Binance DEX, Binance X, JEX, Trust Wallet, and fiat gateways). In case of any inconsistency between relevant terms of use of the above platforms and the contents of these Terms, the respective applicable terms of such platforms shall prevail.[58]

Binance claims to be overseeing a multiple-platform operation or managing an "ecosystem" made up of websites. Yet for the purposes of this legal contract, the ecosystem itself is seen as one big platform that provides clients with services and presents a market as only one element.

Many of these exchange platforms ask for the user's residence and locate themselves in the national jurisdiction of that particular user (figure 3.3). They accept the boundaries of the user's nation-state as defining their operations, even for free accounts.

FIGURE 3.3 A cryptocurrency exchange platform's geographic boundaries.

The place is as important as the agency. These exchanges require the user of their services to be a human or a limited liability company hiring humans to trade on their behalf. Bots, spiders, automatic devices, algorithms, and digital-manual instruments meant to trade in or bypass platform infrastructure are not allowed.

Once users are accepted onto a data money exchange's platform, they can choose any of the services offered there. The buying and selling of data monies, either one for another or for fiat currencies, is a central function of these exchanges. They maintain completely digitalized order books, and by matching buy and sell orders according to a chosen algorithm, they facilitate trade much like any other commodity exchange. Unlike with cotton or barley, however, the "quality" of the data money bought is universally the same, although the security of holding onto and keeping it changes from platform to platform. As my informant from X Exchange said, their Bitcoin was "different" because their exchange was different.

Similar to commodity exchanges that use warehouse receipts to transfer ownership, crypto exchanges use digital representations of the ownership of data monies to transfer that ownership instead of transferring the data money itself. If a client buys cotton, no one ships cotton to the place where the client will open its bales. Rather, the client owns the receipt that represents the commodity. In crypto-exchange trading, when a client buys 1 BTC, the exchange registers that data money in the client's internal account and does not register it as belonging to that client on the Bitcoin blockchain. It remains a custodial asset within the exchange, and the exchange can use it for its own trading and money market purposes. If a client wants to take their data money and sell it in another exchange, they have to "withdraw" it from the exchange where they bought it and pay a withdrawal fee, which can be a substantial amount if this operation is repeated often. Depending on the exchange, it is not uncommon for the client to have to wait for a few days before they can have the data money registered under their name. Platforms prefer to keep data monies in their secure data centers, which are not connected to the internet, as they can use those data monies whenever they want. As long as they hold these data monies, stack economization on their platforms can be richer and more lucrative in terms of fees or prices for their services.

There are five types of fees charged by data money exchanges: the spot transaction fee, interest rate, futures transaction fee, deposit fee (which is usually zero), and withdrawal fee. Whenever a client moves data monies, the platform charges fees for moving data from one place to another. The more users move data, the more money and services move—and the more money the platform makes. In most of these platforms, there is a minimum amount of data money one has to keep, always represented in terms of fiat currency such as dollars or euros. The fees decrease as the account size increases. If a user chooses to buy a lump sum of data money, the price is negotiated outside the platform, and the data monies they buy are handled away from the order books unless the buyer and seller decide otherwise. Someone buying $20 million worth of Bitcoin would not buy it from X Exchange. The owners of X Exchange would arrange a special deal.

In addition to fees, exchanges impose an interest rate if a user chooses to borrow data money to trade it. There are two forms of borrowing. The first consists of an authorization to trade on margins—for example, ten times the user's account balance—as long as their position remains within a range defined by the exchange. Margin trading draws on data monies borrowed from a cryptocurrency exchange and assetizes them by means of a loan that is extended to the user from the same exchange, replicating any other margin trading practice in noncrypto markets. The amount one can lose in these margin trades cannot exceed the original data money one keeps as a custodial asset. The second way of borrowing is similar to contemporary banking, but this time the interest rate imposed is a percentage of the data money one borrows. This emergent form of borrowing, without a systemized and legal framework, may entail multiple data monies, including the one that the exchange itself produces.[59]

Almost all exchanges either issue their own monies or have plans to do so. X Exchange's X-Coin is not a successful data money. It is worth almost nothing in comparison to Bitcoin or dollars, and it is not used by third parties. But there are many other successful data monies minted by cryptocurrency exchanges, usually carrying the name of the exchange where they originate, such as Binance Coin, trading for around $30 as of September 2020. Issued on the Ethereum blockchain, Binance Coin enjoys special consideration on the Binance platform. If a client uses Binance Coin for their transactions, they pay less in fees when compared to those holding other data monies. Platforms offer special treatment not only to customers with a higher balance but also to customers who draw on the host platform's data monies, thus incentivizing the use of their own currencies. Those incentives, fees, other payment vehicles, and the previously mentioned services are all defined and explained in the rich world of the terms of service.

A computational text analysis of terms of services shows that the most frequently used words fall into three frequency categories (figure 3.4). The first category, with terms that are used more than 8,500 times, consists of *user, services, account,* and *information.* It should not be surprising to see such a distribution because these documents define the users of platforms and provide the information necessary to hold them accountable for the services that these exchanges monetize. The second group of terms, clustered around frequencies of 4,500–8,500, helps us better understand the focus of these exchange platforms. These terms are *digital, company, agreement, website, platform, service, transaction*, and *terms*, ordered from the least to the most cited within that range. This string of terms can even be read as a full sentence in itself. In a close reading of these texts, one sees very clearly how these digital companies ask their users for their agreement to log into a website for platform services that entail transactions.

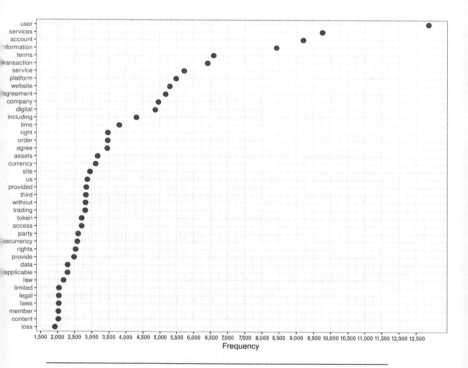

**FIGURE 3.4** Frequency of words used in terms-of-service agreements.

The final group of words, used between 1,500 and 4,500 times, includes *times, right, order, agree, assets, currency, site, trading, token, access, party, cryptocurrency, right, data, law, legal, member,* and *content.*[60] A four-topic modeling of these three sets of frequencies makes visible which four clusters of terms are used more frequently in association with each other. Topic modeling shows that these exchanges focus their institutional legal attention on actors, places, materialities, and, of course, regulation.

Defined as users, the actors have to be either humans or nonhuman but legally formed institutional entities such as companies. Users become members as soon as they sign the contract with the platform and begin to enjoy membership privileges.

Places identify geographies in terms of either states or platforms, apps, and sites as sociodigital spaces that harbor economic interaction. It is important to note that these platforms do not shift all economic activity from material to digital, as it is assumed by many. Rather, they hybridize economization relations by rematerializing and digitizing. Empirically speaking, data money platforms draw on rematerialized spaces of encounter and do not operate along a digital/material divide. Successful economic stacking relies on this dynamic hybridity.

The third topic model suggests that specific terms are gravitating around the forms of things to be exchanged: *(crypto) currency, right, data, content, token,* and *asset.* These exchanges draw on data materialities in organizing their economic universes. The money they mint or trade is data money whose exchange of ownership is made possible by transferring the right to send data privately in a public space. There are two kinds of materiality that are deployed in cryptocurrency exchanges. The first type is a *tangible materiality* associated with infrastructure works and networks of machines, such as cables, signal systems, antennas, and computer hardware.[61] Secondly, *intangible materialities* draw on materially observable orders that representational tools such as data or algorithms produce.[62] The terms of service I analyzed give much space to imagining and constructing a space in which to mobilize a process of entanglement and disentanglement among rights, data, and money. Monetizing the right to send data and then imagining and mobilizing a data money form depend on the simultaneous deployment of such tangible and intangible materialities. In order to ensure a successful transfer of these material things, such as data monies, exchanges construct a framework of meticulous and arduous regulation.

Finally, the last observable cluster of terms refers to the everyday practices of exchange and regulation, such as *trading*, *agreement*, *exchanging*, and *accounting*. These platforms see trading much like older and more traditional commodity exchanges that facilitate trade by exchanging specific representations of the ownership of commodities, not necessarily the commodities themselves. They represent the entire exchange relationship in a new world, this time made up of concepts, and regulate these concepts as they aim at moving digital materialities on the ground.[63]

These exchanges define themselves as intermediary institutions that *undermine* public open-accounting blockchains such as that of Bitcoin. Instead of registering the transfer of ownership of data monies on blockchains, these exchanges mobilize an in-house accounting system to keep track of ownership rights. They register data monies under a user's name only if that particular user decides to withdraw their assets from the exchange. Thus, legally speaking, these exchanges hold onto the assets they help people trade and present representations of transfer instead of transferring the ownership itself. Such an operation requires immense bureaucratic and centralized governance. Therefore, a development that is associated with "the Blockchain revolution," referring to *blockchains* at least ten times less than *platforms* and mostly in the context of *cryptocurrency withdrawal,* also makes visible how blockchains are overshadowed and undermined by the historical emergence of data money markets.

What evangelicals like the Tapscotts define as a revolution in the economic relations of money becomes a vehicle that maintains dollarization and conventional accounting for two reasons: First, the dollar has become the main asset that represents the comparative value of cryptocurrencies, thus opening new economic avenues for it to be deployed in trade relations. Second, by bypassing blockchains as distributed accounting systems and using the exchanges' own double-entry centralized and private bookkeeping, data money markets contribute to the undermining of public open-accounting blockchains like that of Bitcoin. As is seen in figure 3.5, which is based on a comparison of

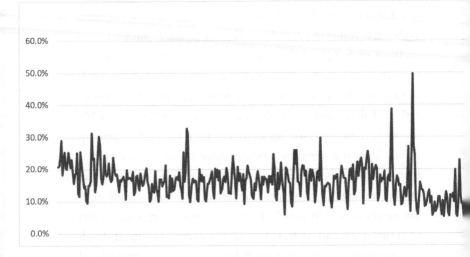

**FIGURE 3.5** Percentage of Bitcoin network transactions in 2018.

internally registered and blockchain-registered Bitcoin trades between January 23, 2018, and January 22, 2019, the percentage of Bitcoin transactions registered in the Bitcoin blockchain is declining. In the future, this percentage may become negligible, making blockchains a simple tool for the final confirmation of data money trades instead of *the* main mechanism of their distributed accounting.

The unsupervised frequencies of the terms within the terms-of-service documents show much, even though they have two limitations. First, one encounters an obvious list of terms. It should not be surprising to see *account, service, rights*, and *users* among the most frequently occurring terms. Second, these unsupervised frequencies do not give us a chance to control for a specific perspective in approaching the data. We can address this challenge by deploying a social sciences dictionary as a lens when we approach the same data and counting the appearance of social-scientific concepts that are used in terms-of-service agreements. With 1,800 entries supported by a comprehensive bibliography, Calhoun's *Dictionary of the Social Sciences* is the most helpful dictionary.[64]

Similar to the results of our unsupervised analysis of general terms, social-scientific concepts are clustered in three groups (figure 3.6). The most frequently used terms are *currency, rights, law, exchange*, and *market*. Used between 1,500 and 3,200 times, these are the central social-scientific concepts that these exchanges deploy to describe themselves and to govern the economic world they inhabit. The obvious frequency of these words, which pop up on virtually every page of these documents, attests to the fact that data monies are marketized by exchanging the right to send data among users, with exchange as the framework for organizing these relations.

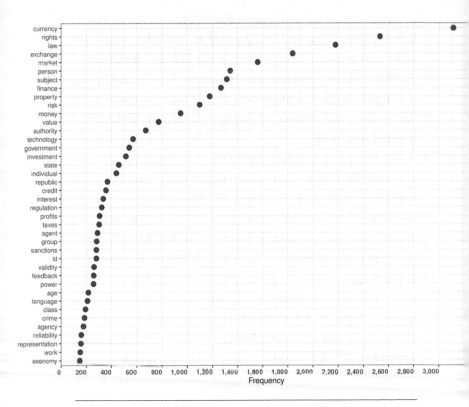

**FIGURE 3.6** Frequency of social-scientific concepts used in terms-of-service agreements.

What is more telling in this cluster is the absence of the two essential terms related to the emergence of these exchanges. A comparison of figures 3.4 and 3.6 makes this absence visible. *Platform*, the central concept that relates to everything that happens in a data money exchange, does not occur even as the least frequent term in figure 3.6 for it does not exist in one of the most popular social sciences dictionaries. If it was there, with a usage of 5,750, *platform* would be *the* most frequently used term, appearing over ten times more often than *blockchain* (538 times), the second crucial term that also does not appear in the social sciences dictionary.

In these terms of service, *platform* refers to the place where every exchange activity takes place. *Ecosystem* (330 times) is also used—but usually in preambles and never as a legal term to regulate these exchange platforms' relations with users. *Place, website, webpage,* and *marketplace* are also used to refer to the place of exchange activities, although less frequently, without legal entanglement, and as colloquially as these texts allow. It is safe to argue that *platform* is the term that these exchanges use to describe, show, and regulate their economic activities. However, much like in the context of other exchanges around the world, it would be erroneous and incomplete to either equate economization with the place where it occurs or accept how market architects describe themselves as *the* main description of exchange practices. This is because these descriptions are, among other things, simultaneous investments in making more money for these exchanges.

If *platform* refers to the place where the relevant economic practices take shape, we need to describe the practices that are peculiar and historically specific to the emergence of economic platforms such as data money exchanges. As is empirically clear and also can be seen in figure 3.1, platforms go beyond being mere markets that bring together supply and demand. This is not because markets cannot be defined only in reference to supply and demand, as a massive and heterodox literature has already shown, but because platforms make possible economic practices that go beyond marketization, such as money making (Binance Coin, X-Coin), infrastructure development (markets built within markets), banking (loan and interest rate servicing), accounting (double-entry bookkeeping and blockchain), barter (among various data monies), gifting (issuing gift data monies for new users), and many other, intersecting modalities of economization that are all stacked and deployed together on a platform. *Stack economization* describes the dynamism and multiplicity of economic practices that take place on platforms better than any other available concept. It refers to the stacked nature of the multiplicity of economization practices that either draw on or enable each other as architectures or infrastructures. The exchange (Binance) is infrastructural to a specific market (ETH-USD), which is infrastructural to futures in ETH, whose trading makes possible margin trading. Furthermore, depending on the user, the ground of activity can be an architecture or an infrastructure. For Electra Coin users, the Bitcoin blockchain is an infrastructure; for Electra wallet users, the Electra blockchain is infrastructural.

Stack economization does not *explain* how a data money exchange platform works. It defines platforms to provide a theoretical basis for understanding, registering, and analyzing the multiplicity of their specific economization processes. Seeing platforms as two- or multisided markets[65] or technologies[66] or megainfrastructural places fails to account for the dynamism and multiplicity of these economization practices.[67] These approaches choose to describe platforms based on the tools they use (technological tools), the limited practices they mobilize (trade), or the place they are located (the stack) and imagine an objective systemic unity in what they call "the platform." Platform is a process, not a bounded object.

Looking at the terms of service of data money markets from the perspective of social-scientific terms also makes visible how platform makers try to control overflows in such an economic universe. The second group of concepts, used between 400 and 1,500 times in these documents, consists of *person, subject, finance, property, risk, money, value,* and *authority.* These terms create a legal structure that governs data monies' transfer and valuation by controlling the risks associated with financial volatility, economic overflows, and fraud. Nonhumans, except for registered limited liability companies, and unauthorized algorithms are not permitted to be actors on these platforms. Without being a human subject, one cannot trade on these sociodigital platforms that are based in part on the values that data monies carry.

Finally, the terms that are used between 100 and 400 times render visible the remaining social-scientific concepts that frequently appear in the terms of service. Two terms that are central in both the four-topic modeling of unsupervised frequencies and this last group of social-scientific terms are *agency* and *representation*. These platforms make and/or trade data monies that depend on certain representational practices. But unlike with metal and paper monies, re-representing data money is very easy. One cannot produce a dime or a hundred-dollar bill without substantial investment; however, copying and pasting data is done easily and without much cost. Thanks to blockchains and cryptography, these digital representations can be individualized and are almost impossible to replicate. The data materiality of cryptocurrencies, then, constitutes a factor that enables new economic agents to imagine, produce, and exchange new monies. Paradoxically, and perhaps even in a contradictory fashion, data money exchanges undermine blockchains and cryptographic frameworks by replacing them with their own accounting systems and using public open-accounting blockchains only if users want to withdraw their monies from exchange platforms.

## CONCLUSION

Despite the frequent studies of cryptocurrency markets and data money prices, there is little literature on how these markets, organized under the umbrella of hundreds of exchanges, work on the ground. Emergent social studies of cryptocurrencies have shown that these monies do not represent a radical rupture from the past in terms of their social and political universe.[68] Yet there has been a tendency to bypass fieldwork in exchanges and research on market actors and instead to draw on anecdotal experiences or the theoretical premises of the very empirical developments under consideration. This propensity has been criticized for accepting the plans and motivations of actors as practices rather than beginning with empirical observation and analyzing how actors mobilize economization practices in the first place.[69] This chapter addressed this gap in that it has empirically analyzed global cryptocurrency markets and exchange platforms simultaneously from within and above by pursuing a two-tiered research strategy.

The first tier rested on ethnographic research at X Exchange and presented an introductory analysis of how a data money exchange platform works from within. I have described how exchange actors see what they do in their everyday practice. These "transparent" places that mobilize "trustless" systems do not trust scientists, as I was asked to sign a multiplicity of legal documents, had my movements monitored, was not permitted to photograph the offices, and had to have HR experts accompany me during my research. Still, one also has to consider that X Exchange has been one of the most respected exchanges in the world, never having been associated with wash trading or illegitimate economic practices. This very exchange is now helping to set the data money trading standards in the world.

A detailed look into the workings of X Exchange has shown us that market actors and designers do not operate along a digital/material divide. For them, data have a materiality that is distributed among tangible and intangible properties. Their job is to build new architectures by using or drawing on these materialities. Making data money counts among these practices. My ethnographical study enabled me to describe the everyday practices in a data money exchange, rendering visible the actors' own understanding of the exchange for which they work and which they make. This discussion has illustrated how exchanges go beyond marketization relations that draw on five general practices: pacifying goods, marketizing agencies, designing the exchange encounter, realizing prices, and managing trade politics. We observed all of these practices in X Exchange, but we also saw that the exchange goes beyond mere marketization and constitutes, as one X Exchange actor called it, "a whole world."

Enlarging the scope of analysis to include all other data money markets has required me to give up the analytical power of ethnography and interviews and to employ a computational analysis with a wider scope in order to take a brief look into these exchanges' "whole world." The first precondition to enter these economic places is to sign a legal document that frames the way in which exchanges see and describe what they do: the terms-of-service agreement. This chapter has focused on 251 exchanges, representing 99.99 percent of data money trading, by analyzing, among other things, their terms of service. A two-step computational text analysis of these documents' corpus facilitated a consideration of their priorities and definitions. As a first step, I looked at the unsupervised frequencies of all terms, whereas in the second step I employed a social-scientific lens so as to discover which social-scientific concepts are used the most.

Surprisingly, terms-of-service texts do not describe these markets as mere markets. Their preferred term is *platform*, one of the most frequently used words in the unsupervised frequency analysis (figure 3.4), although completely absent in the dictionary analysis (figure 3.6). This is in part because the social sciences are still working on making visible and understanding platforms. If *platform* was considered a social-scientific concept in the particular dictionary I used, it would be by far *the* most frequently used social-scientific concept in figure 3.6. These exchanges see themselves as platforms that present their users with a variety of products and services, such as trading, futures trading, decentralized market entry, vaulting, banking, infrastructure, data gathering and interpretation, security, and nonblockchain accounting. The multiplicity of these platform economic practices marks a historically specific and empirically observable economization modality, which I call stack economization. It can just as well be called platform economization or simply platformization.

This chapter has described platform works as stack economization processes. Drawing on an empirical study of data money platforms, it has demonstrated that the economic practices designed and deployed in data money exchanges entail a spectrum of unprecedented economization practices. Such multifunctionality is the result of the material opportunities that gave birth to the possibility of stacking economic relations in the sociodigital universe of data things. On these platforms, one can build one's own market infrastructure, borrow money to trade and buy a car, receive and give gifts, exchange dollars for Ethereum, buy or hire security services, subscribe to a trading algorithm, and, if necessary, even bypass the organized market if one is a special platform customer.

It is true that markets are never just markets. Conventional organized exchanges, such as spot and derivative commodity markets, also entail a multiplicity of functions. Yet their multifunctionality remains within marketization limits and never constitutes a domain of practice that engulfs the commodity exchange itself. On platforms such as those of data money exchanges, we observe a *categorical* multiplication of economization modes and their deployment, not a mere variation of marketization. In the entire world, there is no commodity market with its own mint.

Another reason why platforms cannot be seen as mere markets lies in the fact that with a market, one is more concerned about the quality and price of services and products. With a platform, however, one is concerned about the quality of the platform itself, where one engages in various economization activities from barter to gift giving, from production to exchange. Users chose platforms first, and only then come the rest of the economic practices.

As a term that first emerged in the industrial organization literature, *platform* was initially used to qualify a tangible product, not the processes of economic relations. With the proliferation of computers in economies, a multidisciplinary literature shifted the direction of research from platform things to platform economic relations. Interestingly, however, instead of historically specifying the dynamic sociotechnical universe of platforms, scholars have tended to objectify them with a static understanding of markets, technologies, and places.

One strand of research has described platforms as a new kind of market. For Rochet and Tirole,[70] the platform is a two-sided market that negotiates network externalities in specific ways. For others, the platform is a multisided *framework*,[71] a *technology* of matchmaking intermediation,[72] or a coordination *device* facilitating trades with certain new economic effects.[73] For yet other scholars, the platform draws on the use of data, algorithms, and computing as new tools of production[74] or even as a new capitalist accumulation form.[75] And, finally, the platform is viewed as a system, an economic system, or an ecosystem that qualifies basically everything happening within it.[76] In many other approaches, platforms are discussed as being simultaneously markets, ecosystems, and infrastructures with intersectional functionalities[77] or as being reprogrammable systems: "If you can program it, then it's a platform. If you can't, then it's not."[78]

My empirical research on data money markets has shown that the actors who make, use, and maintain data money exchanges describe them as platforms that incorporate technologies of intermediation in a digital/material space that they also call a market or an ecosystem. Most of social-scientific approaches are accurate in using the concepts also used by the actors of platform economization to describe their universe. However, considering platforms *only* as markets, technologies, systems, devices, infrastructures, frameworks, or places does not represent the ways in which actors mobilize, carry out, and maintain platform works in data money exchanges. If considered stack economization processes, however, the multifunctional and layered geography, devices, performativities, practices, agencies, and technologies of platforms can be better studied and also more thoroughly regulated. As this empirical study has demonstrated, platforms go beyond marketization practices and can be seen as stacked economization processes. One should be careful, however, not to confuse conceptualization with explanation and analysis. Stack economization is a concept we can use to explain the workings and maintenance of platforms. It cannot be used to stand in for analysis. In other words, we need to better understand the stacked nature of economization in platforms, not to describe the platform with yet another concept, for a platform is a platform. Actors call it thus.

This chapter has identified the specificity and empirical novelty of data money exchange platforms. It has thus avoided flattening the rich universe of economic platforms that results when we see them as mere markets and giving a second life to an already shallow and empirically unfounded neoclassical notion of market, this time in the study of economic platforms as two-sided markets. The multipurpose and dynamic universe of platforms expands beyond marketization relations and mobilizes a series of business opportunities that can best be understood as *stack economization*. The latter entails marketization, but it also moves beyond it in pursuing other modes of economization from barter to redistribution, from data valuation to money making.

This chapter has also avoided identifying the process of stack economization with the digital/material geography it makes and where it takes place. Places of interaction have an infrastructural effect on the economization relations of which they are a part, but they cannot replace their very description. The findings of my research do not support a conclusion that data money markets either are a part of the stack-like systemic formation or contribute to its unfolding. Theoretically speaking, imagining static objects (such as the economy, the nation, the stack, and the social) seems to do a disservice to a relational description of dynamic processes such as marketization and economization. Furthermore, this chapter has indicated that what is being stacked in data money exchanges is not *the place* of encounter but the *processes* of economization.

Approaching platforms as stack economization processes has two advantages. First, it makes it possible to isolate layers of economic interaction in their enframed platform universe and to study the making and deployment of their technical operations on the ground. This enables us to focus on the various forms of infrastructure, performativities, agencies, and devices that make platform works instead of focusing on each as a defining variable and then discussing platforms with reference to it. Platforms, as shown in this book, are not mere markets of buying this and selling that with network effects in an ecosystem, even when we consider cryptocurrency *markets*. By approaching platforms as stack economization, we can isolate the consequences of these network effects. We carry out such an analysis not by imagining an externally appropriated *endogenous* effect but rather by focusing on concrete practices that can undermine economization practices *exogenous* to the platform under consideration. For example, here I have shown that an endogenous development that fosters cryptocurrency usage in centralized data-money markets has been undermining blockchain networks themselves while at same time contributing to the dollarization of economic relations.

Second, approaching platformization and platforms as stack economization processes may inform a more nuanced research agenda that can isolate specific threads and functions in platform works and study their consequences. Such a nuanced perspective has the potential to inform social policy and regulation more effectively. For example, centralized data-money platforms that allow data money to be traded for fiat currency are introducing decentralized data-money platforms that can be bridged in one platform. Thus, these platforms are advancing the stacking of economization in order to give actors tools to avoid public accounting systems and thereby are punching holes in traditional taxation and money transfer processes. This development raises serious and urgent questions about accountability and legitimacy. Using stack economization to refer to the mutually supporting and enabling platform-based exchange, production, barter, and representation processes that are qualified by their makers and observers as economic also helps us to imagine more effective economic policy and intervention tools for platform economies. Chapter 6 of this book visits this discussion in terms of taxation and regulation.

The previous two chapters have shown that blockchains are accounting infrastructures that facilitate the transfer of the rights to send data transparently. These data-sending rights are monetized and make possible specific blockchain-based rights for cryptocurrencies such as Bitcoin, Ethereum, and Avax. However, data monies cannot barter, stack, or exchange by themselves; they need human actors doing things on the ground. In other words, without making sense of human communities who make and maintain crypto-economic relations, our understanding of them will be incomplete. Addressing this potential problem, I took a detailed look at a contemporary data money community in two ways. First, I examined the general sociological universe of Electra, and, second, I did an ethnographic study of the same community as it proposed, lost, and reimagined its data money. The next two chapters present the findings of my two research strategies.

# 4

## GLOBAL CRYPTOCURRENCY COMMUNITIES AS DATA MONEY MAKERS

Since their emergence in 2009, cryptocurrencies have been attracting ever more academic attention. Within this burgeoning literature, a thread of research has begun to look at new economic communities that come together around a cryptocurrency in order to realize it. Scholars have argued that these communities have been producing a new money form in legal terms, "the non-sovereign fiat currency,"[1] built on/by an assortment of social institutions, infrastructures, and networks.[2] Approaching data monies as community experiments, scholars have focused on the primary role that collective actors play in making data monies and have analyzed the nature of their forum interaction,[3] ideological tensions,[4] economic imaginaries,[5] patterns of organization,[6] crypto entrepreneurship,[7] community impact on price movements,[8] governance,[9] relations of solidarity,[10] and mining collectives.[11]

Contributing to the recent ethnographically informed research on cryptocurrency communities,[12] this chapter analyzes the sociotechnical universe of a data money community, a group of around ten thousand individuals who live in various time zones all across the world and work around the clock to make a cryptocurrency called Electra Protocol. My research draws on three sources of information. First, I surveyed 254 Electra members, who represented more than half of the core actors that shape the course of action in the community. Their answers helped me examine the demographic characteristics of this community and their general take on cryptocurrency economies. Second, I carried out a computational text analysis of Bitcointalk's Electra forum, which illustrated a variety of concerns that formed the main contours of discussion and contestation in the community. Complementing this, I carried out a network analysis of all Twitter interaction data involving the 18,600 followers of the handle @ElectraProtocol and their 358,000 followers, be they groups, persons, or bots. This analysis enables us to locate the community's more powerful actors and clusters. Third, I carried out fieldwork within the Electra community, beginning in March 2018, as a participant and nonparticipant observer in a variety of group platforms, and I conducted fifty-three unrecorded interviews with central actors in the community, including its anonymous founder, Electra01, who agreed to meet me in person.

The chapter presents three clusters of findings, some illustrated in collaboration with designers. First, focusing on a general sociological approach to the Electra community's networks, the chapter presents a visual representation of all its actors that underlines the concentration of power, one that aligns with the actors' own description of these relations. From an introductory demographic profile of the people who make Electra, we see within this supposedly "open" community the unprecedented dominance of well-educated men who live in the West. We observe that there are clearly identifiable centers of power in this decentralized financial infrastructure, marked by race, education, gender, and geographical location. Yet this community is also open and quick to address such asymmetries: after seeing the survey results, which I made available to participants, the

Electra community decided to take a number of concrete steps toward inclusivity, equity, and diversity by deploying what I call *everyday performativity*. Such a development calls for a rethinking of questions of economic performativity, which takes place between scientific practices and economization processes on the ground.[13]

Second, drawing on a computational text analysis of forum discussion content, the chapter identifies the most frequently used words and interprets the results with a second analysis that plots the most frequently used social-scientific terms in these discussions. We see how the community members were focused on topics such as valuation, prices, and tokenization, given that *community, exchange, market, work,* and *money* were the social-scientific concepts most frequently mentioned in their discussions. The analysis moves beyond a descriptive account of the unintentional distribution of actors' intentional choices of concepts and, by drawing on a big-data analysis of Twitter interactions, renders visible which actors' intentional utterances carry more power. Offering a second visualization of the same community, this time by analyzing Twitter data, the findings present a more nuanced understanding of relations of power. We see that it is not those who post the most frequently or who are followed by the largest group that carry more weight in this economic community; rather, it is those who help build clusters and then bridge them to others.

Third, and rather surprisingly, the findings also show that it is not the most influential actors on the Bitcointalk forum or Twitter who have the largest influence on community affairs; instead, it is the agents who manage to control and shape "the parliament of the community affairs," or the Discord group. We see that the agency of the actors on the Discord platform is so powerful that they were even able to induce a vast digital/material migration of the Electra community. Electra (ECA) collapsed in November 2020 when its anonymous founder dumped his hundreds of millions of ECA, effectively killing the project and pushing the value of its money to zero. Yet within a few days, the community left the founder behind and moved on to a new project, the rebirth to their community money, this time called Electra Protocol (XEP). This entire move was planned by a handful of individuals in the core team and administered by the 369 members of Electra's Discord group.

In conclusion, the chapter discusses fundamental motivations behind the economization practices of crypto-community actors as they pursue their interests and propose ways of describing such interests and practices. We see that in this new money community, actors work many hours a week, mostly for free. Three motives seem to incentivize their unpaid and arduous labor: hope, joy, and knowledge. When asked about the primary reason for working for the community, community members cited (1) the hope of making money (41 percent), (2) enjoyment (21.1 percent), and (3) the desire to learn about cryptocurrencies (20.7 percent). Almost all of these central actors, especially the founders of the core team have full-time jobs with benefits, except for Jenova and MasterDen, who work full-time (around 70 hours a week) for Electra without pay.

We still know too little about these actors in the new economic universes, such as those of data monies, whose market capitalization exceeded $2.5 trillion in May 2021. Who are they? How do we describe them in terms of class, gender, and ethnicity? What motives and interests inform their behavior? How do these dynamics inform the future constellation of economic activity in the world? It is beyond the objectives of this chapter to provide a general answer to these questions. Yet this limited study of the sociotechnical universe of a new financial community presents possible answers, as articulated by the members of the Electra community.

# NETWORKS: A GENERAL LOOK AT THE ELECTRA COMMUNITY

Everything started with an idea developed by a young man and announced using a personal computer. On March 30, 2017, following a year of preparations, Electra01 proposed a new cryptocurrency and its blockchain on a Bitcointalk forum page. Following in the footsteps of Bitcoin's founder, Satoshi Nakamoto, and anonymizing his name using the cryptocurrency he created, Electra01 simultaneously initiated a forum, a money, and a blockchain. His aim was a successful valuation of the money that he proposed. For this to happen, an accounting infrastructure needed to be constructed for its transactions. The blockchain made such transactions possible. Yet he knew that, without a community, monies could not be made. And without a forum, communities could not gather. Much like Nakamoto, he needed them all. It is not a coincidence that Nakamoto had also started his project with the trilogy of forum, money, and community. It worked for Bitcoin, and it was going to work for Electra—for a while.

Electra01 drew on an interesting idea: instead of implementing a slow and energy-costly mining process like that of Bitcoin, he planned a mining big bang that would take place in a matter of hours. At the end of this process, 95 percent of all proof-of-work Electras would emerge and be owned by miners. If people found the idea interesting, then they would rush into what he called a Super Rewards Bonanza, thus beginning to value the money. This push effect would then be balanced by a pull device: if miners kept their Electras, they would earn a very high interest rate, initially set at 50 percent, thus incentivizing them to keep a stake in the money. This proof-of-stake currency would then have enough time to build its community because whether people loved or hated it, they still conversed about it in its forums.

Everything went as planned. The value skyrocketed for a short while, making Electra01 a theoretical billionaire. As the effect of the Bonanza faded, the pull mechanism kicked in, convincing miners to keep a stake in the money and wait for a while. In the meantime, Bitcointalk's Electra forum pages became more active, bringing together dedicated followers. Eventually, a new leadership began to form, with Master Den emerging as one of the leaders of this community-building process or, as one Electra -owner described him, the "glue of the community." He had approached money making from another angle:

> I realized that technical stuff was secondary to cryptos. What comes first was the community. So I decided to build a community for a crypto project, instead of offering a new crypto by myself. It was easy to code a crypto; it was very difficult to make a community money. One had to bring together digital infrastructures, tools, filters, organizations, and people. This was similar to the power projects that I led as an electrical engineer.

Building and developing a community required an interaction infrastructure. Securing Electra01's support, Master Den reached out to other active members and began to contribute to making a community out of followers. He opened Telegram, Facebook, and Twitter accounts. He built the project's group on Discord, a popular platform with interactive chat and video- and audio-conferencing functions, as well as specialized meeting rooms, a toolbox for developers, and file-sharing links. As these networks and devices were made and/or adopted, more followers turned into community members. As the number of members grew, a core team emerged, using the analogy of a system or a planet with a center.

A term used by many other data money and gaming communities, *core team* refers to a handful of very active members who maintain community relations, develop and repair tangible and intangible infrastructures and networks, write and improve the code and data infrastructures, and represent the community in forums. In short, the core team members are responsible for the management of the entire project, and in the case of Electra, they even planned and executed the community's digital emigration. As the next chapter analyzes in detail, following a fundamental controversy between the founder and the core team on the project's future, Electra collapsed in value as Electra01 sold off all of his Electras in November 2020, effectively killing the money that he had helped create. Within a short period of time, however, the community left the founder behind and moved on to a new project, disassembling and remaking all infrastructural formations and bringing about the rebirth of their community money, this time called Electra Protocol.[14]

The core team also identified a second tier of people who led collaborative projects but did not have the time to meet every Sunday. These "Electrans" took on many responsibilities and reported to the core team. Over two years, the core team increased to 14 persons; the community now included a professional editor, designers, community managers, a head moderator, 25 Electrans, and more than 430 members who had the privilege of joining Electra's strictly moderated and controlled Discord group, of which I had been a member. Also, there were 18,600 Twitter followers; 8,000 Telegram users distributed across thirteen channels, each using one of eleven different languages;[15] and many Facebook, Reddit, Medium, LinkedIn, and

WhatsApp groups or pages, as well as a few advisers, including myself. Reading my work, they decided that the money they were making was indeed data money and asked me to advise them, giving me an opportunity to observe their everyday life more closely.

Figure 4.1, created by the design strategist Nishant Wazir and myself, is a visualization of the Electra community, using varying unit sizes, shapes, and hierarchies that draw on the data I collected. With 32,800 users, the largest amount of community activity in terms of interactions, mentions, information gathering, and production takes place on Twitter, Telegram, Reddit, and Facebook. Yet these platforms are not used for decision-making. Thus, we chose to represent one hundred users of these platforms as one node. Electra's Discord group takes the center stage for leadership, along with 430 others who are allowed to join in those conversations. This platform operates like a general assembly of individuals who have proven their commitment to the project. All major decisions are shaped and made there. Aiming to better visualize platform hierarchies, we chose to represent eighty of these actors as one node in figure 4.1, use a larger representative symbol, and locate them at the core of Electra's world, in accord with how interviewed Electra community members viewed their place as close to the core team.

Wazir and I also placed two individuals among other nodes and clusters. Electra01 never chose to be an active member in any community subgroup, participate in the core team, or attend the hundreds of community meetings, even though he held much power, thanks to the 1 billion ECAs he owned. We represented the author of this book, since I had been a member of all these platforms and joined in conversations but never took part in decision-making. I was the only participant in the community who did not own cryptocurrency. We chose not to represent the Electra Foundation, discussed in detail in chapter 5, for two reasons. First, the core team proposed and established the foundation as an organizational device to support Electra's move toward greater transparency. Second, the core team was using it to counterbalance the anonymity of the founder, which was now perceived as a liability for the growing project. It was more of a tool than an actual actor in the community. Another platform we chose not to represent is the original forum, Bitcointalk's Electra page, because it had become outdated after a short while and was used almost like a personal communication channel, mostly by Electra01, whose messages were simultaneously broadcast on other channels.

Following the community's discussion and critique of the first prototype of our visualization, we arrived at our current iteration, which proposes many paths outside this world, thus connecting Electra to other crypto communities. The four edges in each corner of the visualization are populated by nodes that leave and join communities such as Electra. It would be misleading to imagine these communities as a mere coming together of platforms, for each individual keeps an assortment of platform memberships. It is not uncommon to be a member of all platforms simultaneously. My data suggest that 97.5 percent of the platform usage by the community comes from Telegram's thirteen subgroups (58.2 percent), Discord (29.5 percent), and Twitter (9.8 percent). This is also why I focus on the activity on these three platforms in the following section.

Who are these people? Ninety-six percent are men, with an average age of 37.5, and 75 percent were living in Europe, the United States, or Canada. They cited three reasons for joining the community: to make money (41 percent), to find enjoyment (21.1 percent), and to learn about cryptocurrencies (20.7 percent).

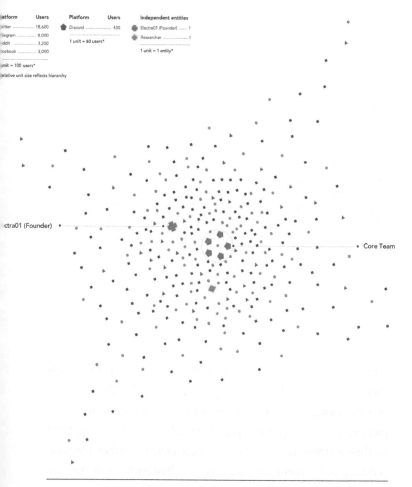

FIGURE 4.1 A visualization of the Electra community.

This is a mostly white, male, and Western data-money community that claims to be global, open, and transparent.

The members of the Electra community are well educated: 73.2 percent have a college degree, and 31.2 percent have a graduate degree. The majority (57.1 percent) use only a pseudonym or

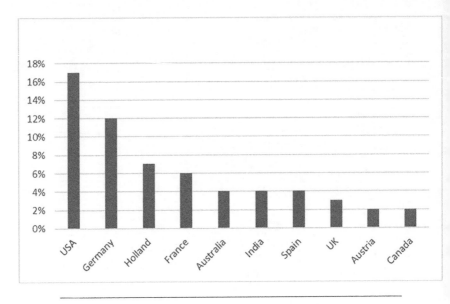

**FIGURE 4.2** Top ten countries of origin.

a nickname in their correspondence, and 22.2 percent use only their legal name, whereas 20.6 percent use both. All core team members except for Asmoth post their legal names and their pictures on the project webpage.[16] Members of Electra are loyal to their community. Unlike members of many other unstable cryptocurrency communities, Electra followers tend to stay. Of the community members, 57 percent have been active almost since the emergence of Electra in 2017, while 92 percent of active members joined Electra by 2018, providing evidence that the community has been successful in incorporating and retaining anyone interested in what they do.

How active are these members? On average, a community member uses a platform at least once on 2.8 days per week and receives and sends at least one instant message about Electra on 3.5 days per week. Survey respondents estimate the community's active membership to be 5,437, of which 210 are very active,[17] 683 are moderately active,[18] and 4,544 are less active.[19] Yet members who are active at least 4 days per week and are thus more informed about the community estimate the total size to be 10,970.[20]

We can approach the size of the Electra community from another angle: Theoretically, it cannot be more than 26,032, which is the total number of memberships for the platforms that the community uses. However, we know that most users are members of more than one of the platforms used in the Electra community. Twitter is a good indicator of follower population, and we can assume that the Electra community numbers less than 20,000 persons. Twitter data show that those who follow Electra have 358,000 Twitter followers of their own. These followers of followers are informed about what is going on in the Electra community on a daily basis, but they are not even inactive members of this community.

What keeps these economic actors in the community? One might think that Electra is their key investment in life; therefore, they are actively participating in the community on a daily basis because they have put their money in the project. Surprisingly, this is not the case. An average Electra community member keeps only 38 percent of their entire financial assets in Electra. More than 75 percent of Electra members invest only 22 percent of their wealth in the data money they make. They are not paid to make this money. They do not keep most of their assets in it. Why, then, are they so active? To address these questions, we need to shift our attention from who the members are to what they do and talk about.

## REPRESENTATIONS: COMMUNITY DISCUSSIONS AND PERSPECTIVES

Looking at where it all started, the Electra forum in Bitcointalk, is a good point of entry to identify and analyze specific ideas and representations that the community produces. Bitcointalk had been one of the main forums that brought Bitcoin followers together, giving them an opportunity to imagine their community and invent forms of agency and tools of realization with which to pursue their goals. Originally operated on bitcoin.org and then moved to its current domain, which Nakamoto created, Bitcointalk gave birth to Bitcoin to the extent that the first Bitcoin transaction took place not in a market but in this forum. It also introduced myriad other cryptocurrencies and forums. Economic actors used the Bitcoin blockchain to create their own blockchains and the Bitcointalk pages to build their community forums. Electra was one of them.

Electra's Bitcointalk forum emerged on March 30, 2017, with Electraoi's genesis message. During the formative period, this forum served as the main vehicle for the members' interaction; later, as the community grew, as we saw in the previous section, the members began to use many other platforms. The discussions on the Bitcointalk Electra forum can thus be seen as indicative of the emergent community's priorities. If printed, the forum's text corpus of around 200,000 words and 1.2 million characters would fit on about 1,000 U.S. letter-size pages. A computational text analysis of these pages illustrates the relative frequency of words used by the community members (figure 4.3).

The most frequently used words in Electra's forum discussions are *coin, wallet,* and *exchange*—for a number of reasons. First, crypto communities usually refer to cryptocurrencies as coins because it is short and thus easy to type. It is expected

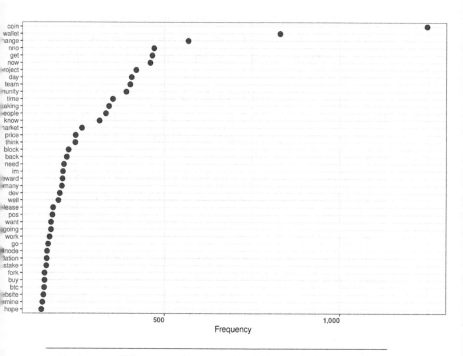

**FIGURE 4.3** Frequency of words used in the Bitcointalk Electra forum.

that a data coin community will mention *coin* all the time, since the forum is built to discuss a coin in the first place. Second, community members are primarily concerned about security, even more than about the value of the coin, for valuation does not matter if one fails to keep the material in which the value is imagined. The intangible material that data monies are made of is the right to send data on a digital/material infrastructure. The wallet is the place where the data leave and arrive as one sends or receives them, making their security even more important than that for a leather wallet, where many people keep their paper monies. One cannot fit much into a paper money wallet, but a digital wallet can hold an unlimited value of money. One can fit all cryptocurrencies of the world in only two wallets, for the materiality of data money is relational: one wallet is not enough to maintain the relational possibility of transferring the right to send data if one lacks a place to send it.

*Exchange* is the third most frequently used word because forum conversations revolve around this concept: as cryptocurrencies are accepted in more exchanges, it is more likely they will gain value. The possibility of being accepted to a new and vibrant exchange attracts great attention from forum participants. As we saw in chapter 3, exchanges are platforms that mobilize stack economization; thus, they offer a variety of economic services to actors. Such an openness may also entail security risks because platforms invite actors to use channels to enter them, thus also providing thieves with multiple channels to reach wallets—something that happens often in exchanges. That is also why community members talk about exchanges very frequently.

The second group of most frequently used words is clustered around two themes: (1) actors, such as *team, people,* and *community*; and (2) valuation, such as *day, staking, project, price,* and *Coinmarket.* Actor-oriented concepts, including less frequently used ones such as *dev* and *foundation,* mark the agencies referred to in most of these discussions. Community members typically converse about the ways in which the Electra price can be valued and protected on exchange-related webpages such as Coinmarket. Time-related concepts such as *day* are used frequently in the context of valuation because time is for a cryptocurrency value what a glass is for water. One can give shape to fluid, digitally represented values only by using the intangible material order of time to mark uniqueness on otherwise identical representations. Without time stamps, it is almost impossible to mark a unique identity on data monies and their transactions.

Searching for frequencies is helpful, but they have limitations. What will we see in this corpus text of interactions if we pursue a controlled analysis and search for the relative frequency of concepts that social scientists use in their research practice?

Presenting the conceptual infrastructure of the forum discussion, figure 4.4 shows that the *community* (top concept) makes itself by talking about itself as a community. Such a performative effect is materialized as the emergent community discusses its money's place in *exchanges* (the second most popular concept). *Good* appears as the third most frequently used term, for it operates as a positive reinforcer in a community of individuals who work on a voluntary basis.[21]

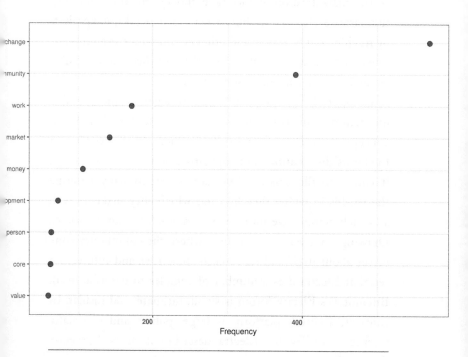

FIGURE 4.4 Frequency of social-scientific concepts used in the Bitcointalk Electra forum.

Forum discussions are never mere chats. Much like in other economic contexts, actors carry out everyday research about their financial universe by being active in these forums and thus work to imagine, make, and trade value. They also use this discussion platform for the purpose of reinforcing certain perspectives. They use *good* very frequently to incentivize others and *bad* relatively less frequently to disincentivize a disliked behavior or perspective.

The second group of most frequently used social-scientific terms is *work, market, money*, and *development*. Electra's economic actors conceive of their contribution as work, not a mere hobby or insignificant activity. Their primary purpose is the successful marketization of Electra as money. For this, they continuously develop devices, infrastructures, networks, and projects by reaching out to people and other communities around them. The core team works as the coordinator of these efforts, which entail discussion, planning, and outreach.

Computational text analysis gives us a general picture of an unintentional distribution of the actors' intentional choice of concepts. It is useful for putting together a bird's-eye view of the terms' distributions and popularities, but it is limited when it comes to illuminating how actors intentionally describe the worlds in which they live and which they make, as well as which actors have more power in reaching out to others. Drawing on a variety of forums where the community converses about itself and its projects, practices, and futures, we see that Electra uses a number of vehicles to describe itself. Bitcointalk's Electra forum is small, intimate, and insular. In contrast, Twitter's platform is large, public, and externally oriented. On Twitter, Electra describes itself as "a secure, decentralized, open-source, community driven cryptocurrency project" (figure 4.5).

**Electra Protocol**
@ElectraProtocol

$XEP is a secure, decentralized, open-source, community driven cryptocurrency project that is lightning fast at near zero fee Supports #womenincrypto #DataMoney

⊚ Worldwide  🔗 electraprotocol.com  🗓 Joined October 2017

**160** Following  **19.1K** Followers

Not followed by anyone you're following

**FIGURE 4.5** Electra Protocol's Twitter handle communication.

Two interesting references on Twitter underline the centrality of the performative aspects studied in this chapter and the realities it tries to understand. First, after seeing and discussing the raw data from my project, the core team members realized how male-dominated their community was and decided to present Electra as supportive of women's participation in crypto communities by incorporating #womenincrypto into their Twitter handle's byline. They had been aware of the problem of not having as many women as they wanted to have in their community, but they realized how serious the discrepancy was only after looking at this chapter's survey data. Their action to pursue a #womenincrypto agenda was made possible in part because of this research.

Second, they began to present their cryptocurrency as #DataMoney, following the first paper I published on crypto-currencies.[22] Already aware of the recent social-scientific stud-ies that my paper discussed, they gave me extensive comments and thus contributed to the making of the scientific statements that, in turn, had a performative effect on them. Needless to say, many community members had been following the social-scientific and technical literatures about cryptocurrencies and blockchains, drawing on an evidence-based decision-making process, everyday research, and data-driven planning for their planning strategy. After all, this is one of the hundreds of com-munity money projects in the world that describes itself with an academic-looking white paper in the first place.

How do we make sense of such an interaction between pro-fessional research and economies? Studies of performativity have shown that economic knowledge contributes to the making of economic realities on the ground.[23] Empirical studies concerning these developments usually focus on larger economic universes and institutionalized actors who can deploy such economic knowledge in the real world and who sanction those who do not use it, as we observe in exchanges such as the Chicago Board of Trade and the options pricing algorithms it uses to build its trading platforms. What we observe in the Electra community is *everyday performativity*, which is different from institutional performativities.

Everyday performativity is similar to institutional performa-tivity in that it still shapes the ways in which an entire project works, such as by informing organizational devices to increase women's participation. But naming its entire community money project after a social-scientific concept, such as data money, exemplifies the more engaged nature of everyday performativity. Institutional performativity is more about the institutional infrastructure-building of markets and their auction mechanisms. Everyday performativity in a cryptocurrency community can be defined as a practice that incorporates scientific or popular representations in order to change an element of the community's universe. For this, they reach out to a spectrum of representations from entrepreneurial discourses to social-scientific studies. Community members carry out research all the time and incorporate anything that works or that they find appealing.[24]

Publishing three white papers in two years, the Electra community became the first data-money community that wrote a paper without the original founder's contribution. These white papers are a good example of how research and money making go hand in hand in crypto communities. The first paper was published on January 31, 2018, ten months after Electra first emerged.[25] Much like a social science research paper, it runs around 6,000 words and introduces the money, its community, and the sociotechnical scaffolding surrounding them. It views "traditional financial structures" as "darkness," much like many other crypto projects that emerged following the 2008 financial breakdown. Yet it is neither antimarket/anticapitalist nor anarchist in its political aspiration. Identifying Electra as "an ecosystem," the paper stresses the importance of collaboration, solidarity, and transparency. That ecosystem is imagined as a community built by individuals who believe in Electra and offer their services in changing forms.

Aiming to present Electra as "the electric current of the cryptocurrency community" (p. 1), the white paper uses tangible material infrastructure metaphors, such as the electric power grid, to describe the process of building an intangible material infrastructure in order to operate as a blockchain accounting mechanism for a global payments system. In the community's imagination, the main problem with the "traditional system" is its limited infrastructure, which fails to incorporate "everyone" in its making. By "return[ing] the power to the people, and assign[ing] members of the community an active role in the evolution of . . . economic and monetary systems" (p. 5), Electra wants to create "a global people's money" to serve as an alternative to the assortment of sovereign fiat currencies. Yet the main problem is not structural; rather, it involves the accessibility of money transfer infrastructures. The paper identifies the Electra project as a market collective actor and describes its "products," their qualities and uses, and how they are made by the community itself. But it does not imagine Electra to be a cooperative or socialist economization project. It is a collaborative marketization project run by individuals who have the power to govern the direction that the project takes.

## ACTORS AND AGENCY IN THE ELECTRA COMMUNITY

Who are the followers of @ElectraProtocol? Who follows these followers? Whom do they mention? How do we identify the most influential actors and their relationships within this community? Electra had 18,600 Twitter followers when I received the authorization from Twitter Inc. to download the data from its databases in January 2021. These followers in turn had 358,000 followers, be they groups, persons, or bots. Many of the followers had less than 1,000 followers and thus had only a limited reach. However, an analysis of followers who had more than 1,000 followers makes visible the interactive universe of Electra's Twitter community.

An analysis of the followers and their mentions identifies several patterns.[26] We can see a number of clusters whose members are more connected to each other when compared to other clusters. We can then compare similar clusters in terms of the direction of their interactions. In other words, we can see who is mentioning whom more often than not. Following these directions, we can locate *bridge actors*, who connect one cluster with another. Bridged clusters are more effective in community discussions than distant and unbridged clusters. By analyzing the timing and frequency of intercluster mentions, we can measure the proximity of the actors in each cluster, whose relative size can be measured in terms of its active members. Such interactions also help locate the most influential actors in Electra's Twitter community. Follower counts are not necessarily a powerful indicator of influence in the community because an Electra follower with a very high follower population may not be followed at all *within* the community, may not have an interactive cluster, or may not play a bridging role between various clusters.

It is not useful to look at every interaction between thousands of actors, since this makes it difficult to identify effective interactions. For a community such as Electra with its 18,600 actors, it is useful to look at the interaction of nodes with 1,000 or more followers. Such a filter helps to identify effective mentions instead of all mentions because nodes with a larger number of followers are more likely to initiate a discussion that has a larger impact on the community. Figure 4.6 illustrates all the interactions between all actors with 1,000 or more followers.[27] These 626 nodes play an effective role compared to the rest of the 17,974 actors, who have a very small number of followers and thus are less likely to play a central role in Electra's Twitter community.

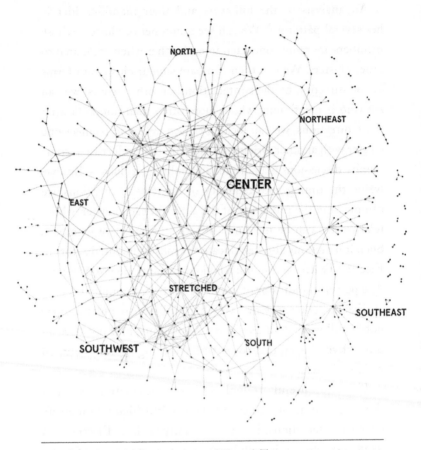

**FIGURE 4.6** A visualization of Electra's Twitter community.

Figure 4.6 renders visible three dynamics.[28] First, it isolates those actors who interact with each other more often and plots them closer to each other. This ability to illustrate actors' interaction clusters also makes it possible to position various groups in the digital community closer in terms of geographical distance. Needless to say, geographical closeness pertains only to the digital/material geography of Electra. Figure 4.6 shows seven clusters, located arbitrarily in this universe-like design. The number of clusters would change if I changed the criteria for identifying these groupings. In this analysis, I aimed at analyzing an optimum number of clusters with the maximum number of interactions; this allowed me to identify seven clusters that carry 93 percent of all mentions in the Twitter conversations of Electra followers. Following the analogical universe of the figure, I chose to name these clusters with reference to their location. These clusters seem to be of two types. The central clusters, composed of the Center Cluster and the Stretched Cluster, have a widespread reach and carry 43 percent of all interactions in the community. They also connect all other clusters to each other. The second type can be called peripheral clusters, which carry the rest of the interactions. They dot the periphery of the community and are composed of the Southwest, South, Southeast, Northeast, North, and East Clusters.

The second dynamic we can observe in the analysis concerns the most influential actors, the directionality of their mentions, and their locations. A closer look at these seven clusters shows that the actors with the Twitter handles humoalex, linkcrypto1, ElectraPanther, Htmlbunker_Boy, Tapatrade, bitcoins_future, pumpingAltcoin, Verge Girl, and didencu1 play a central role. One might think that an actor in a more central cluster would have a larger effect than one in a peripheral cluster. This is not the case. We can analyze the impact potential of a certain actor with reference to two variables: connectedness and betweenness. The former indicates the number of connections an actor has, whereas the latter refers to the frequency of mentions an actor makes or receives.

Observing connectedness and betweenness dynamics in the Electra community helps us articulate several conclusions. It is not the follower count or the centrality of actors that makes them

### TABLE 4.1 MOST INFLUENTIAL ACTORS IN ELECTRA'S TWITTER COMMUNITY

| Connectedness | Betweenness |
| --- | --- |
| ElectraPanther | humoalex |
| bitcoins_future | davidgokhshtein |
| PumpingAltcoin | RoyCavalera3 |
| humoalex | LinkCrypto1 |
| devnullius | devnullius |

more influential in digital communities such as that of Electra. For example, ElectraPanther might not considered an influential actor if one checks their followers. Having 1,658 followers and following only 777 actors, they could be considered completely negligible. Yet, ElectraPanther is the most connected actor in the community (table 4.1).

Analyzing the nature of betweenness gives us an additional hint. humoalex is followed by and follows less than nine thousand actors. Yet they are one of the two most central actors in the community in terms of betweenness—that is, the number of mentions they receive and make. Anything that ElectraPanther and humoalex share has the largest possibility of being seen by the largest number of actors in Electra's Twitter community. There are actors with more than half a million followers in the community, but even the actor with the highest follower count of 1 million is not on the list of the one hundred most influential actors.

Finally, the centrality of a cluster does not say much about the centrality of the actors in that cluster. Four of the top five actors in terms of connectedness and three of the top five actors in terms of betweenness are from peripheral clusters. One can be a central actor in a peripheral cluster, and a central cluster can be composed of less influential actors. It is the coming together of an actor's place, connectedness, betweenness, and location that matters the most, not a static count of followers per se.

However, one should not confuse the interactive universe of Electra's twitter community with the community itself. Twitter interactions are important when making sense of communications within the community, but it would be a mistake to exaggerate the role that Twitter actors play in making and maintaining the community itself. For instance, Electra01, the founder of Electra, and Aykut Baybaş, the most central community builder, have almost no presence in the Twitter community. Except for RobertSB84, or Robert Bakker, there is no member of the core team among the ten most influential actors in the community based on Twitter data. Where, then, should we look for the central actors in the government of Electra community?

I asked this question to every community member I interviewed. Their unanimous answer was Discord. The holding company of Discord describes it as a "platform designed for creating communities" and claims to give its users "the power to create your own place to belong."[29]

On Discord, one starts building a community by first creating a space for it: the "server." Discord provides tools to craft and design "your community" with templates, enabling the community founder to build audiovisual or text-graphic channels for group and subgroup interaction. Thanks to Discord's tools for constructing hierarchies of privilege, it is possible to build a modular community interaction platform on a single communication infrastructure. Electra has many communities on Discord, and only those who introduce and develop the community can distribute these rights.

Electra's "parliament" is located on Discord. While one is only a click away from membership on forums such as Twitter and Bitcointalk, it is difficult to get accepted onto Electra's Discord. One needs to be invited and then has to prove that they are who they say they are. After the invitee enters, they become an ordinary member of the assembly, with no privileges other than reading and posting general messages.

Discord's internal architecture illustrates the distribution of powerful actors better than any other platform. At the top of the hierarchy sits the core team. Its membership changes, depending on the availability of participants and their engagement levels. Unlike the *representational* leadership of Electra's Twitter community, the *administrative* leadership of Electra on the Discord forum has the most power to shape community decisions. These leaders decided to move the community away from Electra and to introduce Electra Protocol, the same community money under a new name. They are the members who decided the timing of the upgrades, the nature of changes, and the future direction of the community.

Yet Discord chat is not sufficient to serve the core team members' self-assigned duties as the administrators of community affairs. Taking time away from their families, they meet every Sunday over Discord's audio and/or visual core team channel, at times with the participation of an invitee or two, to discuss and carry out decision-making.

In addition to their own take on community money affairs, it is the general Discord discussions, private WhatsApp group chats, Telegram correspondence, and other things that they read and discuss over a myriad of forum channels that inform their decisions. The professional life of a core team member of such a voluntary initiative involves everyday research, analysis, and decision-making. The deliberative process of Electra's Discord forum is carefully moderated and managed by specific actors such as discussion moderators, who are coordinated by a head moderator. They are responsible for the "order" of the community discussions by, for example, trying to control "impulsive reactions by mostly anonymous and too excited community members," as one moderator explained his job.

THE AUTHOR: What do you do if a member disrupts the order in the community?

MODERATOR: First, we contact the unruly member via private chat; if it doesn't work, we call or try to meet anonymously. If this fails, we have sticks to use.

THE AUTHOR: Sticks?

MODERATOR: I mean punishment. I can sanction a member by preventing him from posting any messages. We can even throw him out from Discord.

THE AUTHOR: How many times have you sanctioned anyone?

MODERATOR: One or two times. It doesn't happen often.

Actors and agency change as one changes the interaction platform. Twitter's influential actors and their groups are different from those on Discord. As actors and their groups change, so does their agency. The agency of actors on Discord is so powerful that they can even induce a digital/material migration of the community. Yet such a migration would not be successful if the actors on the Twitter platform did not find it necessary. To be able to pursue different forms of agency, actors build and use a variety of platforms that maintain a distributed yet hierarchical placement of agency. The smaller and the more controlled a platform is (such as Discord), the more powerful its actors' governing agency is. The larger and the less controlled the platform is (such as Twitter), the less powerful its actors' governing agency is.

Yet it is not necessarily the number of followers on less controlled platforms that make for stronger agency; rather, it is who you follow and who follows you. Representational power and the effectiveness of one's communication depend on their place in a cluster and the way in which they bridge clusters.

## CONCLUSION

Drawing on a variety of research strategies, such as computational text and big data analysis, ethnographical fieldwork, and sociological survey, this chapter has described and analyzed a cryptocurrency community whose members are dispersed across all time zones and continents. Such a global community that operates a decentralized financial infrastructure has immediately invisible centers and hierarchies. The Electra community is run by a predominantly Western, well-educated, and male membership, and its very organization represents centers and concentrations of power and leadership that are articulated in different ways on different platforms. Twitter data analysis shows us that representational power is distributed to a handful of actors who have the potential for more effective communication—not because of the number of their followers, but because of their location in a cluster and their bridging role between different clusters.

Yet the power distribution becomes less anonymous and more easily identifiable when we change the platform to be analyzed from Twitter to Discord. The Discord platform brings together a tool kit and a digital/material space that help the community build hierarchies and specialized leadership groups that can imagine and organize an effective division of labor among themselves. We observed that none of these central actors with administrative power are among the actors with the largest representation power in the Twitter community.

Located on changing platforms of power that have varying degrees of outreach potential, these actors also carry out everyday research to make (sense of) the world around them. The volatility of data money prices and the novelty of the financial infrastructure (in which) they operate push them to be agile researchers on economic developments. They listen to talks, meet people, attend scientific and professional conferences, read, and write social- and economic-scientific papers, mobilizing research as an important instrument of their everyday activity. Informing a new type of performativity, whatever they learn can promptly be turned into a prototyped new interaction with the world around them. The research that informed this chapter is no exception. Learning about the power asymmetries surrounding their community, the members of Electra's core team decided to address them by planning an outreach drive to increase its diversity and inclusion.

Therefore, one of the three motivations behind working for free for a new money project is knowledge. The other two are the hope of making money and enjoyment. Also identified by other researchers,[30] such overdetermined motivations are the emotional fuel that makes a new money community possible. The hope of making money and the fear of losing it render this community similar to other everyday trading communities.[31] However, the element of enjoyment makes it quite different. All the core team members and all the actors in the community told me how much they enjoyed designing, making, and building things economic on the ground. Of the survey participants, 21.1 percent cited enjoyment as the main reason behind their participation in the Electra project, and 91 percent said it was among their top three reasons for participating.

"Building a new economic thing," as Jenova, one of the core team members, described it to me, was new in the sense that, unlike infrastructurally passive day traders who use already existing trading platforms, Electra community actors take pride and joy in designing, developing, or using everyday instruments of new economization. Michel Callon and I have defined economization as the assembly and qualification of actions, instruments, and representations as "economic" by actors who are active in the sciences and/or economies.[32] Electra community members use a variety of instruments of new economization—such as various forms of voting, scientific and nonprofessional research, announcements, games, campaigns, gifts, and tokenization—on a variety of platforms—such as Twitter, Signal, WhatsApp, Bitcointalk, and, of course, Discord—in order to make and maintain their money-making community.

One would imagine that whatever they do is all about money. Surprisingly, in their everyday life, they talk very little about money and its value. In contrast to the global hype about the skyrocketing or collapsing value of popular cryptocurrencies such as Bitcoin and Ethereum, active members of the Electra community are not too preoccupied with the immediate value of their or other people's monies. As we saw before, a great majority of them do not necessarily invest in cryptocurrencies, and even when it comes to Electra, they keep only 38 percent of their assets in their own money.

Predominantly occupied with making economic things possible in a new way, Electra community members and their activities present the social sciences with a unique window to investigate how cryptocurrency-maker communities make monies and their transaction infrastructures possible. Despite the empirical findings of this study, we are still far from making sense of the vast new economic terrain of more than ten thousand cryptocurrencies, traded in thousands of centralized markets and hundreds of decentralized exchanges. We still do not know how these new communities that create nonsovereign fiat currencies in the form of data money will interact with old financial institutions that control sovereign fiat currencies, how old and new money-making devices will produce hybrid forms and instruments, and, finally, how these new communities will shape and be shaped by centralized and decentralized cryptocurrency exchanges.

# 5

# THE EMERGENCE AND DEMISE
# OF A CRYPTOCURRENCY
# COMMUNITY

This chapter presents an analysis of the rise and fall of Electra. In the process, it considers the distributed interaction of actors, representations, networks, organizational frameworks, and devices that contributed to the making, maintenance, and death of a data money project.

Earlier approaches to cryptocurrencies argued that these new money types have revolutionized the ways in which monies are made. For Dan and Alex Tapscott, cryptocurrencies and their blockchains created revolutionary economic contexts without the need for intermediaries to maintain relations of trust.[1] Blockchains and cryptocurrencies were expected to decrease the costs of transactions and increase the efficiency of market mechanisms by eliminating a chain of institutions and simplifying transactional spaces.

This did not happen. Instead, we saw a big bang of new institutions as thousands of new markets emerged over a few short years. As we saw in the previous chapter, founder Electra01 proposed Electra (ECA) in 2017, and thanks to its unique valuation instrument, the new data money gained great value quickly in a short period of time, even exceeding Bitcoin's market capitalization for a moment. The money was designed to lose value quickly too, but not enough to destroy it so that there was time for its community to form. Electra01's plan worked, and Electra's community began to emerge a few weeks after he proposed the new data money. Yet following a forty-four-month ride, Electra collapsed in value as its founder began to sell off all his Electras off in November 2020. What went wrong? What can we learn from the rise and fall of Electra with regard to new monies and their communities?

Almost all studies focusing on cryptocurrency projects have selected their empirical examples from the successful ones. I had done this also when I originally approached Electra's founder in 2018. Yet the unfortunate collapse of Electra during my fieldwork gave me the unique opportunity to analyze the conditions under which a project can be killed, despite an active and dedicated community, strong institutional foundations, and widespread market presence and valuation.

My research draws on fieldwork within the Electra community beginning in March 2018; a series of meetings with the anonymous Electra01, who agreed to see me in person; thirty-four unrecorded interviews with the founder and core team members; participant observation in the group's Discord rooms; and a computational and interpretive text analysis of Bitcointalk's Electra forum, which the founder had opened in 2017.

Drawing on an ethnographically informed historical discussion of the rise and fall of a cryptocurrency, this chapter analyzes the proposal, emergence, community building, institutionalization, success, and failure of Electra as it was imagined and made by its community. It also shows how a blockchain network and its money, presented to conclusively address questions of trust, collapsed following a crisis of trust between its founder and core team members. Attempts to prevent such a collapse centered on a chain of institutions and frameworks. Yet the very political and economic nature of the contention between the founder and the core team, caused by a disagreement regarding who would control funds and decide the future direction of the project, fueled a series of reactions that brought about the end of the money itself. In a surprisingly short period of time, however, the community proved that it would not disappear, even if its money did. In the final section, the chapter shows how the very same community left the founder behind and moved on to a new project, using the same network infrastructures and devices to develop a new money built on the old one. The chapter ends by briefly discussing the community transitioning efforts of Electra Protocol (XEP), the effective rebirth of Electra under a new name.

## A YOUNG INTROVERT IN BRITAIN

Electra01 was twenty-five years old when he first began mining Bitcoin (BTC). He had learned about it from a BBC story on the demise of Silk Road, a dark-net exchange platform that drew on Bitcoin to facilitate the anonymous trading of goods and services. Its founder, Ross Ulbricht, had been arrested and would later be sentenced to life in prison without the possibility of parole. Managed and owned by Dread Pirate Roberts, a pseudonym used by Ulbricht, the Silk Road marketplace helped its founder amass unprecedented wealth in just two years. Ulbricht was twenty-five years old when he built Silk Road; when he found himself in prison, he had more than 173,999 BTC, an amount that would be worth around $10 billion in February 2021. The U.S. Marshals Service seized all the Bitcoin they could find in Ullrich's secret accounts and began selling them at auction, thus contributing to the legitimation and public acceptance of the world's first data money.

Electra01 became acquainted with blockchains and crypto-currencies thanks to this traumatic story of monies and markets. Then two years younger than Dread Pirate Roberts and with a major in economics from a top British university, he decided to deploy his minor—computer science—to make some money. Bitcoin was worth around $13 then. It would increase in value by 92 percent before the year ended.

In part inspired by Bitcoin's legendary founder, Satoshi Nakamoto, he decided on the pseudonym Electra01 and began to think about making "his own Bitcoin." There was another, even more fundamental reason for his choice to remain anonymous: he was a young introvert living at a time when data money mate-riality allowed individuals to amass an extraordinary amount of wealth in the form of very small materialities, such as a cell phone or a representation such as data, without needing a bank account. If someone knew how much money he had, it would be a challenge to protect that wealth and himself. For instance, if he was kidnapped, everything could be taken from him. His "Bitcoin" was going to be worth several million dollars soon. In our last meeting, in December 2020, he said, "I would become a theoretical billionaire in a couple of years, but of course I didn't know about that. I was only dreaming."

After studying the computing infrastructure of data monies during 2015 and planning the launch of his own money dur-ing 2016, Electra01 took the first public step in 2017, around ten months before our first meeting. Over the next three years, I was the only person in the entire Electra community he would meet in person.

Electra01 thought that for data monies to be valuable, they had to offer a novel economic service, and people had to find that service valuable. For him, without something real and new and without a community, data monies were worthless. In his mind, a data money community was composed of two kinds of people: miners and transactioners. His business plan was to appeal to miners in order to attract the attention of transactioners. After he achieved this, he wanted people to keep the money that he had created without an enormous mining operation, like that of Bitcoin, which needed huge amounts of electric power and an expensive computing infrastructure. He found a way to achieve this when he turned his eyes away from the computer screen and toward people.

He thought that he needed an organizational device to attract attention to his Electra, the name that he and the money share. He had researched the history of monies while searching for a name and had learned that electrum—a natural mixture of gold, silver, and other metals—was used to make the first fiat metal money, minted in Anatolia by the Lydians in the sixth century BCE. Moreover, he thought that as a well-known character in Greek mythology, Electra would hold global appeal.

Electraoi decided to organize a fast mass-mining operation that would take place over twenty-four hours, during which 95 percent of all proof-of-work Electras, except for the 1 billion premined Electras that he controlled, would be mined. Miners from all around the world would be invited to a marathon of computing, which would give them hundreds of millions of Electras within a matter of hours. If his plan it worked, what he called a Super Rewards Bonanza would attract miners, people would start talking about Electra, and the sudden public interest would skyrocket the money's theoretical market capitalization. Following the mining of billions of Electras within a single day, the money would jump onto users' radar.

Immediately following the Bonanza, Electra's market value would fall sharply as markets began correcting such an induced and unsustainable explosion of value based on an innovative pricing prosthesis. Yet Electra01 would be prepared for this. He had already attached another valuation and accounting device to his money: a proof-of-stake mechanism. Unlike Bitcoin, which has to operate on proof of work and has no mechanism to incentivize its accumulation in a user's wallet as the user keeps a stake in it, Electra was born with an interest rate incentive. Mimicking fiat monies and conventional banks' interest rate mechanism, Electra owners would earn 50 percent more Electras if they did not sell their currency for a specified period of time and *staked* it. Such a large interest or stake rate, as it is called among data money communities, would convince users to keep Electra instead of dumping it, thus creating an upward move in the money's value. The interest rate would then automatically decline almost all the way to 0 percent as more Electras were mined. When the total circulation supply reached 30 billion ECAs, mining would stop.

## ELECTRA IS ANNOUNCED TO THE WORLD

Electra01 uploaded the information regarding the new coin to a free webpage service,[2] and on March 30, 2017, he sent his first message to the world by opening the Electra thread on Bitcointalk: "Super Rewards Bonanza." Here he was drawing on a colonial term used by miners to describe significant deposits of valuable metals such as silver or gold and borrowing the name of the globally popular TV series *Bonanza*, whose last episode had aired fifteen years before he was born. His stated objective in the message was to create a "gold rush effect."[3] Then he waited anxiously to see whether his money would be accepted.

His plan worked. Miners rushed to Electra as the new money gained value. As people bought more Electras, a data money community began to emerge, and as it emerged, Electra became money. Among the leaders of this community-building process was Master Den or, as one board member of Electra Foundation described him, the "glue of the community."

Master Den had been looking for a promising project without a community. In July 2017, he saw Electra, liked it, and dropped a line to the anonymous founder through the Bitcointalk messaging system. He asked whether he could work with others who might be interested in supporting Electra. Receiving a green light from Electra01, he reached out to other active members and began to contribute to making a community out of followers. In addition to opening Telegram, Facebook, and Twitter accounts, he started a Discord group. This was shortly after the Bonanza, and there were billions of Electras in the world, in the hands of thousands of people. For Master Den, a money needed a community to grow and live:

> It's a lot of work. You can't just issue a money and expect people to use it. One has to maintain it every day. Wallets don't work. You need to be there to fix it. People would trash it; you need to be there in the forum to pick up the trash and clean conversations. You need to update and maintain the computing infrastructure, make people trust and respect your community, so that they can see value in its money. Once people begin to accept that value, money begins to move upwards. Blockchain does not address issues of trust, people do.

Soon the community decided that Electra did not have a trustworthy webpage. A free Weebly site was not enough. They needed designers to create a visualization of the invisible networks that produce Electras and enable their transactions. More importantly, Electra did not have a white paper, an informal requirement to be taken seriously in the crypto world. The community began working on it in late 2017 and published it on January 31, 2018. Electra01 chose to remain in the shadows, not participating in the white paper's writing and contributing a short statement only when he was approached.

## THE COMMUNITY EMERGES

Master Den had come to be seen by many community members as the project leader who devoted all of his working hours to Electra. It was not a coincidence that one of his nicknames is Admin.[4] He never accepted such a description and denied that the community had a leader. He was correct; instead of a leader, I observed a contracting and expanding core team in the short history of Electra. And it was that core team that could make and repair the community, that could make Electra a money.

Actors need to create, borrow, and use economic devices and organizational frameworks to increase the valuation of whatever they do in economization relations.[5] Discord began to serve as a helpful organizational framework that provided the community with the capacity to develop a modular and easy-to-tweak division of labor and hierarchy. The community was using economic devices and representations such as reports, papers, tweets, and visuals in order to create an image of professionalism. The members were reaching out to the world to recruit followers, sympathizers, investors, and team members. Yet without being recognized by a representational authority such as Coinmarketcap and being accepted into markets that organize the trading or barter of monies such as Bitcoin, the value of Electra could not increase.

By the end of 2018, the community and its money passed both thresholds. Electra was listed in Coinmarketcap, indicating it had been accepted into the global arena of cryptocurrencies. One immediate result of this was that it was considered for cryptocurrency exchange markets. Electra had one major advantage: it was an early comer. Today it is very difficult to get listed in a major exchange, and new money projects are charged from $75,000 to $2 million, depending on the popularity of the exchange. There are other requirements too: for example, daily volume must be above a certain amount, such as $50,000. In actual data marketization relations, markets and communities precede the emergence of successful monies.

Markets can also be fatal to objects of exchange, especially in data money worlds. Cryptocurrencies are based on monetizing the right to send data from one node to another. Money is not a passive record in the blockchain; without the possibility to send data to a place that can receive it, the right to send data cannot be monetized—thus, money disappears. Therefore, any technical glitch that makes data impossible to send—as a result of either a tangible material problem, such as the failure of the hardware where one keeps their digital wallet, or an intangible material problem, such as a coding bug in the wallet itself—can make a cryptocurrency obsolete.

Note that one does not send a passive representation in the form of data as money, a common misunderstanding about cryptocurrencies. What is being transferred is *the right to send*, and such a right is possible only if one's wallet is accepted as a node in the blockchain. Imagine that you have a unit of data money, the blockchain has a fork, and the entire community moves to that part of the fork that does not recognize your wallet as an active node. You no longer have money on record anywhere. Because you lose the right to send data, your cryptocurrencies are gone, or *burnt*, the term used in data money communities. Data money is not code that one keeps in a memory device. It is the right to send data, not the data itself.

Furthermore, one does not need a blockchain to own data money. Marketplaces receive data monies on behalf of their customers and keep them as custodians. These places look like giant wallets full of cash. If the wallets are not secured well, someone may grab the money. When one "holds" their money in a market, however, they do not own the data money itself; rather, they have a receipt that represents their ownership that the market accepts. As long as one does not withdraw it, the data money is kept by the market as a custodial asset. Hence, if one faces a problem with wallets and markets, one encounters an enormous problem.

Electra experienced both problems multiple times. In the beginning, its Bitcoin-based blockchain froze as result of a coding problem. This meant that it became impossible to move data as money because accounting could not be carried out, much as if one had a double-entry book but no pen to write in it. When people could not move their money, they moved their bodies and began to protest. Electraoɪ had to learn about this very early on. When the blockchain froze, people rushed to sell Electras, but they failed, for the blockchain was not working. Only the ones who could sell them in markets did so, pushing the value of Electras to zero. Electraoɪ looked around for help and found Bumba, who had his own data money, Bumba Coin. They worked for days on a fix and managed to get the blockchain going once again. Electraoɪ told me:

> Bumba saved my life. He is someone whom I have never met, I have never seen. We worked on a strategy and convinced the community and saved the project. The community supported our decision; they downloaded the new wallets, and we moved on.

I will never forget Bumba's help. These things happen in the cryptocurrency world. People support each other because they like what they do.

The Electra community's second challenge came from the second major market where its money was listed, coinsmarkets.com. The money was also listed on exchanges such as cryptopia and coinexchange.io—but with smaller trading volumes. In terms of trading volume, coinsmarkets.com hosted the largest turnover. One day in 2018 everything stopped. As with many other hacks, the market representatives lied and told users that there was a problem with their servers. They wanted to gain some time to get their act together. The coinsmarkets.com hack turned out to be a real life-and-death struggle for Electra. Many Electra owners who had just lost their money associated the market with the Dutch members of the Electra core team and went so far as to threaten them. The hack cost Electra users around 1 billion ECA. Later there were other, smaller hacks, but none has been as detrimental to Electra as the coinsmarkets.com hack. It took at least three months of hard work by the core team to leave it behind and move on with the project.

A few months after this hack, the community members decided to introduce an upgrade to the wallets, in part because they wanted to better secure personal wallets. Two developers prepared the transition, but as a result of a small, yet avoidable structural problem, the new wallet lost millions of Electras. The community began to move again, sending hundreds of emails per hour, cursing and threatening Electra01 and the core team members. Electra01 decided to step in to cover all losses from the premined Electras that he controlled and the interest that they had generated. He told me that he sent 150–200 million ECA from the premined monies (an amount that was then worth about $70,000) to cover the losses that the community members had incurred as result of the "hole in the wallet."

Following the last hack, @RobertSB84 became concerned that Electra01's anonymity was creating a liability, and he came up with a very old idea in a very new financial universe. As noted earlier, his real name is Robert Bakker. As a career retail banker, he had worked in leading financial institutions in the United States and the European Union for sixteen years and was at the time leading an investment team in a private company. In 2017, he had received a tip from a friend in Australia and had begun to research Electra. Seeing great potential in its community, he started to work with the emergent core team. Together with Master Den and The Revolution, he proposed a new form of institutionalization for Electra using one of the oldest economic institutions in world history—a foundation:

ROBERT BAKKER: Electra01 is a controversial figure in the community. Nobody knows who he is. He proposed Electra and then stepped back to watch people give value to it. Because he has more than 1 billion ECAs, he has great power. He is like a Satoshi Nakamoto figure. This anonymity takes away from the project. Why? Imagine he dumps all his ECAs. The value will collapse. But no one knows who he is in reality. We had to fix this problem and thought that instituting a foundation in the Netherlands would be a good way.

THE AUTHOR: Why a foundation, a very old type of institution?

ROBERT BAKKER: A foundation is a trusted institution. It's nonprofit, it's legal, it's transparent. We were bartering our labor power and time to create a new money. So we thought that a nonprofit institution would increase the legitimacy of the project and balance the liability of having an anonymous founder with a known and trusted institution.

Incorporated in 's-Hertogenbosch, Netherlands, the Electra Foundation had a board that included The Revolution and @RobertSB84, appearing as Bob van Egeraat and Robert Bakker, respectively. They used their legal names and actual photographs as they alternated as chair of the board, and they also asked many other core team members to use their actual names in public statements regarding Electra. Following their call, all core team members except Asmoth—including Admin or Master Den, aka Aykut Baybaş—began to use their legal names in the project in addition to their nicknames. They also talked to me without anonymizing themselves, although they referred to each other by their nicknames in their everyday conversations and team meetings.

The foundation played another role in the evolution of the Electra community. With this institution established, the members of the core team asked Electra01 to turn all of his premined coins and their stakes over to the foundation, which would then be the primary institution responsible for the development of the Electra platform, and they discussed the community's new road map with him. Electra01 was not convinced and refused to send all the premined Electras. Instead, he sent 300 million ECA, around 30 percent of the entire premined amount, excluding the interest he had earned by staking.

## THE FOUNDATION MAKES A DIFFERENCE

It was after the foundation's emergence that fault lines began to emerge between Electra01 and the core team. Deep at its center lay fundamental questions about money and power: Who owned the project? Who would call the shots? Electra01 saw it as *his* project, despite the fact that he believed that the community made money, not just he himself.[6] The core team thought that Electra01 had a responsibility to join them and to contribute to making and maintaining Electra, but also that if he stayed away, he should have no final say or veto power merely based on the fact that he had proposed Electra in the beginning.

This rift would then turn into a storm and take down Electra. Yet despite such a central problem in their community, during all these months of fieldwork both parties were kind and just to each other. Electra01 had been proud of the community and had never tried to exaggerate his role in Electra. He himself introduced me to the community and asked them to include me on Discord, Electra's core administration platform. The core team and the foundation's board members were also courteous. In my presence, they always spoke respectfully of Electra01 until he started selling off his assets in a variety of markets.

At the center of contention between the core team and the founder was a fundamental difference concerning the future of (their) money. The core team's dream was to turn Electra's blockchain into an economization platform with a variety of instruments, from payment systems to distributed accounting of supply chains. In short, the team members wanted to stack various economization processes by building an Electra platform that would be very similar to the platform I analyzed in chapter 2. Electra01, however, believed that the money he had proposed should not be used as a project of advanced economization. Electra's successful, yet limited, marketization was his main objective. He even objected to making the blockchain faster, in order to decrease the waiting time for transactions, at a time when the core team was trying to make Electra Pay into a worldwide payment vehicle. Thinking about Electra as a personal investment project, limited to "a valuable asset," he wanted the community members to respect his conservative take and follow his road map.

But it was too late. The project had already moved in a new direction. In voluntary projects such as Electra, new developments are locomotives that move people. Without them, it is not rational to expect people to run and maintain a community. For their continuous attendance and care, they receive compensation in the form of either money or enjoyment, as we saw in the previous chapter. Electra was not valuable enough for the community to maintain it and to secure their livelihood by cashing in their Electras. Thus, novelty had to be an essential aspect of a project like Electra, a reality that Electra01 did not see or accept. The core team had already built a payment infrastructure with atomic swaps that allowed interchain operability and had begun to work with an oyster company in order to move its supply chain management to the Electra blockchain. More importantly, the team applied to join the Electronic Transactions Association (ETA), the global payments industry association representing five hundred companies such as PayPal, Visa, Mastercard, Apple Pay, and American Express.

In 2019, Electra became the first cryptocurrency initiative to be accepted into ETA. The core team members began to sit on a variety of commissions and working groups, helping to imagine the future of payment relations. They wanted to turn their already very agile blockchain into a global payments system accounting architecture and change their money from a data money as asset to a data money as everyday currency. Their Electra Pay system was being used to transfer money at almost no cost. They were imagining instruments of marketization and dreaming of starting a stack economization that required colossal organizational power—power of such a magnitude that Facebook had tried and failed to build it. The core team members were dreaming big, and it was their dreams that fueled their continued and growing engagement with Electra. As their commitment to Electra increased, their loyalty to the founder's road map declined. The core team members had always been together, but Electra01 had never been with them. He was estranged and distant.

As new economization steps were taken, the anonymous spirit and amateur excitement around Electra began to change. The core team increased to 14; the community now included a professional editor; designers; community managers; a head moderator and various other moderators; 25 "Electrans," who were closer to the core team but also very active in the community; and more than 430 members who had the privilege of joining Electra's strictly controlled Discord group.

The Revolution explained the necessity of increasing professionalism and transparency: "Imagine I am calling a bank and asking for a meeting to discuss a credit to upgrade wallet systems: 'Hello, sir. I am The Revolution. Can I meet you and see whether I can secure a credit of 1 million Euros?' They would hang up on me. I would do the same. Who would trust a guy with the name The Revolution?"

As their professionalism increased, the Electra core team members also became more popular in global crypto communities. Various projects asked to consult with Electra's experts to solve their own problems. The Electra core team was there to help others. The members did not see making data money as a competitive practice among various projects. Cooperation and solidarity were their key values. Asmoth, a key member of the core team, was responsible for community relations. He said, "We are empathy builders, we need to reach out to people, teach what we learn, learn what we don't know. Calm and assured, we are a community that everyone loves and respects."

He was correct on this point, and this would be confirmed by cryptocurrency communities around the world. Binance, the world's largest data money exchange, uses various outreach tools to keep itself at the center of cryptocurrency trading. It has research and academy divisions and publishes reports and educational digital pamphlets on cryptocurrencies and blockchains. Binance prefers to write its globally popular reports only about cryptocurrencies with very large trading volumes. However, it also organizes annual votes to identify the most popular cryptocurrency project that, like Electra, does not make it to the top one hundred list in terms of market capitalization. The prize is a report written by Binance Research, an elevator to move a lesser known data money up to the main stage of the crypto world.

Excited about the 2020 "Oscars" of crypto communities, the Electra core team members found out that people around the world were voting for them, which increased their hope of winning. The team members began to reach out in a more systematic fashion, testing their global outreach. Now they had a community with members on every continent. The core team was composed of people living in five time zones, creating a difference of up to twelve hours. Yet their money was only one among seven thousand other active projects—only a drop in a lake, as one member put it.

Yet Electra was voted "the best project" of the year by thousands of people who had joined the Binance campaign. Becoming a sensation among crypto communities, Electra was then approached by four reporters from Binance Research who wanted to study the project inside and out. The audit was conducted six days a week for two weeks, with about four hours of meetings every day. Jenova (Antoine Aimé), Ruru (Ruanne Lloyd), Master Den (Aykut Baybaş), and Asmoth represented Electra in this process of intense scrutiny. Then, on July 27, 2020, Binance announced its publication of the Electra report over Twitter, accepting Electra into the world of major global data monies.

Now the core team knew that Electra had joined a new league. At the beginning of summer 2020, before the Binance campaign had begun, Electra's total market capitalization had been $3 million. At the end of the same summer, it was were worth around $13 million, representing an increase in value of 433 percent over a mere three months. In the same period, Bitcoin's market capitalization had increased by only 75 percent. A new chapter in the history of Electra was about to emerge. Yet no one could predict that Electra would soon collapse. If it had not died, it would have easily reached a market capitalization of $35 million and perhaps even more, following all other cryptocurrencies' rally in February 2021.

## THE FALL OF ELECTRA

At the time of the Binance report's publication, Electra had a very active core team of fourteen members with clear mandates and roles in the maintenance of the cryptocurrency and its blockchain and around twenty thousand users active around the money's orbit. They formed a money-maker community whose members worked without being paid. They had two full-time core team members who worked pro bono, and many of the core team and ancillary team members, fueled by passion for Electra, were working twenty to thirty hours a week without pay. This activity was taking place at a time when Electra01 was not joining any team meeting. Overall, he had joined only 5 of the 130 meetings that the core team had held since 2018.

Figure 5.1 summarizes Electra01's contribution to the community deliberation process. He used Bitcointalk's Electra pages as a medium to reach out to the community, but the community was mostly elsewhere. The most active members, numbering around 430, used Discord, and others were dispersed across Twitter, Telegram, Facebook, and Reddit. Even on a channel he built himself, he was very private and silent. He wrote a total

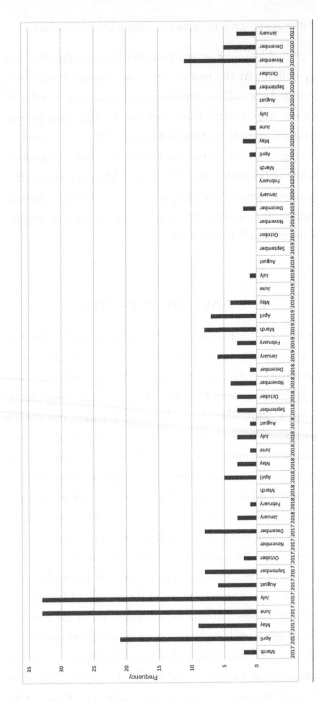

**FIGURE 5.1** Monthly frequency of Electraoi's Bitcointalk messages.

of 205 messages in forty-four months, or less than 5 messages per month. For a total of thirteen months, he did not write anything public to address the community.[7] During the seventeen months immediately before he started the sell-off, he wrote only eight messages. His last message, one month before the collapse, was a congratulatory note to the core team members for their hard work. The message prior to that was dated three months earlier; in it, he had copied and pasted what was then old news that Electra had been accepted into a new market. The message before that was also a note about the markets and had a congratulatory tone. For someone afraid that the core team would exclude him from the project, he had been strangely silent for almost two years, until he had begun to sell off his Electras.

Despite the core team's deliberative and collaborative decision-making process, Electra01 stayed away from discussions and chose to draw only on his implicit veto power, which he derived from being the founder, as well as controlling a massive amount of premined and staked Electras, the sudden dumping of which would kill the project. There was no one who had more Electras than Electra01.

Electra01 knew that his contribution to the making of Electra was limited to founding and supporting it with a very small amount of cash and mostly premined Electras. He was aware that, without a community, Electra was merely an idea, not money. He knew how much the core team worked and frequently showed his appreciation for their hard work. He was proud of Electra's global success, and he was also aware of the fact that the community saw his anonymity as a problem. The charm of the "Satoshi of Electra" had turned into a liability. Electra01's first name and private email had been leaked by a crypto market he once used, and although a few core team members later learned about this, they had not made this information public, even at times when their rift had become difficult to navigate.

I had observed the Electra community, interviewed Electra01 and a number of the community members many times, joined their team meetings, and enjoyed access to their cell phone numbers (which facilitated a direct WhatsApp channel to a few of them). Nevertheless, I was surprised about the events of the last week of November 2020, when I received a private Discord message from Asmoth, the other anonymous central figure in the community:

> Good morning Koray, and Happy Thanksgiving to you and your family. Something very big just happened to Electra . . . we just took a kick in the pants at our value of ECA. I, as well as others, have a lot of fiat into this, and we just watched it tank . . . so that's enough to churn your stomach . . . but, with what has been going on . . . we didn't know what else to do.

I immediately checked Electra's value. It was like someone was pushing Electra off a cliff. The money was taking an enormous dive in value (figure 5.2). No one I knew other than Electra01 had such a power. At that moment, I realized that he had decided to sell all of his Electras and leave the community. I had difficulty believing what he was doing. He had drawn a sword no one believed he would touch. Electra01 was dumping Electra.

The core team's two central members, Asmoth (community relations leader) and Robert Bakker (chair of the Electra Foundation), had talked with the founder regarding the premines and stakes under his control. Electra01 had already pledged this capital for the development of the community, mentioning that he would take out only his personal cash investments. Now the foundation was asking for the rest of the premines to cover project expenses and investments. Furthermore, Ruru and others had been working on a new update to carry the Electra community to its new chapter, as described in the third version of the

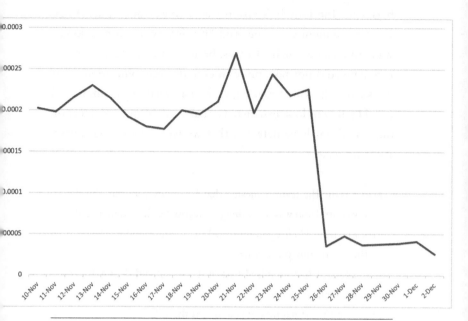

**FIGURE 5.2** The fall of Electra.

*Source*: Coinmarketcap, https://coinmarketcap.com/currencies/electra/.

white paper, which Electra01 had approved, albeit with second thoughts about it. For a long time now, the community had been pushing for changes that Electra01 did not wish to make; yet he did not have the social power or the willingness to join the team to change the members' decision. He had been enjoying the community's success and the brilliance of his original plan, as well as supporting the community in times of crisis by spending premines that he said he had earmarked for support in the first place. He had already sent the foundation 300 million ECA from his premined holdings.

From the perspective of Electra01, the team's incessant thirst to improve and develop Electra had to be checked and balanced. The founder's vision was a conservative one. As an Electra community member said, "Eo1 is very risk averse, doesn't want to change much." In this, he was correct. Eo1, his other nickname, did not take pride in everyday economization. Four weeks after he killed Electra, we had a WhatsApp audiovisual call. He did not look exhausted or battered; from his demeanor, one could not have detected that we were conversing during Electra's wake.

ELECTRAO1: The team requested that I hand over all funds under my control and was not willing to negotiate. They wanted it all.

THE AUTHOR: Hadn't you promised the premine and its stakes to the community previously?

ELECTRAO1: I had promised part of it. Not all and definitely not the stakes.

THE AUTHOR: What moved you to start the sell?

ELECTRAO1: When I saw the team Twitter update about progress made on the new code, I posted a message of praise on Bitcointalk. The team responded by removing my Bitcointalk forum link from Coinmarketcap and me from the team page that week. A week later or so I get a message from the team asking me to hand over all funds under my control and they were not willing to negotiate. The recent actions against me had already made me bitter and the latest request made me suspicious of a coup in the upcoming update. I subtly and politely asked to see the code multiple times over two months to ease my suspicions, but my requests were ignored. After a certain point, I had enough of waiting and decided to reduce my risk.

THE AUTHOR: What could they have done with that code?

ELECTRAO1: They could have excluded my wallets and burnt all the premined and staked ECAs I controlled if I wasn't cooperative. And this was the first move they did after I refused to cooperate and started to sell. They excluded my wallets during the airdrop.

He was right in that they excluded his wallets during the airdrop—a process during which a new cryptocurrency project gives the new money that comes with the new project to all the (old) wallets of another project, as if the monies were dropped from the air into the old wallets. However, the exclusion was a response to Electra01's sale of his Electras, thereby taking down the entire value of the community money. Ruru, or Ruanne Lloyds—the director of the IT hub of a South African corporation who leads seventy coders in her full-time job—had been one of the two leaders of Electra's coding team. In an interview after Electra01's sell-off, she challenged the founder's story:

RURU: It is not true that we were hiding anything. We meet every week as a team, he was invited to join us. He never asked myself for access to the code. I myself did not have access to the code whilst it was in development. We followed the same pattern for each release. It is an open-source project. The current block-chain source code is public so any person can join and see it.

THE AUTHOR: Were you planning to exclude Electra01?

RURU: I assure you that we were not. First, we never had an idea of airdrop; it came after E01 began dumping. Second, we were already negotiating with him regarding the premined ECAs. There were disagreements, but nothing major looking at it from our perspective. He dumped while we . . . were still in negotiations.

On January 3, 2021, I joined an Electra core team meeting that included Asmoth, Robert Bakker, Greg, Kai_2007, Ruru, The Revolution, and Master Den, and I heard the same sentiments from the team members. I asked about Electra01's concern, which had sounded legitimate to me:

THE AUTHOR: Electra01 thought that you would burn his ECAs, and you did this immediately, didn't you?

ASMOTH: We didn't do it immediately. We had no plan for an airdrop. Not even a single proposal or discussion about it. We had no plan to fork ECA and create XEP. When he killed ECA, we lost trust in him. So the community did not want him again. Why would you include someone who sold everything and left? He forced us to exclude him. We realized on November 18 that someone started selling ECAs; it was him. We asked him to buy them back. He did not even bother writing back. He, Robert Bakker, and I were negotiating, and we thought that it was in good faith.

ROBERT BAKKER: I want to add something. Eo1 never lied to me. I thought of him as an honest man. He always thought that Electra was his baby. He wanted the baby to follow his own footsteps. He never acknowledged the fact that the baby grew up. And then the community made it money—and real. He realized that he did not have a future in Electra.

THE AUTHOR: He acknowledged this to me, too. He said without a community, Electra would not be Electra.

MASTER DEN: This is good that he did this. But he never joined the community. He stayed away from us. He would even say things like he didn't have a mic to talk to you. He chose to use a veto power in a community who makes every decision by deliberation. He wanted to dictate his preferences. I believe he realized that this would be impossible in the future. If he really wanted to see the code, Ruru would show him. He is using this as a pretext for his terrible move.

RURU: Yes, I would show him. Why wouldn't I?

After reading the minutes of this conversation, Electra01 disputed what was said with an email:

I have never believed in holding all the power or influence and this is not the motive behind my actions. As a person who is very exposed to ECA, I simply found it uncomfortable being left in the dark about what is going on with the code and the existing possibility I could be forked out. The team wanted control of both the pre-mine and stakes and was not interested in negotiation which made me fear that they could, if I did not grant their request, take it by force with the upcoming team fork. The team's big demand, zero negotiation and decision to hide the code from me is what led to my breakdown in trust. Shall I send you the private messages where I asked to see the code multiple times?

People make mistakes all the time. For a variety of reasons, Electra01 was mistaken in his belief that his Electras were going to be burned by the core team. First, I had never sensed even the slight chance of such a possibility in team meetings and individual interviews with community members. Second, Electra01 had told me about his concerns regarding the fact that he was not shown the code. But later I learned from Ruru and Jenova, the two leaders who had wanted to include him in the first place, that he had not addressed his request to them. Third, he had not been a part of the community and was not in a position to read the signals coming from that community. His interpretations drew on the game theory assumptions about human behaviors that he studied in college economics courses. He thought that the community would take a "rational" step to eventually get rid of him. As a risk-averse introvert, he thought that it was time to leave the project before it left him. Thus, killing his money was his rational step. Yet, on the other hand, I don't think it was a big deal to let the founder see the new code of the money he proposed in the first place. It is not rational to think that he would accidentally delete something. He was not just anyone; he was Electra01. The community members had a chance to keep him, but they missed it.

Forty-four months after he had introduced Electra to the world, Electra01 killed it by selling off hundreds of millions of Electras in a variety of markets. The sell-off consisted of the premined Electras and the interest they had earned, an amount he had promised to use for "projects that improve accessibility, reliability and usage of Electra" in the third Bitcointalk message he sent on the day he announced the project.[8] He had also written on August 23, 2017: "I am staking in order to cover the initial, and possibly, future investments I have/will put up for this project from my own capital. The pre-mine was not sold or claimed at all for any of these investments. My personal costs add up to more than $1,000 which is about 100,000,000–200,000,000 ECA with the current market valuation."[9]

The foundation was asking him to honor his word. But if he, as the founder of Electra, gave back the premine and the interest it had earned, he would have nothing left to his name. Electra01 would be a nobody in the Electra project. Furthermore, he had never promised to give everything to a foundation. He thought that Electra was still a young project that he had to support with a variety of instruments. Giving away all the premines would take all of these instruments away from him. He would be an actor without any influence in the community. He decided to take his ball and leave, calling the game over.

Market actors in a variety of exchanges did not know what was going on; they saw that their buy orders were filling fast, and they ended up owning millions of Electras. Then they panicked and began to sell too. But it was too late. There was no one to buy. Electras were worth almost zero within a few days, as illustrated in figure 5.2.

Electra01 continued to write on Bitcointalk's Electra page, trying to help people who still wanted to keep their Electras, which had no value at the time I wrote this chapter. He did not disappear and continued working on what was now "his" project. A good man at heart, he tried to reach out to a few people who still showed some interest in the now defunct Electra. I asked him about his plans for the future:

ELECTRAOI: I am doing my best to help people claim their ECAs. But I am also very exhausted.

THE AUTHOR: How do you feel about the death of ECA?

ELECTRAOI: ECA did not die yet. The blockchain is still moving. A project only truly dies if the blockchain stops. The core team of ECA was behaving suspiciously from my perspective. I moved before they did. I decided to sell my stake in the project before they rid of me. That's it.

## THE BIRTH OF XEP

The core team members took from Electra every infrastructure and device they had built for the old money and then used them to build their new one, Electra Protocol. They were not prepared for such a digital community migration. They found a method used by other projects and organized an airdrop. They changed the contents of their website, removing the foundation webpage entirely. All that remained was a sarcastic link to Electraoi's Bitcointalk page. Electraoi learned about this last move from me. I felt that he was already detached from the project, although he himself did not consider it dead quite yet. The GitHub page where the core team kept all the code was also cleared—but well after Electraoi had copied the code. All platforms except for one Weebly page had been built and operated by the community.

Working without much sleep, the core team members managed to migrate the entire universe that they had previously built for Electra and reconstruct it for Electra Protocol. In a survey I conducted with 246 respondents after the fall of Electra, 93.8 percent of those who filled out the questionnaire did not support Electraoı's move and joined the core team in the new project. When I conducted the survey again among those who stayed in Electra, 65 percent still believed that the core team was right. The community had left the founder behind.

The core team also continued as it was, joined later by the foundation, which then decided to close its doors. The community had lost all the networks, markets, and data but had gained a new platform, one no longer in the shadow of an anonymous founder. Electraoı might have thought that the core team would not choose the drastic measure of leaving the project behind and moving on to a new one. He might even have strategized about deploying a buyback of the Electras that he had sold if the community had stayed. He would even have made money by this move, kept the community together, and continued to enjoy the de facto veto power he had held over the years. If his dumping of Electras was a big surprise, then the core team's departure was a shock.

The community's new money, Electra Protocol, emerged following a forking of their own code, which was a fork of the original Bitcoin. Immediately after Electra Protocol emerged, it had zero value, but despite not being traded in any major market and thanks to the community's backing, the new money was worth 115 times more than the old one on January 14, 2021, a month after the sell-off. At the time of writing, the team had been working on entering the markets. I have been observing their work closely, as they have been observing mine.

One day on Twitter I saw that the community had begun to use the term *data money* to describe the cryptocurrencies around them, and the members wanted to consult me about the sociological universe of their community. They had read a paper I published about cryptocurrencies[10] and had agreed with me about the specific materiality of the money they were making. Such an unexpected performativity had two consequences: First, an actual project began using a new social-scientific proposition to describe itself. Second, they also used that concept as a marketing device, marking Electra Protocol's difference from other projects that were, in fact, also data money projects.

The community members were very interested in the research I was conducting about their community. I had already made my surveys transparent and had allowed two core team members to see the real-time raw data as the community addressed my questionnaire on Google Forms. They were surprised, for example, to see the minuscule contribution of women in their project. They knew that the making of data money communities was male-dominated. Yet seeing that more than 90 percent of the community consisted of men was still a surprise to them. They learned as much from me as I learned from them, an exchange that happens in all fieldwork.[11]

I took joy in observing their meetings and reading their correspondence and communiqués sent to the expanding community. At one team meeting during the last week of my fieldwork, the members decided to invite me to become their strategic adviser. I told them that I would be happy to see my name on their Discord webpage. I already had Discord privileges; however, seeing my name next to the list of team members as an adviser was new. They knew that I did not hold any cryptocurrency because of ethical considerations relating to my fieldwork, and they accepted me as the only person in their community who did not hold any of their data money.

## CONCLUSION

This chapter has investigated the rise and fall of Electra, a crypto-currency project proposed by its anonymous founder, Electra01, and developed by a community of dedicated individuals. Focusing not only on a story of success but also on a case of failure, an analysis of the short history of Electra shows how a data money is developed, proposed, valued, and killed.

Electra was proposed as money by Electra01; it became money, and thus became valuable, after a series of valuation interventions and strategies were deployed by the founder and the community. A well-planned Bonanza created buzz about the new project, which was emerging among thousands of other cryptocurrencies. A staking rate of 50 percent complemented the Bonanza's buy wave with the interest rate's keep wave.

Then a few core members picked up the project from there and began to work on it diligently every day in order to build and maintain a community that would add value to the data and make it money. If Electra01 was the founder, then people like Master Den, Ruru, Asmoth, Jenova, The Revolution, Robert Bakker, and many others were the invisible founders of the community. As the founder himself acknowledged, it was this collective and distributed agency that made Electra money, not his original idea and opening interventions.

The core team used a series of organizational devices and platforms to help people imagine themselves as a community and act like one. Using the U.S. minimum wage as a standard, a core team member estimated that over the first two years of the project, the community used around $1 million worth of person-hours in making, using, and maintaining Electra's devices. In the meantime, Discord became the main administrative platform of the project, providing the community with a framework to define working groups, hierarchies, and specialized communication and collaboration channels. Other platforms—some of which were integrated into Electra's Discord page, such as Telegram, Twitter, Facebook, Reddit, and WhatsApp in multiple geographies and languages—were also used extensively to expand the number of followers. It is in these conversations that the community members began to imagine what they wanted and what directions they wanted to take. As they conversed, they became.

Soon the core team members chose new routes of marketization, such as payment systems and atomic swaps, but they realized that the founder's anonymity constituted a liability, especially for institutional partners. To counter this factor, they decided to use one of the oldest economization institutions— a foundation—to strengthen their new cryptocurrency project. Established as a nonprofit legal entity with a board, the Electra Foundation soon was seen as the project's legitimate governing and representative body. The community members then began to use the foundation to reach out to their absentee founder, who was not interested in the day-to-day affairs of their money community.

As the community grew stronger and more institutionalized, the founder began to conceive of and experience them as a well-defined core. Now it was no longer a mere community but a developed community with a functional differentiation and a variety of organizational devices. Confident in their power, the core team members then asked the founder to do what he had pledged to do in the first place: to send the premined Electras to the foundation to be used for the development of the project. Electraoi sent 300 million ECA to the foundation but kept both the remaining "capital" and the interest earned, or the staked amount. He had pledged money not to a foundation but to the project. For him, the Electra project was larger than the foundation. The community members were the factor that had made the money in the first place, while the foundation was a mere instrument that they had built and used.

Operating on the wrong assumption that the core team was getting ready to dump him, Electra01 dumped his money. As soon as the first batch of 60 million ECA arrived in the marketplace, the core team members, in a last-ditch effort to save the project, reached out to try to convince him to buy them back. They even considered buying everything. But they were not sure how many Electras the founder held and whether he had premined under other names during the Bonanza. They had lost complete *trust* in him while they had developed a project that *The Economist* called a "trust machine."[12] In the meantime, Electra01 had already stopped responding to the core team and used his only remaining channel, the Bitcointalk pages, to describe the team members as "rogue players." As they watched Electra01 kill their money, they decided to move on and to re-create the entire project under a new (yet mnemonic) name.

Electra01 might have been thinking that he was teaching them a lesson, but the core team members knew that they had learned their lesson in money making. As they parted ways, the new Electra Protocol picked up in value immediately, whereas the old Electra nose-dived to zero value, proving once again that money is a social process of valuation. Without a community of makers, monies are nothing but valueless objects, whether they are metal, paper, stone, or data transfer rights.

In accord with the existing literatures that have underlined the social universes of monies, this chapter has demonstrated that Electra, a data money built on a Bitcoin fork, was created by its emergent community using a variety of instruments of economization, from formal organizations such as a foundation to community-building practices such as voting. Chronicling the emergence and development of the Electra community, this chapter has rendered visible the milestones of community building in a cryptocurrency project.

Following these milestones, we saw how two key actors, the founder and the core team, found themselves developing not only money but also differing ways of imagining the project's future. The founder was conservative, wanting to keep Electra as data money as asset. The core team members imagined new economic horizons for their data money as nonsovereign fiat currency, seeing it as a medium for a global payment structure operating on a superfast blockchain. They all were working on making money without being paid. In the place of money, they had something more precious: the motivation and joy of creating something new and valuable. This need to innovate fueled their excitement, and the project came to require more complex institutional buildings and more people to maintain it, as well as more resources to keep it going.

Electra01 needed the community to realize his idea of turning data transfer rights into money. Yet the community members needed to innovate as they mobilized a barter economy in making money. This embedded contradiction fueled a grievance that then turned into a disastrous conflict. The strength of the Electra community turned into its major weakness. Realizing that his absentee yet powerful status in the community would not be tolerated, Electra01 cashed out all the Electras he owned and left.

Contemporary money makers are no longer limited to mints, central banks, or governments. Communities have always been making or earmarking monies, differentiating and personalizing their meaning, use, and materialities in a seemingly impersonal monetary economic universe.[13] However, data monies have created an unpreceded economic universe and have succeeded to the extent that, as of January 2021, their combined market capitalization was larger than the GDP of 92 percent of all countries in the world.

One of those money communities, Electra, affords social researchers an opportunity to study the microcosm of a data money community. This chapter uses the milestones of the rise and fall of Electra to examine the role of economic devices and organizational frameworks in mobilizing the upward valuation of data money. Using Discord as its main organizational framework has enabled the community to build a modular and easy-to-tweak division of labor. Yet we are far from understanding how the very architecture of platforms such as Discord contributes to the substantial shaping of communities such as Electra.

The community members have also been using economic devices such as reports, papers, tweets, visuals, algorithms, and code architectures to pursue their economic objective, and these devices are not of their own making. Thus, we do not know how the deployment of these economic devices on the ground affects the making and changing of new economic communities.

Yet, as this chapter has shown, the collective agency of economic actors, such as the core team of Electra, was stronger than any other single factor in money making. When Electra01 started the sell-off of Electras, the community members lost everything—from the value of their data money to the very founder himself, from their markets to a substantive presence in the cryptocurrency universe. What remained was their belief and enjoyment in making economic things possible. They gave birth to Electra Protocol and now stand at the beginning of an exciting future, thanks to their accumulation of experience, economic devices, and networks. As Master Den put it, "the rest is hard work and good luck."

# 6

## A NEW FRAMEWORK FOR CRYPTOCURRENCY TAXATION AND EXCHANGE PLATFORM REGULATION

Reminiscent of the parable of the blind men and the elephant, we seem to approach cryptocurrencies from a variety of vantage points and propose different descriptions for the same thing. As we have seen in previous chapters, for social scientists, cryptocurrency is digital cash, an electronic currency, a crypto asset, or virtual money.[1] For the Securities and Exchange Commission (SEC), it is a digital asset that behaves like a security.[2] For the Commodity Futures Trading Commission (CFTC), it is a commodity.[3] For the Internal Revenue Service (IRS), it is property.[4] For legal scholars, it is money,[5] not money,[6] fiat currency,[7] not fiat currency,[8] or pseudo-currency.[9] Like in the parable, it seems that we are trying to comprehend the shape of an elephant in the dark.

Such a rich variety in the perceptions of cryptocurrencies in the social sciences and law creates new opportunities for making sense of new monies, their emergent communities, and the proliferation of their markets.[10] However, the same wealth of definitions also contributes to regulatory confusion and a variety of missed taxation opportunities when these conflicting approaches are deployed in designing policies that (fail to) govern crypto economies. Never has another taxation and regulatory topic created a wider spectrum of policy proposals and disagreements than cryptocurrency. Most countries fall into one of the following categories. Some choose not to regulate cryptocurrencies, while many choose to tax them without regulating their markets. Others ban or limit their trading or mining, whereas a few do not even recognize their existence as money. China banned using, investing in, and mining them across the board. El Salvador made a cryptocurrency its legal tender when its government chose Bitcoin as its national currency.

Yet none seems to be exactly sure about what to do with cryptocurrencies and their markets. This confusion gives birth to the varying and, at times, even conflicting definitions of cryptocurrency used by different regulatory institutions, even within the same country, as we see in the United States.

How do we to address this problem? Drawing on the United States as a case study, this chapter argues that we can benefit from the variety of social-scientific perspectives to imagine a unitary and more effective framework for the regulation of crypto economies and the taxation of income accruing from cryptocurrencies. Most confusion regarding the nature of cryptocurrencies emerges from a failure to acknowledge their specific and historically new material ontology.

The intangible yet material nature of new data-money making and blockchain accounting technology creates fundamentally new economic opportunities and thus leads to new regulation and taxation challenges. Overlooking the materially novel universe of data monies, most approaches draw on old regulatory frameworks to address the challenges of new economic realities. As a result, instead of designing a new way to deal with emergent economic realities, these approaches expect such novelties to fit into regulatory regimes designed to address old problems in the first place. Therefore, a cryptocurrency is seen as a commodity by the CFTC, a security by the SEC, and property by the IRS.

This first weakness of the analogical approach gives birth to another and more serious problem. The cryptocurrency exchanges are also understood to be a new version of old markets, this time imagined as entailing two- or multisided exchange relations.[11] We have seen in chapter 3 that these exchange platforms go beyond market relations in that they have multiple functions— such as banking, exchange infrastructure development, minting, payment system maintenance, software development, security, and centralized extrablockchain accounting. Proposing *stack* as a theoretical construct to describe the new sociodigital economization process taking place in these data money exchanges, chapter 3 showed that these exchange platforms can best be understood as economization stacks of multiple interactive layers with a supporting relationship. This is because they deliver an empirically observable range of economic functions, all of which forge or take place in taxable events and thus need to be scrutinized from the perspective of regulation for the common good.

Unlike underdigitalized economic relations that draw on the unitary exchange infrastructures of auctions, outcries, computerized transfers, and the like, hyperdigitalized crypto-platform work takes place in digital sociotechnical spaces where users and makers simultaneously imagine, build, operate, and invert stack economization with invisible taxable events and underregulated yet substantial economic activities.

These two novel economic concepts, data money and stack economization, can help us more effectively address contemporary challenges associated with the new economies based on cryptocurrencies. First, stack economization allows us to identify taxable events more easily and accurately by making visible all economic activities that take place on an exchange platform. Such an enrichment of perspective makes it possible to apply stack regulation to a platform's economic activities. Furthermore, limiting our analysis to a two-dimensional demand-and-supply universe limits our imagination of taxation to the moment when data monies and all other economized assets, properties, and commodities are cashed and transferred to fiat currencies. As we will see later, such a limitation decreases net tax revenues, complicates taxation processes in the name of simplifying them, and prevents regulatory agencies from effectively addressing consumer-investor protection issues in ways that would not curb innovation. By taxing data monies in terms of the same materiality of money, taxation authorities can simplify tax compliance, increase their revenue, make visible a more comprehensive taxable event portfolio, and, finally, foster new crypto-economic innovation.

Would this cause fiat currencies to become less important in world economies and undermine states' democratically accountable governance of economic life? This book has shown that the proliferation of crypto economies did not curtail but rather fostered the dollarization and euroization of trade. Furthermore, the platformization of crypto economies in centralized exchange contexts surprisingly undermined blockchain accounting systems and encouraged almost complete reliance on double-entry bookkeeping. Third, the very organization of seemingly decentered and disintermediated blockchains is based on centralized economic and political relations that are governed by new intermediary institutions.[12] We are witnessing an order-creating economic innovation, not an anarchic one. Finally, various fiscal logics are already embedded in blockchains and their design, making them readier for regulation than many observers expect.[13]

We live in an age that is witnessing an explosion of network effects in platforms, an expansion of data money relations, and an unprecedented stacking of economic relations—to such an extent that even millennium-old definitions of corporeal and noncorporeal property are changing. A webpage, an exchange platform, a universe in the metaverse, and a header space on a webpage are all intangible but can be observed and sensed. The very platforms that economize these new spaces—through everything from online bidding to cryptocurrency trading on centralized and decentralized platforms—now create colossal economic growth that requires a new perspective on platform regulation.

This chapter concludes by discussing concrete taxation and regulation instruments, as well as examples of their deployment on the ground. The emergence of data monies and the platformization of their economic treatment have blurred the boundary between commodities, properties, inventories, capital assets, and securities, on one hand, and exchange, barter, rent, and production relations, on the other. Our taxation philosophy and regulatory perspective have been built from and mobilized by the building blocks of the predigital economic age. Therefore, neither the SEC nor the CFTC has the jurisdiction and power to regulate the entire universe of cryptocurrency markets, as both of their chairs confessed in 2018 in their testimony to the U.S. Senate's Committee in Banking, Housing, and Urban Affairs.[14] Following the proliferation of digital materialities and the hybridization of economic relations around us, we also need to hybridize, enrich, and reform our understanding of taxation and regulation. We cannot continue to address new economic problems with political solutions that were designed for predigital economies.

## OLD AND NEW WAYS TO TAX CRYPTOCURRENCIES

How do we tax these categorially novel monetary developments and regulate cryptocurrency platforms? Currently, the United States is leading among the world's crypto economies in terms of crypto ATMs per person, acceptance of cryptocurrency by the banking sector and other institutional entities, government regulation of cryptocurrency, transparency, and cryptocurrency spending.[15] This leadership position comes with an irony. Government agencies that are supposed to be regulating and taxing cryptocurrency economies do not know how to regulate these crypto economies, let alone what exactly a cryptocurrency is.[16]

The IRS deploys a limited and analogical approach to data monies and treats cryptocurrencies as virtual currencies that are assumed to be operating like property.[17] Pursuing the analogy of property, the IRS defines two different types of such property ownership. "Individuals who hold cryptocurrency as a capital asset and are not engaged in the trade or business of selling cryptocurrency"[18] have to report cryptocurrency income if they keep it for 366 days or more. Any income generated by this cryptocurrency is treated as long-term capital gain and is taxed at a rate between 0 and 20 percent, depending on the taxpayer's ordinary income tax rate. If the cryptocurrency is sold less than 366 days from the date of purchase, any income is treated as short-term capital gain and is taxed at a rate between 0 and 37 percent, depending on the underlying volume of the gain. Companies or real persons who engage in cryptocurrency business as their primary business are treated differently: their crypto assets are treated as inventory.[19]

There are exceptions. If one receives cryptocurrency as payment for goods or services provided, they have to report it as monetary income by calculating the dollar equivalence of the payment received.[20] The amount of cryptocurrency the taxpayer receives as payment is calculated vaguely, using "the fair market value" of the virtual currency in dollars as of the date of receipt. The IRS chooses to depend on the receiver's subjective judgment of fairness. However, if they keep the cryptocurrency for the following tax year, it becomes property again and can be taxed only if the receiver converts it to dollars.

The IRS's detailed account of crypto taxation masks an irony. Its logic draws on a false analogy because cryptocurrency is not property, even when using a very broad definition of such. The philosophy of taxing properties draws on the high transaction cost of corporeal and real properties. Corporeal properties are defined as visible, tangible, and thus perceptible by the senses, such as touch or sight. Real properties, such as a house or land, are also immovable.[21] Because it is very difficult to move these tangible things, their transaction costs are high. A cryptocurrency is not corporeal and real property. As we saw previously, data monies are intangible yet material; they consist of the right to transfer data privately on a public accounting system called a blockchain.

However, the IRS may have been thinking of incorporeal properties, defined as things that cannot be seen or handled, such as a trademark.[22] Still, these things over which actors have a legal claim need to be nonfungible for their right to be seen as property. Owning a fungible dollar as paper money or a Bitcoin as data money is not owning an incorporeal property. It is owning money itself. Hence, data monies are neither corporeal nor incorporeal properties. Yet nonfungible tokens (NFTs), which are essentially data certificates or titles of ownership, can operate in relation to intangible yet material properties that are produced and exchanged on metaverse and nonmetaverse webpages such as Decentraland and Somnium Space. Yet the IRS does not distinguish digital properties and their new corporeal characteristics.

The IRS's decision to treat data monies as property is informed by the legal universe in which they establish their position. Bound by the federal government's assumption that only metal and paper monies and their digital representations can be accepted as fiat currency, the IRS cannot to treat data monies and currencies as monies or currencies. The irony of not accepting cryptocurrency as a currency emerges from this legal constraint.

Avoiding the challenge of reforming our legal framework as we are dealing with new economic realities, we are currently addressing economic novelties by forcing them to fit into our old legal frameworks. This is not very different from insisting on taxing paper money income with metal monies, as happened in Kublai Khan's era in the thirteenth century. There exists an alternative based on a precedent. Much like taxing paper money with paper money, data money income can be taxed with data money. But how?

There are two ways we can carry out such a task. The first draws on legitimizing cryptocurrencies as nonsovereign fiat currencies and thus treating them much like other foreign currencies, such as the euro in the U.S. context. One may argue that the volatility of cryptocurrencies makes them unsuitable for treatment as foreign currencies. It is true that many cryptocurrencies are volatile, but many fiat currencies are even more volatile than Bitcoin—for example, the Turkish lira, the Venezuelan bolivar, and the Lebanese lira in 2021. We cannot infer that cryptocurrencies are volatile simply because they are not made by states. As community monies, their value depends on the ways in which their community values and makes them. By treating cryptocurrencies as nonsovereign fiat currencies, the IRS can identify an entirely new universe of taxable events. Pioneering legal scholars such as Josephine Nelson have already proposed the validity and the historical legitimacy of treating data monies as nonsovereign fiat currencies and have called for taxation and regulatory agencies to start imagining the design of new frameworks.[23] Similarly, for G. E. Kalbaugh, cryptocurrency is foremost a currency.[24]

The second way—that is, taxing data money with data money—is simpler but requires the Federal Reserve to take a radical step. The IRS can use the dollar form of a central bank digital currency (CBDC-USD) as a benchmark to identify the taxpayer's gain and loss without expecting a formal sale of a cryptocurrency as if it were corporeal and real property. Thus, a novel form of data money tax can be collected without treating cryptocurrencies as property and without necessarily waiting for the taxpayer to "sell" them. If a taxpayer has one hundred various data monies that are worth 10,000 CBDC-USD in March 2021 and if they are worth 12,000 CBDC-USD when the time comes to pay taxes, their taxable income is 2,000 CBDC-USD. In this way, the IRS can identify income without specifying the currency source of income. Much like with stock-agnostic taxation of securities income, as long as income can be monitored by a data money form, the IRS will be in a position to more accurately identify taxable events.

Currently, in the absence of a Fed-issued CBDC-USD, the vacuum is filled with imitations of data dollars—i.e., *stablecoins* such as Tether (USDT) and USD Coin (USDC). The problem with these monies is that they use the credibility of the dollar without sharing the cost of maintaining that credibility and they enjoy colossal market capitalizations by using the trust that people have in the dollar.[25] Their large-scale adoption creates systemic risks for fiat currencies,[26] since a currency that mimics its original is a derivative instrument that has to be regulated to control for its effect on the original asset. If not, the pegged currency may destabilize the currency on which it depends. Because the dollar is a sovereign fiat currency, it can be legitimately derived only by a sovereign intervention. USDT and USDC are nothing but data money imitations of the dollar's metal and paper versions. Their issuers' claims that they deposit an equal amount of dollars to back and "stabilize" their imitation of the underlying fiat currency do not change the fact of imitation. More importantly, for some, these imitations can be regarded as blockchained collateralized forgeries. The Fed has already started to prototype its own CBDC-USD,[27] which would stabilize the dollarization of world trade, control the possible adverse effects of dollar-based stablecoins, economize on the printing of dollars, and, finally, help increase the federal government's income by implementing tax collection via a central bank data money.

## STACK REGULATION OF CRYPTOCURRENCY EXCHANGE PLATFORMS

The IRS does not regulate economic relations; it imposes taxes on income that accrues from those relations. The two agencies that can regulate data money markets are the SEC and the CFTC, neither of which seems to be sure about how to deal with cryptocurrencies. Economic relations that take place around the exchange of securities are regulated by the SEC. Since the U.S. Supreme Court decided the famous case of *SEC v. Howey*,[28] a three-step Howey test has been applied to see whether an asset is a security: if money is (1) invested in a common enterprise (2) with the expectation of a profit (3) that emerges from the economic activities of a third party, then the investment is regarded as a security. For example, buying a company stock is buying a security. Buying gold is not; it is buying a commodity. What about buying data monies?

If a data money is proposed as an initial coin offering (ICO), it can be regarded as a security, for it is bought with money with the expectation of profit and the organization that offers the

ICO is managed by others. However, not all cryptocurrencies are ICOs; the combined value of all ICOs in 2021 made up only 2.8 percent of the 2021 cryptocurrency market capitalization. As of January 2021, 5,728 ICO projects raised $27 billion, making them a mere drop in the sea of all cryptocurrencies' centralized exchange economy worth of $1 trillion.[29] It seems that the ICO hype is over. The SEC's decision to view the ICO as a form of security in order to regulate cryptocurrencies is not only radically limited but also misses a great majority of crypto-economic activities that need to be regulated.

More importantly, data money is not a security because when one buys Bitcoin, the profit does not come (if it ever does) from the managerial effort of an organization that supplies Bitcoin. First, there is no company, and, second, no managerial practice is associated with the Bitcoin supply. This is why the SEC is correct to have second thoughts about its willingness to regulate cryptocurrency markets except when they are framed as ICOs.

In contrast to the vagueness of the SEC regarding the nature of cryptocurrencies, the CFTC claims to know what a cryptocurrency is—namely, a commodity. The CFTC draws on the Commodity Exchange Act (1936), which does not define but lists commodities:

> The term "commodity" means wheat, cotton, rice, corn, oats, barley, rye, flaxseed, grain sorghums, mill feeds, butter, eggs, Solanum tuberosum (Irish potatoes), wool, wool tops, fats and oils (including lard, tallow, cottonseed oil, peanut oil, soybean oil, and all other fats and oils), cottonseed meal, cottonseed, peanuts, soybeans, soybean meal, livestock, livestock products, and frozen concentrated orange juice, and all other goods and articles, except onions . . . and motion picture box office receipts (or any index, measure, value, or data related to such receipts), and all services,

rights, and interests (except motion picture box office receipts, or any index, measure, value or data related to such receipts) in which contracts for future delivery are presently or in the future dealt in."[30]

Needless to say, the list does not include cryptocurrency. However, in 2015, the CFTC decided to view cryptocurrencies as commodities—not because data monies had any intrinsic qualities that would render them commodities but because economic actors were planning to offer derivative instruments that mimic Bitcoin's price movements. One of those actors, Coinflip, experienced a controversy with one of its customers about a Bitcoin derivative. Issuing an order on this controversy, the CFTC wrote: "Section 1a(9) of the Act defines 'commodity' to include, among other things, 'all services, rights, and interests in which contracts for future delivery are presently or in the future dealt in.' . . . Bitcoin and other virtual currencies are encompassed in the definition and properly defined as commodities."[31] This definition is so broad that only onions and movie ticket receipts were specified as remaining outside of its definition. It is this legal fait accompli—not a philosophical definition or a serious legal argument—that included Bitcoin in the CFTC's jurisdiction. Pork belly and Bitcoin . . . they have futures, so they should be commodities. Interestingly, the CFTC chair who pulled data monies into the CFTC's jurisdiction in 2015 has argued in one of the best articles on cryptocurrency regulation that cryptocurrencies should most likely be regulated not by the CFTC but by the SEC, for they do not have commodity properties.[32]

Yet the CFTC has an interesting jurisdictional limitation. It cannot regulate spot commodity markets; it has the power to regulate only the trading of any instrument that is derived from a commodity, such as cotton or oil futures.[33] Showing exceptional institutional creativity and choosing to approach the nature of cryptocurrency from its derivatives, the CFTC ruled that cryptocurrency futures fall under their regulatory authority. This is no different from arguing that money may not be a commodity but its future contract is.

Thus, we arrive at a fascinating bureaucratic megacrack—or even perhaps a canyon. The SEC can regulate crypto markets if they behave like securities markets, as in the case of ICOs. But ICOs are no longer significant. The CFTC can regulate cryptocurrency markets only when they trade futures contracts, leaving aside actual spot markets. The result is that cryptocurrency markets in the United States are not regulated at all at the federal level. With their global capitalization passing $2.5 trillion in 2021, this regulatory hole might be among the largest in recent economic history.

Seeing this gap, many state regulators have stepped in. Wyoming and Illinois are working on a new legislative framework. Ohio experimented with receiving state tax payments in cryptocurrency in 2018 but then discontinued the experiment the following year. Hawaii decided to curb crypto markets by asking them to collateralize the dollar equivalent of all the cryptocurrencies that they traded. This was akin to asking banks to actually own all the dollars that they lend. Exchanges left Hawaii. New York took another route, as its Department of Financial Services took action to regulate virtual currency under the state's Financial Services Law. Instead of legally defining cryptocurrency, the law defines market activities that draw on cryptocurrencies as follows:

> Receiving virtual currency for transmission or transmitting virtual currency, except where the transaction is undertaken for non-financial purposes and does not involve the transfer of more than

a nominal amount of Virtual Currency; storing, holding, or maintaining custody or control of Virtual Currency on behalf of others; buying and selling Virtual Currency as a customer business; performing Exchange Services as a customer business; or controlling, administering or issuing a Virtual Currency.[34]

This innovative move made it possible to regulate cryptocurrency cash markets for the first time, albeit only for New York City residents. Furthermore, this law has not been tested in the U.S. Supreme Court yet because the markets that facilitate cryptocurrency trading in the city have supported and welcomed regulation since their inception and have openly cooperated with the state legislature.[35] They know that the legitimation of cryptocurrencies as financial instruments increases their chances of making money from them.

The SEC and the CFTC cannot regulate crypto economies—not because they are failing to do their job but precisely because they are doing their job well. They are not designed to operate in this novel geography. The SEC works with securities, while the CTFC focuses on commodity derivatives. In order to be able to do anything about cryptocurrencies, they had to treat them either as a security or as a commodity derivative. And so they did.

The time has come to name the baby. A cryptocurrency is a money form with a new materiality: data. This chapter has shown that data monies should be treated as nonsovereign fiat currencies and approached as such. Yet this is not sufficient for regulation. Because of the data materialities' innate material characteristics, these new monies create a broad economic opportunity infrastructure on which diverse financial and economic architectures can be built. Thus, it is only when we incorporate an analytical tool to illustrate such economic richness that we can start to identify the spaces for platform regulation.

Stack regulation may be the answer. Instead of treating platforms as mere markets, stack regulation can locate all platform businesses that an organization manages within a single frame of analysis. Figure 3.1 summarized the variety of economic functions and practices that centralized cryptocurrency exchanges organize in six major areas of interaction. Once made visible, these areas help us to identify economic events that require regulation. It is impossible to list all the activities that should be regulated on a cryptocurrency exchange platform here; however, we can still identify several rules of thumb to help imagine a general framework for regulation design.

Exchanges are operating like banks, running substantial custodial services as their customers deposit billions of dollars' worth of data monies. Such services create two crucial risks for economic actors. First, in case of a hack, the exchange can lose all the data monies customers have entrusted to them. However, the terms-of-service agreements do not set out any legal obligation for the exchange to pay back the customers' data monies. When banks keep customers' monies, their security is guaranteed by the state; exchanges operate like banks but without any guarantee. Second, because exchanges technically and practically control the data monies that their customers buy from them and, in return, provide them with in-exchange rights to trade with them, these exchanges can also trade with the money that is entrusted to them.[36] Data monies are fungible; therefore, they can be traded at will and for very short periods of time—as short as a few seconds in the case of flash lending. There is no law or regulation that makes trading with customers' data money impossible. For every person who makes money, there is another who loses it, and exchanges are no exception, for they lose too. As has previously happened to many other exchanges such as QuadrigaCX and Bitfinex, these platforms at times fail to send the data monies that they claim to keep on their customers' behalf. An organizational intervention with a precedent can address these problems of security and market ethics.

Until the late 1960s, stock trading was taking place by transferring paper stocks of companies between traders. These paper stocks were then sent to the buyers' physical addresses. When trading volumes increased, material limitations began to constrain the trading activities themselves to the extent that exchanges had to close one day a week for purposes of bookkeeping. The solution was to digitally represent all paper stocks and keep them in a single place. The new Depository Trust & Clearing Corporation (DTCC) began to serve as the custodial clearinghouse for all paper stocks, and the federal government guaranteed its integrity and security. This move also prevented these same stocks from changing hands without authorization.

Drawing on the precedent of the DTCC, a Central Cryptocurrency Depository (CCD) could be created to supply customers with a custodial service in the form of wallets that secure their crypto assets while at the same time providing security services to customers who choose not to withdraw their crypto assets into their own wallets. In this way, cryptocurrency exchanges could be covered by a public guarantee, and their customers could feel safer when platform trading. One can object to this idea in that it undermines the very definition of blockchains. This is correct, but blockchains are already being undermined by the central authority of cryptocurrency exchanges. Customers are choosing to keep their money in these exchanges, even without security and a guarantee. With the CCD, these assets would be under public protection. Furthermore, the CCD could also contribute to greater transparency regarding the movements of data monies.

Another advantage of the CCD is that it could prevent exchanges from using their own or customers' data monies in trading. Exchanges usually deny that they trade on the platforms they operate. My fieldwork and interviews suggest the opposite. When asked whether they trade on their own platform, almost all my respondents (98 percent) denied that they do. When asked what percentage of other platforms' representatives trade cryptocurrencies with or without their customers' data monies, all traders stated that *all* other trading platforms trade on their own platforms.

The CCD could address the question of security but could not address possible problems regarding trading ethics. For this and other issues, a new regulatory agency is needed. Instead of taking an analogical approach to cryptocurrencies or enlisting agencies that are designed to regulate other things, such as securities and commodity derivatives, Congress should design a commission specifically to regulate cryptocurrency exchange platforms. A Data Money Exchange Commission (DMEC) would be the only organizational solution to the problems that emerge from a huge regulatory canyon that cannot be covered by existing agencies. Cryptocurrencies are data monies and need to be regulated as such.

Currently, data money exchanges operate like banks and lend money for trading. They also mint their own money and incentivize the use of their own monies in trading, thus creating unfair competition for other community or corporation data monies. This is not very different from operating an exchange while at the same time trading in it. Such a clear conflict of interest reduces trust in exchange institutions and decreases their long-term income as a business—and could be avoided with DMEC regulation.

The DMEC could also work to regulate the financial bridges between centralized exchanges (CEXs) and decentralized exchanges (DEXs). CEXs sell data monies by accepting fiat currencies and thus contribute to the dollarization and euroization of trading. DEXs such as Uniswap do not accept fiat currencies and only allow customers to barter an assortment of data monies among themselves. However, it is possible to buy data money such as Ethereum from a CEX and barter it for other data monies at a DEX. In this way, users can continue to make money from their Ethereum and keep it outside the regulatory and taxation domain while at the same time enjoying all the benefits of a working financial and economic universe that allows for DEXs in the first place. The DMEC could address this invisible regulatory gap by bringing DEXs into the economies' regulatory framework.

Laying out all the details of a framework for the regulation of cryptocurrency exchanges and the taxation of cryptocurrency income goes beyond the objectives of this book and should be prioritized by Congress in collaboration with industry actors, the Federal Reserve, the SEC, and the CFTC. But before such work can begin, we have to acknowledge that we are witnessing a historically new and materially novel money form. Cryptocurrencies as data money provide economic actors with the opportunity to engage in innovative economic practices that hybridize barter, trade, and gifting in centralized institutional settings. This chapter has argued that we have to design a new regulatory approach to mimic the innovative economic stacking that we observe in exchange platforms. Furthermore, stack regulation of cryptocurrencies and their economic institutions can work only if we tax them with the money materiality that they make and use—that is, data money. The data money tax can be deployed with or without a Federal Reserve data money, the CBDC-USD. With the Fed's contribution, such a taxation practice would increase the government's regulatory capacity and tax income more effectively. Without the Fed's stablecoin, the data money tax is still possible but would require a more complex regulatory environment and increase the government's organizational and financial costs.

## CONCLUSION

This chapter has shown that regulators are facing two failed approaches, both resulting from analogical thinking. First, they treat data monies as commodities, securities, or properties. This chapter has shown that a cryptocurrency is a new form of money that is made by monetizing the right to send data. It is not money made of data, for all digital monies are made with data anyway. Thus, it has to be treated as such if we do not want to perpetuate the irony of arguing that a cryptocurrency is not a currency. Second, they view exchanges as mere markets. However, cryptocurrency exchanges are not mere markets. These exchanges stack various economization practices and businesses on the platforms that they operate. For us to be able to regulate them effectively, we need to stack our regulatory capacity and mobilize a dynamic stack regulation.

Deploying the concepts of data money and stack economization as scientific tools and organizational devices addresses the colossal regulatory gap in the United States. The taxation of data monies can be carried out with the data monies themselves. Taxation can be performed with or without CBDC-USD. If the Federal Reserve joins the rest of the world by making dollars as data money, it can create a revolutionary regulatory and taxation instrument, in addition to making its own money-making process more economical and up-to-date. Then the IRS can collect taxes that it fails to identify now and make its taxation practices more effective. Furthermore, a new regulatory agency designed by Congress, the DMEC, could collaborate with the industry, the SEC, and the CFTC to propose design principles for formalizing decentralized and centralized exchanges and for bringing them into the modern regulatory universe of contemporary economies.

Drawing on the analysis that a cryptocurrency is data money, the chapter has shown that the specific intangible materiality of this new type of money defines a new spectrum of economizing behavior for actors. Actors can monetize nonsovereign fiats without a central authority; they can tokenize almost all human practices from art to politics, from accounting to social movements; they can account for these economization practices using blockchains; they can bypass these blockchains and trade cryptos without registering them on blockchains by leaving them in the custody of exchanges; they can give, barter, track, and exchange them and their copies; and they can turn art forms into registered and account-trailed nonfungible data monies such as NFTs. This is an expanding and novel economic world. Using old concepts, we have failed to regulate and make sense of this new world.

At the most general level, this chapter has proposed a metachange to policies on regulation and taxation in relation to data money economies. Drawing on an analysis of the historically novel materiality of data money and its new accounting infrastructures on blockchains, the chapter has shown that platform economies work as stack economization processes. These new economization practices are made possible by the new materialities of data monies and computational industries. In terms of regulation, such a change requires us to imagine stacked forms of regulation that target various economization relations on exchange platforms in a separate yet interrelated manner. This is because these exchange platforms go beyond being mere marketization relations. Regulation has to align with the empirical nature of platformization. We cannot regulate platforms as if they are mere markets. Regulation should be stacked.

This change in strategy has two advantages. First, it avoids the flattening effect of seeing platforms as markets and opens up the regulatory imagination to a series of new contributions that are keyed to the nature of whatever is intended to be regulated. Second, stack economization allows regulators to empirically map numerous functions of cryptocurrency exchanges and clearly mark areas of regulation, such as the minting of new data monies. Currently, one can buy Ethereum to the tune of several million dollars from an underregulated market in the United States and then send it anywhere in the world to be changed to any fiat currency. Refusing to acknowledge the stacked nature of data money markets, China decided to ban them. This led to an increase in Bitcoin adoption, pushing the data money's value up and moving data money industries outside of China.

Another possibility is to incorporate data monies in our current regulatory framework with the introduction of the CCD, which could operate as a state-regulated and -secured constellation of digital wallets. Such a reform would entail imagining economic agency not only in terms of individuals or legal entities but also as digital wallet groups registered under the names of real persons or organizations. Therefore, income could also be identified in terms of data money, and financial transactions could be regulated and controlled without necessarily limiting data money movements. A practical application of such an approach could associate digital wallets with tax identification or social security numbers so that unique economic persons could be identified, thus bringing all crypto-economic activity within the reach of regulation and, at least in democratic countries, under the control of democratically elected agencies and their appointed representatives.[37]

Such a shift in the regulatory mindset would not only address societal needs more effectively but also help us imagine new forms of taxation such as the data money tax. This book has proposed that approaching platforms as stack economization processes can help the public conceptualize new forms of taxation. Currently, taxation draws on digital representations of metal and paper money. We do not tax (with) data money. This is comparable to taxing exclusively with metal money in the thirteenth century, at a time when many economic actors had already begun using paper monies.

Because regulators currently register income only in terms of fiat currency, they need economic actors to sell their assets and return them to fiat currency to identify taxable income. Such an insistence narrows regulatory options to a spectrum between two extremes: either banning all usage of crypto assets or closing certain economization functions of exchange platforms. Yet there is another way. If regulators imagine tax collection in terms of data monies, they can still register income without requiring a conversion to fiat currency.

We live in an economic era when all our economization activities are hybridized with digital materialities. From cryptocurrencies as nonsovereign fiat currencies to the platformization of exchanges, we are witnessing a stacking of business functions, at times by introducing banking to trade relations via cryptocurrencies. The time has come to be as innovative as the economic life that surrounds us. The time has come to stop treating new economic things with analogical thinking, as if they were a version of old things, and instead to analytically design tools for their proper characterization and regulation in a new taxable events universe.

# 7

## WHAT IS TO BE DONE WITH CRYPTO ECONOMIES?

This book has analyzed the sociotechnical universe of data monies, as well as how their exchanges work and how new financial communities make, exchange, and account for data monies by using blockchains. I argue that in order to comprehend the historical specificity of cryptocurrencies, we have to first consider their materiality and its deployment in money making. If we skip this necessary step, we may confuse them with other digitally represented monies, such as the monies that one sees on a bank's ATM screen displaying sovereign fiat currencies like the dollar. Moreover, we may confuse their exchange platforms with conventional spot and derivative money markets. This book has shown that we are witnessing currency as *data money* and money exchanges as *stack economization* processes for the first time in history. We need to take a closer look at these historically new monies and their exchange platforms in order to better understand, benefit from, and regulate them.

Furthermore, we need to better understand the new communities that make and use these monies. An unprecedented number of people are joining the world of finance every day, in an around-the-clock economization process of data money markets and communities. Such a new era of pop finance will have effects on our economic futures in ways we do not even know how to study yet.

The first decade of our century witnessed the emergence of the third hegemonic materiality of money in history: data. Previously, we imagined and exchanged fiat value on metal and paper. We built economies around these monies, drawing on technologies that turned these materials into devices harboring monetary value. Money materials are not neutral instruments. They contribute to the ways in which monies are made and exchanged, as well as the ways in which economies and markets are designed and maintained around them. With the emergence of Bitcoin (BTC) in 2009, and then around ten thousand more data monies in the following decade, we have figured out a way to make money and imagine its value in the intangible materiality of the exclusive *right* to send data.

Usually misunderstood as a passive and solitary data entry in a memory device, in reality data money is an active and relational right to send data from one place to another. These places are defined by the specific blockchain network where these rights are registered. If a network removes your node from its universe, you may still have data about your cryptocurrency in your memory device, but these same data cease to work as money. To work, data money needs actors, devices, and networks that are operational. A data money is not digitally *represented*, as the dollars in your checking account are, but is computationally made with the infrastructural possibility of a blockchain. That is why it is impossible to comprehend the making and workings of data monies without also understanding their accounting systems— that is, blockchains.

Before Bitcoin, monies were digitally represented and exchanged. These relations had to be governed by banks. Banks are controlled by the state, which also serves as a guarantor of the account balances that the banks keep. Unless a legal dispute arises or tax documentation is needed, the documentation of these transfers between accounts owned by human persons (for example, you) or legally defined persons (for instance, a company) are kept private.

The emergence of blockchains proposed a new accounting system and a novel way to transfer money without needing a bank or a state by defining new actors that can claim responsibility for accounting. Replacing banks and states as guarantors and double-entry bookkeeping as accounting, miners began to document all transactions on a digital ledger that we call a blockchain. But how? The answer may look complicated, yet it rests on a very simple logic.

There is no free lunch in any accounting system. Accountants are paid to keep the books in order. In crypto economies, miners are paid to keep the blockchain accounting working. As described in the second chapter, blockchain accountants— or miners, as they are called in crypto economies—invest their time, energy, and infrastructure to ensure that transactions are approved and registered in the space of blockchains. Once registered and accounted for, a transaction is safe and can be checked for validity in every computer that forms part of that operational blockchain system. Everyone can download a copy of this ledger, and every ledger has every transaction that has been approved by miners. In exchange for their successful work, miners receive a unique gift, a payment from the blockchain network. This payment is then used as currency in this new crypto economy— hence, cryptocurrency.

In the beginning, mining was easy. There were not many people transacting. No one could imagine that Bitcoin was going to reach tens of thousands of dollars in value. People would buy pizza with 10,000 BTC—which, at the time of writing this book, are worth half a billion dollars. As Bitcoins have turned into money and have begun to serve as asset or exchange vehicles— and in the case of El Salvador, as a unit of national account— more accountants are needed to register its transactions, thus decreasing the Bitcoins you can make with your mining opera- tions. Such slowing down is achieved by making it more difficult to carry out computational operations, an automatic response conditioned by the coders who wrote the blockchain algorithms. Increasing difficulty has been addressed by increasing the number and capacity of the processors that the miners use; thus, mining has become a very energy-intensive computational industry.

That is why the Bitcoin network burns a lot of energy to operate an accounting and transactional architecture that is now criticized as slow and energy-inefficient. First-generation block- chains built their own services, algorithms, and programs on the specific computational infrastructure of the Bitcoin blockchain. They were slow, massive energy-burner networks that did not provide users with any capability to treat computer programs as money. The Bitcoin network still had some capacity to allow simple programming to be imagined as money; yet the more complex it grew, the slower the network became.

The emergence of second-generation blockchains, with the then superfast and cost-efficient Ethereum network, addressed Bitcoin's problems in a variety of ways. First-generation block- chains facilitated the sending of data as money, whereas second- generation blockchains did so only if certain conditions were met, thus embedding computer programmatic conditions in the materiality of data money making. This allowed for imag- ining contracts made of data as value and transferring a short computer program as a contract, thus changing the nature of accounting from checking for value to checking for a working contract or a program. Essentially, this is still monetizing the right to send data—but in the form of a program and within a very fast network that consumes less energy.

But over time, the Ethereum network also began to face the same challenges that Bitcoin had faced half a decade ago. The Ethereum blockchain was faster and more energy-efficient; still, as more people began to use it and as Ethereum's value increased vis-à-vis the dollar, the Ether cost of transactions (called gas) began to increase in value, too. The extreme volatility of the cryptocurrency markets made it more desirable to execute buy and sell decisions quickly; thus, actors needed transactions to be faster, which could be carried out only by increasing the gas fee one pays for moving data monies. In addition to the increasing costs and decelerating accounting services, Ethereum's and Bitcoin's blockchains were not interchains, which allow other chains to work together. One could build a new blockchain on Ethereum or Bitcoin; however, it was not feasible to build a chain that would connect different blockchains.

The new generation of blockchains—such as Cardano, Polkadot, and Avalanche—sometimes called platforms, provide actors with opportunities to build an entire market or interchain network, as they put mutually exclusive blockchains with varying computing protocols into contact so they can transact with each other. Now it is possible to bridge structurally dissimilar blockchains and carry out transactions on them. It will be immensely difficult for the Bitcoin and Ethereum blockchains to protect their competitive edge if they do not pursue a radical change.

Despite this evolution of blockchain accounting, an actor-based taxonomy of blockchains remains unchanged. Based on fieldwork among crypto-economic actors and a computational analysis of the white papers for the one hundred most valuable data monies, this book has proposed an actor-based taxonomy.

There are two types of blockchains based on who can *transact* in them (private and public) and two types of blockchains based on who can *account* for them (open-accounting and closed-accounting).

These differences are important in approaching and regulating blockchains and their ecosystems. For instance, it would be truly revolutionary for a central bank to offer a cryptocurrency with a public open-accounting blockchain because this would require the central bank to decentralize money-making, transactioning, and accounting services. This move would effectively turn that bank into a *de*central bank, thus making it impossible to change the money supply and circulation without convincing a majority of the miners who validate transactions. However, it would be completely normal and easy for a central bank to use a public closed-accounting blockchain with data monies that can be used by anyone but that cannot be accounted for by the general public. Keeping such a taxonomy in mind is essential when approaching blockchains and their cryptocurrencies; without such a taxonomy, discussing the blockchain of cryptocurrency in general would yield no reliable results in terms of analysis and regulation.

Nevertheless, such a taxonomy is not adequate to make sense of crypto economies; one of the surprising findings of this book is that centralized cryptocurrency exchanges are replacing blockchains as the location of cryptocurrency transactions. Contrary to popular assumptions, most cryptocurrency trades are not registered and accounted for on blockchains. Imagine buying 1 BTC from a cryptocurrency market. If you do not transfer it to your own wallet, it is kept by the market as a custodial asset; thus, it technically "belongs" to the market itself. The owner of that market then can and does use this asset for other purposes, such as trading or marketing, most of the time without you even knowing about it.

As demonstrated in chapter 3, data comparing internally registered versus blockchain-registered Bitcoin trades show that the percentage of Bitcoin transactions registered in the Bitcoin blockchain has been declining. In the future, blockchain accounting may become negligible in centralized exchanges that draw on conventional double-entry bookkeeping, thereby making blockchains a mere tool of final confirmation in trading data monies instead of the primary institution of their transactions.

How then should we understand these new crypto markets? This book has demonstrated that one cannot make sense of them as markets only. Today platforms such as the X Exchange, which I analyzed here, are generally approached as markets with two or multiple sides. In this theoretical approach, *side* refers to a cluster of agents with a singular economic motive. Platform owners, operating like owners of conventional exchanges, provide infrastructure to buyers or renters of services and commodities, whereas sellers use the same infrastructure to supply their commodities to those who want to buy or rent them. Adding a new platform owner to the conventional understanding of markets as mechanisms that bring together supplier and demander, this analysis of platforms as multisided markets is supported by one supplementary observation on the *network effect*. This concept is, once again, borrowed from an older debate on how users of a larger system create a value that was not intended in the first place. Presented by Theodore Vail, the president of American Telephone and Telegraph Company, as "the Bell System" as early as 1909, invisible network effects increased as the number of users increased.[1] Following this central observation, a more mature literature on network effects began to find them mostly in communication and transportation systems, again in association with "the Bell System" and at times in company social science reviews such as the *Bell Journal of Economics*,[2] later to be popularized and developed in the 1980s and 1990s by an ever-expanding literature.[3]

My empirical study of the X Exchange platform showed that there is a fundamental flaw in seeing platforms as multi-sided markets with network effects. Drawing on an analysis of 251 exchanges, which represent 99.99 percent of world's data money trading, and fieldwork in one of the largest crypto exchanges in the world, the book shows that platforms go beyond marketi-zation relations. Describing themselves as *exchange platforms*, they are many things at once: digital mints that make data mon-ies, banks that lend money for trading and charge an interest rate, security service providers that offer their users wallets and vaults, insurance agents that sell insurance against digital theft, data centers that market and produce information, clearinghouses that facilitate various trades, accounting agencies that pursue internal double-entry bookkeeping, and, in a few cases, even courthouses that run arbitration cases.

Seeing platforms as simply a new kind of market not only prevents us from analyzing the economic practices organized under their metaphorical roofs but also makes it impossible to imagine and deploy new regulatory instruments to make them work better and for the common good. This book has offered an alternative vision that calls for approaching platforms as *stack economization* processes. In these exchanges, a variety of econo-mization practices work simultaneously under the same roof, all designed and deployed by the same company. Such multifunc-tionality is a consequence of the material opportunities associated with the possibility of stacking economic relations on a platform made and maintained by computational industries.

Actors can build various market architectures, borrow or lend money to buy a car or a crypto asset, flash lend their assets or flash borrow billions of dollars' worth of data monies for extremely short periods of time (such as a few minutes), lend their data monies to traders who post changing interest rates and maturities, buy or sell derivative crypto assets, send and receive gifts, organize barter, trade dollars and Ethereum, consume security services, subscribe to a trading program, or demand arbitration in case of a disagreement. A platform is not a mere market, and it cannot be regulated and understood as such by imaging it as having sides, as if it was a supply-and-demand mechanism moved by sets of actors.

Approaching platforms as stacked economization processes presents three advantages over approaching them as multi- or two-sided markets. First, we can better observe the multiplicity of *all* economization processes with their changing logics of interaction. Second, such a wealth of processes facilitates analysis with the theoretical capacity to imagine more-effective regulation strategies. Finally, stacked economization helps public agencies imagine new taxation possibilities that go beyond fiat money–based tax. These new forms of taxation can be based on nonfiat currency or data assets and may claim part of nonmonetary income as the responsibility of stack economization companies to share with the public. Seeing platforms as mere markets and treating all other platform economic activities as effects or secondary economization practices misleads analysts and prevents the public from pursuing more effective regulation and taxation practice. Furthermore, it also hinders economic actors in imagining and designing economic devices and networks without the fear of breaking specific laws.

Chapters 4 and 5 have provided a detailed study of the most important dimension of crypto economies: the individual and collective human actors that make up hundreds of global crypto communities. Blockchains are accounting infrastructures, data monies are material devices of economization, and white papers are scientific and/or popular representations. However, without human agency, data monies cannot barter, stack, or exchange by themselves. Addressing this potential gap, this book has taken a detailed look at contemporary data money communities in two steps. First, it has described the general sociological universe of Electra, a data money community that was chosen the best community by a global voting process organized by the world's largest crypto exchange, Binance. Second, it has presented an ethnography of the same community as it proposed, lost, and reimagined its data money. During my two years of fieldwork, Electra collapsed in value as a result of a central controversy in its economic community, giving me the opportunity to observe not only the rise but also the fall of a crypto project.

Chapter 4, an ethnographical analysis of the Electra community, has drawn on four research activities: (1) a survey of 254 Electra members, representing more than half of the core actors who shaped the course of action in the community; (2) a computational text analysis of Bitcointalk's Electra forum, which made visible the contours of discussion and contestation in the community; (3) a computational network analysis of all Twitter interaction data among the 18,600 followers of the handle @ElectraProtocol and their 358,000 followers; and (4) my fieldwork among the actors who make and maintain the Electra community.

Providing the literature with a demographic snapshot of a global data-money community, the chapter has shown how a seemingly transparent, open, trustless data community is dominated by an unprecedented hegemony of well-educated men who live in the West. Underlining this concentration of power, which is in accord with the actors' own descriptions of these relations, the chapter makes visible the centers of power in these "decentralized" financial infrastructures marked by race, education, gender, and geographical location. Needless to say, this detailed study concerns only one community and cannot represent the rest of a large and diverse global sociological universe. Yet it hints at the potential emergence of an unprecedented patriarchal dominance in crypto economies even more acute than in noncrypto-economic relations, where glass ceilings now display many substantive dents.

A focus on discussions within the Electra community has illustrated the members' internal focus and the conceptual devices that they deployed as they designed new economic devices and activities. The analysis of these discussions, distributed in a variety of forums from Twitter to Bitcointalk, showed that it is not those who post most frequently or who are followed by the largest group that carry more weight in the community; rather, it is those who help build clusters and then bridge them to others that are more influential.

Representational influence matters but cannot automatically translate into administrative power. We saw that the most influential Bitcointalk forum or Twitter actors are not necessarily the people who influence the concrete steps that the community takes. The actual leaders are the ones who govern the community on Discord. These people are so powerful that they can even organized a vast digital/material migration of the community.

Chapter 5 has moved away from the general view of a global data-money community and focused on an analysis of Electra's collapse and Electra Protocol's emergence in order to explain the dynamics of continuity and transformation in two ways. First, the discussion has presented the organizational tools, novelties, tactics, and strategies that data money communities deploy as they economize on their various platforms. These tools include gifts, barter frameworks, design sprints, conferences, workshops, prizes, and a variety of architectural, infrastructural, and platform practices—such as forking and air-dropping. Such novelties are hybridized with prior economization devices as old as any institution in the world. Instead of an organizational transformation, we witness an enrichment of organizational innovation that brings together tangible and intangible material orders, devices, and networks, at times facilitated by various human and nonhuman agencies such as foundations, anonymous or pseudonymous actors, and social media handles. Unlike many other analyses that have seen a revolution of trustless systems around blockchains, we have seen that digital innovations do not address questions of trust: for instance, we witnessed how the collapse of trust between Electra's founder and the community leadership led to the phenomenal collapse of the very data money itself. The blockchain did not help them fix this fundamental issue of trust.

Second, the chapter has analyzed what happens if trust and cooperation collapse. When market prices took a dive, the community actors did not sell everything they had and move on to other markets. Refusing to "exit," they decided to use their platform as an economic tool kit, along with their properties such as the webpage, the white paper, the Twitter handle, the Discord infrastructure, and various WhatsApp and other messaging networks, to make a new money based on their experience with the old one. They chose to use the entirely novel economization strategy of starting up a new infrastructure altogether so as to remake Electra, this time as Electra Protocol. Such a move constitutes further evidence that economic actors mobilize choices that go beyond the narrow spectrum of action presented by a neoclassical understanding of markets.

Chapter 6 deployed the concepts of data money and stack economization as scientific tools and organizational devices to address the colossal regulatory gap and invisible taxable events in the United States. We saw that the taxation of data monies could be carried out with the data monies themselves. If the Federal Reserve would join the rest of the world by minting dollars as data money, it could create a revolutionary regulatory and taxation instrument, in addition to economizing and updating its own money-making process. Hence, the Internal Revenue Service would be able to collect taxes on income that it has failed to identify and to better economize its taxation practices. Data money should be taxed with data money. This is the only viable way for the future.

Furthermore, a new regulatory agency that Congress can design, the Data Money Exchange Commission, could collaborate with the industry, the Securities and Exchange Commission, and the Commodity Futures Trading Commission to propose design principles for formalizing decentralized and centralized exchanges and for bringing them into the modern regulatory universe of contemporary economies.

In terms of regulation, the chapter pointed out the urgent need to imagine stacked forms of regulation that target various economization relations on exchange platforms in a separate but interrelated manner. We saw that regulation has to be keyed to the empirical nature of platformization; thus, it has to be stacked. In this way, regulators can empirically map numerous functions of cryptocurrency exchanges more accurately and clearly see areas of regulation, such as the minting of new data monies. These "new" markets are also minting their monies. They are not mere markets but stacked places with their own mints.

If this is the case, we can then imagine a new organization, the Central Cryptocurrency Depository, which can work for a public bank of digital wallets, associating these wallets with tax identification numbers. Thus, the colossal crypto-economic world could move to more transparent and democratic control.

Looking at our discussions about cryptocurrencies, it seems as if we are trying to decide what to do with them, whether they are good or bad, and whether we should embrace or ban them before we truly understand what they are. As we do so, we are attracted to analogical thinking to address analytical problems. We treat data monies *as if* they were mere digital representations of previous monies. We approach their platforms *as if* they were mere multisided examples of previous markets. This book has shown that it is problematic to deploy such analogical thinking and has proposed a radically new and more useful alternative for understanding cryptocurrencies and their centralized exchanges.

As they have created an economic universe that is worth trillions of dollars, crypto economies can no longer be seen as weak and transitory formations that are used for speculation and illicit economic affairs or organized by nerds with strange ideals. In the second decade of data monies, it is time to acknowledge that they are made and valued by people and institutions that monetize the right to send data among themselves. These people are not necessarily technology enthusiasts. They are teachers, students, farmers, accountants, and white- and blue-collar workers. They make and trade data monies. They account for their transactions. Institutionally, their around-the-clock exchange relations have already accumulated almost half a century of crypto trading hours when compared to the trading hours of conventional bourses.

Understanding the data materiality of cryptocurrency opens up an entirely new way to make sense of, benefit from, and regulate data monies. Comprehending their accounting systems on blockchains and the ways in which their exchanges operate will allow us not only to understand their economic universe more accurately but also to imagine more effective ways to regulate them.

Many regulators seem to understand cryptocurrencies as digital currencies and their exchanges as two-sided markets. Such analogical thinking, supported by microeconomic approaches to cryptocurrencies, results in a misleading or partial analysis of cryptocurrencies, their markets, and the people who make and exchange them.

This book has shown that cryptocurrency is not merely a digital currency. It is data money. The specific intangible materiality of this new type of money defines a new spectrum of economizing behaviors for actors. They can monetize nonsovereign fiat currencies without a central authority; they can tokenize almost all human practices from art to politics, from accounting to social movements; they can account for these economization practices using one of the four mutually exclusive kinds of blockchains; they can trade cryptocurrencies without registering them on blockchains by leaving them to the custodial services of exchanges; they can give gifts, stack, barter, and exchange cryptocurrencies and their copies; and they can turn art forms into registered and account-trailed nonfungible data monies such as nonfungible tokens. This is an expanding and novel economic world. We cannot regulate and make sense of this new world based on old concepts.

At the most general level, this book has proposed two radical policy changes in cryptocurrency regulation and taxation. First, drawing on an analysis of how platform economies work on the ground as stack economization processes, the book sheds light on the new materialities of data monies and computational industries. This new perspective requires us to design regulation also in a stacked manner, targeting all economization relations in platforms.

Such a change would also help us better incorporate data monies into our current regulatory framework, only if we design and deploy of a state-registered electronic metawallet. This second novelty entails imagining economic actors not in terms of individuals or legal entities but as digital wallet constellations that may be linked with tax identification or social security numbers so that unique economic persons could be identified in order to bring all crypto-economic activity within the reach of regulation.[4] This way we can start taxing data money income with data money itself.

We are entering an era of radical financial change. Like all other great transformations, this one entails innumerable forms of continuity and change. And as in other periods of change, we have chosen to understand novelty in reference to mnemonic things from the past. Unfortunately, this strategy does not always work well. Paper and metal monies, as well as their digital representations—the main money forms of our past and present—cannot help us now to make sense of data monies. We need to stop approaching data monies as digital currency and move beyond seeing their exchange platforms as mere markets. This book has presented a novel way to understand these new monies, their markets, and their communities. What we decide to do with them will be determined by public discussion and the state's innovative regulatory framework. This can be carried out by moving beyond *analogical* thinking and deploying an *analytical* framework to better understand them.

# NOTES

## 1. THE HISTORICAL NOVELTY OF DATA MONEY AND ITS MAKERS, MARKETS, AND REGULATION

1. Michel Aglietta, *Money: 5,000 Years of Debt and Power* (London: Verso, 2018), 89.
2. For the composition and weight of U.S. metal monies, see https://www.usmint.gov/learn/coin-and-medal-programs/coin-specifications.
3. Aglietta, *Money*.
4. Aglietta, *Money*; David Graeber, *Debt: The First 5,000 Years* (Brooklyn, NY: Melville House, 2011).
5. Christine Desan, *Making Money: Coin, Currency, and the Coming of Capitalism* (Oxford: Oxford University Press, 2014).
6. Nigel Dodd, *Money in Social Theory: Economics, Reason, and Contemporary Society* (Oxford: Polity, 1993); Keith Hart, *The Memory Bank: Money in an Unequal World* (London: Profile, 2000); Viviana A. Zelizer, "The Social Meaning of Money: 'Special Monies,'" *American Journal of Sociology* 95, no. 2 (1989): 342–77.
7. Finn Brunton, *Digital Cash: The Unknown History of the Anarchists, Utopians, and Technologists Who Built Cryptocurrency* (Princeton, NJ: Princeton University Press, 2019); Nigel Dodd, "The Social Life of Bitcoin," *Theory, Culture, & Society* 35, no. 3 (2018): 35–56, https://doi.org/10.1177/0263276417746464; Quinn DuPont, "Experiments in Algorithmic Governance: A History and Ethnography of 'The DAO,' a Failed Decentralized Autonomous Organization," in *Bitcoin and Beyond: Cryptocurrencies, Blockchains, and Global Governance*, ed. M. Campbell-Verduyn

(London: Routledge, 2019), 157–77; Lana Swartz, "What Was Bitcoin, What Will It Be? The Techno-economic Imaginaries of a New Money Technology," *Cultural Studies* 32, no. 4 (2018): 623–50, and *New Money: How Payment Became Social Media* (New Haven, CT: Yale University Press, 2020).

8. Throughout this book, dollar ($) refers to U.S. dollars (US$).

9. Digibyte, Dogecoin, GAS, Huobi Token, and Monacoin have no formal white papers.

10. These cryptocurrencies are Aelf, Aeternity, Aion, Allsports, Ardor, Ark, Augur, Bancor, Basic Attention Token, Binance Coin, Bitcoin, Bitcoin Cash, Bitcoin Diamond, Bitcoin Gold, Bitcoin Private, Bitshares, Bytecoin, Bytom, Cardano, Centrality, Cortex, Cryptonex, Cybermiles, Dash, Decred, Dentacoin, Digibyte, DigixDAO, Dogecoin, Dragonchain, Elastos, Electroneum, Enigma, EOS, Ethereum, Ethereum Classic, Ethos, Funfair, Fusion, GAS, Golem, Gxchain, Huobi Token, Hypercash, ICON, Internet of Services, Kin, Komodo, Kucoin Shares, Kybernetwork, Lisk, Litecoin, Loom Network, Loopring, MaidSafeCoin, Maker, Miota, Mithril, Mixin, MOAC, Monacoin, Monero, Nano, Nebulas, Nem, NEO, Nexusi, Nuls, OmiseGo, Ontology, PIVX, Polymath, Populous, Qash, Qtum, Rchain, Reddcoin, SiaCoin, Skycoin, Status, Steem, Stellar, Stratis, Substratum, Syscoin, Tether, Theta Token, Tron, Vechain, Verge, Veritaseum, Waltonchain, Wanchain, Waves, Waykichain, XRP, Zcash, Zcoin, ox, and Zilliqa.

11. The data can be found in Koray Caliskan and S. Ilker Birbil, "White Papers of Top 100 Cryptocurrencies and Their Blockchains," Github, 2020, https://github.com/sibirbil/DataMoney.

12. The data can be found in S. Ilker Birbil and Koray Caliskan, "Terms of Service Agreements of 251 Cryptocurrency Exchanges Representing 99.99% of Centralized Data Money Transactions," Github, 2020, https://github.com/sibirbil/TermsofService.

13. The forum discussions can be found at https://bitcointalk.org/index.php?topic=1848351.0.

14. The data can be found in Enis Simsar and Koray Caliskan, "Twitter Interaction Data of Electra Cryptocurrency Community's Twitter Handle Followers and a Code for Follower Interaction Analysis," Github, 2021, https://github.com/enisimsar/DataMoney.

## 2. THE MATERIALITY OF DATA MONEY AND THE INFRASTRUCTURE AND TAXONOMY OF BLOCKCHAINS

1. This statement draws on www.coinmarketcap.com closing price data, cross-checked with Chicago Board of Trade and Chicago Mercantile Exchange data. The data on GDP come from World Bank, National Accounts Data, 2020, https://data.worldbank.org/indicator/NY.GDP .MKTP.CD?year_high_desc=false.

2. "The Guardian View on Cryptocurrencies: A Greater Fool's Gold," *The Guardian*, January 7, 2018, https://www.theguardian.com/commentis free/2018/jan/07/the-guardian-view-on-cryptocurrencies-a-greater -fools-gold.

3. Edward Castronova, *Wildcat Currency: How the Virtual Money Revolution Is Transforming the Economy* (New Haven, CT: Yale University Press, 2014); Dan Tapscott and Alex Tapscott, *Blockchain Revolution: How the Technology Behind Bitcoin Is Changing Money, Business, and the World* (New York: Penguin Random House, 2016).

4. *Brave the World* (blog), "We Declare Bitcoin's Independence," August 13, 2014, http://bravetheworld.com/2014/08/13/declare-bitcoins -independence/.

5. Nina Bandelj, Frederick F. Wherry, and Viviana A. Zelizer, eds., *Money Talks: Explaining How Money Really Works* (Princeton, NJ: Princeton University Press, 2017); Nigel Dodd, *The Sociology of Money: Economics, Reason and Contemporary Society* (New York: Continuum, 1994); Keith Hart, *The Memory Bank: Money in an Unequal World* (London: Profile Books, 2000); Bill Maurer, "The Anthropology of Money," *Annual Review of Anthropology* 35 (2006): 15–36; Lana Swartz, *New Money: How Payment Became Social Media* (New Haven, CT: Yale University Press, 2020); Viviana A. Zelizer, *The Social Meaning of Money* (New York: Basic Books, 1994).

6. Henrik Karlstrøm, "Do Libertarians Dream of Electric Coins? The Material Embeddedness of Bitcoin," *Journal of Social Theory* 15, no. 1 (2014): 23–36, https://doi.org/10.1080/1600910X.2013.870083; Bill Maurer, "Blockchains Are a Diamond's Best Friend: Zelizer for the Bitcoin Moment," in Bandelj, Wherry, and Zelizer, *Money Talks*, 215–29.

7. Ole Bjerg, "How Is Bitcoin Money?," *Theory, Culture, & Society* 33, no. 1 (2016): 53–72; Sam Dallyn, "Cryptocurrencies as Market Singularities: The Strange Case of Bitcoin," *Journal of Cultural Economy* 10, no. 5 (2017): 462–73, https://doi.org/10.1080/17530350.2017.1315541.

8. Nigel Dodd, "The Social Life of Bitcoin." *Theory, Culture, & Society* 35, no. 3 (2018): 36, https://doi.org/10.1177/0263276417746464..

9. Quinn DuPont, "Politics of Bitcoin: Software as Right-Wing Extremism," *Journal of Cultural Economy* 10, no. 5 (2017): 474–76, https://doi.org /10.1080/17530350.2017.1322997; David Golumbia, "Bitcoin as Politics: Distributed Right-Wing Extremism," in *MoneyLab Reader: An Intervention in Digital Economy*, ed. Geert Lovink, Nathaniel Tkacz, and Patricia DeVries (Amsterdam: Institute of Network Cultures, 2015), 117–31.

10. Lana Swartz, "Blockchain Dreams: Imagining Techno-economic Alternatives After Bitcoin," in *Another Economy Is Possible: Culture and Economy in a Time of Crisis*, ed. M. Castells (Cambridge: Polity, 2017), 82–105.

11. Taylor C. Nelms, Bill Maurer, Lana Swartz, and Scott Mainwaring, "Social Payments: Innovation, Trust, Bitcoin, and the Sharing Economy," *Theory, Culture, & Society* 35, no. 3 (2018): 13–33, https://doi.org/10.1177 /0263276417746466.

12. Pavel Ciaian, Miroslava Rajcaniova, and d'Artis Kancs, "The Economics of BitCoin Price Formation," *Applied Economics* 48, no. 19 (2016): 1799–815, https://doi.org/10.1080/00036846.2015.1109038; Huisi Jang and Jaewook Lee, "An Empirical Study on Modeling and Prediction of Bitcoin Prices with Bayesian Neural Networks Based on Blockchain Information," *IEEE Access* 6 (2018): 5427–37.

13. Eli Noam, "The Macro-Economics of Crypto-Currencies: Balancing Entrepreneurialism and Monetary Policy" (Entrepreneurship & Policy Initiative Working Paper Series), Columbia University School of International and Policy Affairs, New York, accessed November 28, 2021, https://sipa.columbia.edu/sites/default/files/25222_SIPA-White -Paper-MacroEconomics-web.pdf; David W. Perkins, "Cryptocurrency: The Economics of Money and Selected Policy Issues," Report No. R45427, Congressional Research Service, Washington, DC, 2020, https://crsreports.congress.gov; Eswar S. Prasad, *The Future of Money: How the Digital Revolution Is Transforming Currencies and Finance* (Cambridge, MA: Belknap Press of Harvard University Press, 2021).

14. Koray Caliskan, "The Meaning of Price in World Markets," *Journal of Cultural Economy* 2, no. 3 (2009): 239–68, https://doi.org/10.1080 /17530350903345462; Michel Callon, *The Laws of the Markets* (Malden, MA: Blackwell Publishers/Sociological Review, 1998); Vincent Antonin Lépinay, *Codes of Finance: Engineering Derivatives in a Global Bank* (Princeton, NJ: Princeton University Press, 2011); Donald MacKenzie, *An Engine, Not a Camera: Financial Models Shape Markets* (Cambridge, MA: MIT Press, 2006); Timothy Mitchell, *Rule of Experts: Egypt, Techno-politics, Modernity* (Berkeley: University of California Press, 2002); Fabian Muniesa, "Market Technologies and the Pragmatics of Prices," *Economy and Society* 36, no. 3 (2007): 377–95; Janet Roitman, *Fiscal Disobedience: An Anthropology of Economic Regulation in Central Africa* (Princeton, NJ: Princeton University Press, 2005); Don Slater and Fran Tonkis, *Market Society: Markets and Modern Social Theory* (Cambridge: Polity, 2001).

15. Brian Larkin, "The Politics and Poetics of Infrastructure," *Annual Review of Anthropology* 42 (2013): 329, https://doi.org/10.1146/annurev-anthro -092412-155522.

16. My point here does not assume an essentialist nature of digitality but rather draws on analyses of materialities of representational objects like digital things. For an illustration of such materialities, see Paul Dourish, *The Stuff of Bits: An Essay on the Materialities of Information* (Cambridge, MA: MIT Press, 2017).

17. Yet for the actors that cannot be defined by the computer code, infrastructural inversions are almost always the norm. For a rich discussion of the possibilities of inversions, see Casper Bruun Jensen, "Power, Technology and Social Studies of Health Care: An Infrastructural Inversion," *Health Care Analysis* 16, no. 4 (2017): 355–74; Atsuro Morita, "Multispecies Infrastructure: Infrastructural Inversion and Involutionary Entanglements in the Chao Phraya Delta, Thailand," *Ethnos* 82, no. 4 (2017): 738–57, https://doi.org/10.1080/00141844.2015.1119175.

18. Dodd, "The Secret Life of Bitcoin"; Kristopher Jones, "Toward a Political Sociology of Blockchain" (PhD diss., Queens University, 2018); Maurer, "Blockchains Are a Diamond's Best Friend"; Lynette Shaw, "The Meanings of New Money: Social Constructions of Value in the Rise of Digital Currencies" (PhD diss., University of Washington, 2016); Swartz, "Blockchain Dreams"; Matthew A. Zook and Joe Blankenship,

"New Spaces of Disruption? The Failures of Bitcoin and the Rhetorical Power of Algorithmic Governance," *Geoforum* 96 (2018): 248–55.

19. Koray Caliskan and Michel Callon, "Economization, Part 1: Shifting Attention from the Economy Towards Processes of Economization," *Economy and Society* 38, no. 3 (2009): 369–98, https://doi.org/10.1080/03085140903020580, and "Economization, Part 2: A Research Programme for the Study of Markets," *Economy and Society* 39, no. 1 (2010): 1–32, https://doi.org/10.1080/03085140903424519.

20. Nikhil Anand, "Municipal Disconnect: On Abject Water and Its Urban Infrastructures," *Ethnography* 13, no. 4 (2012): 487–509, https://doi.org/10.1177/1466138111435743; Hannah Appel, "Offshore Work: Oil, Modularity, and the How of Capitalism in Equatorial Guinea," *American Ethnologist* 39, no. 4 (2012): 692–709; Andrew Barry, *Material Politics: Disputes Along the Pipeline* (Chichester, UK: Wiley-Blackwell, 2013); Laura Bear, *Lines of the Nation: Indian Railway Workers, Bureaucracy, and the Intimate Historical Self* (New York: Columbia University Press, 2007); Brian Larkin, "The Politics and Poetics of Infrastructure," *Annual Review of Anthropology* 42 (2013): 327–43; Julia Elyachar, *Markets of Dispossession: NGOs, Economic Development and the State in Cairo* (Durham, NC: Duke University Press, 2005); Michel Foucault and Colin Gordon, *Power/Knowledge: Selected Interviews and Other Writings, 1972–1977* (New York: Pantheon Books, 1980); Penny Harvey and Hannah Knox, *Roads: An Anthropology of Infrastructure and Expertise* (Ithaca, NY: Cornell University Press, 2015).

21. Bruno Latour, *Science in Action: How to Follow Scientists and Engineers Through Society* (Cambridge, MA: Harvard University Press, 1987), and *Reassembling the Social: An Introduction to Actor-Network-Theory* (Oxford: Oxford University Press, 2005).

22. In the list of the one hundred most valuable cryptocurrencies, there are five—Digibyte, Dogecoin, GAS, Huobi Token, and Monacoin—without formal white papers. However, even those currencies' websites include a scientific-looking page and/or discussion that can be analyzed as a white paper. The current analysis excludes any data or text concerning these five data monies from the corpus of white papers but includes them in general calculations such as that of the one hundred top cryptocurrencies in terms of market capitalization.

23. These cryptocurrencies are Aelf, Aeternity, Aion, Allsports, Ardor, Ark, Augur, Bancor, Basic Attention Token, Binance Coin, Bitcoin, Bitcoin Cash, Bitcoin Diamond, Bitcoin Gold, Bitcoin Private, Bitshares, Bytecoin, Bytom, Cardano, Centrality, Cortex, Cryptonex, Cybermiles, Dash, Decred, Dentacoin, Digibyte, DigixDAO, Dogecoin, Dragonchain, Elastos, Electroneum, Enigma, EOS, Ethereum, Ethereum Classic, Ethos, Funfair, Fusion, GAS, Golem, Gxchain, Huobi Token, Hypercash, ICON, Internet of Services, Kin, Komodo, Kucoin Shares, Kybernetwork, Lisk, Litecoin, Loom Network, Loopring, MaidSafeCoin, Maker, Miota, Mithril, Mixin, MOAC, Monacoin, Monero, Nano, Nebulas, Nem, NEO, Nexusi, Nuls, OmiseGo, Ontology, PIVX, Polymath, Populous, Qash, Qtum, Rchain, Reddcoin, SiaCoin, Skycoin, Status, Steem, Stellar, Stratis, Substratum, Syscoin, Tether, Theta Token, Tron, Vechain, Verge, Veritaseum, Waltonchain, Wanchain, Waves, Waykichain, XRP, Zcash, Zcoin, Ox, and Zilliqa.

24. This date is arbitrary in the sense that it marks the day I began carrying out research on white papers but not arbitrary in the sense that it is temporally distant from too bullish and bearish episodes of cryptocurrency trading.

25. Many blockchains do not offer any data money. This chapter focuses only on cryptocurrency blockchains.

26. For an interesting comparison of silver mining and Bitcoin mining, see Zac Zimmer, "Bitcoin and Potosi Silver Historical Perspectives on Cryptocurrency," *Technology and Culture* 58, no. 2 (2017): 307–34.

27. For Nakamoto, mining referred to the computational search for a nonce—i.e., a number used once that would be attached to the registering of a certain number of transactions, which would correspond to a hash.

28. The analysis was carried out on R with the collaboration of Ilker Birbil. For a more detailed analysis of these white papers and the data source, see Koray Caliskan and Ilker Birbil, "Computational Text Analysis of Cryptocurrency Blockchain White Papers," 2019. For a discussion of methodological concerns, see Fran Tonkiss, "Analysing Text and Speech: Content and Discourse Analysis," in *Researching Society and Culture*, ed. C. Seale (London: SAGE, 2004), 367–82; Kasper Welbers, Wouter Van Atteveldtb, and Kenneth Benoit, "Text Analysis in R,"

*Communication Methods and Measures* 11, no. 4 (2017): 245–65, https://
doi.org/10.1080/19312458.2017.1387238.

29. Blockchain development and maintenance are made possible by a variety of actors such as wallet designers, wallet providers, security architects,
speculators, mining pool operators, engineers, investors, application
developers, forum editors and writers, trolls, academics, regulators, and
lawyers. My focus here is on the two sets of actors defined and enabled
by cryptocurrency blockchains. For a discussion of the actor-network
approach to blockchain forks, see Najmul Islam, Matti Mäntymäki,
and Marja Turunen, "Understanding the Role of Actor Heterogeneity
in Blockchain Splits: An Actor-Network Perspective to Bitcoin Forks"
(paper presented at the fifty-second Hawaii International Conference
on System Sciences, Wailea, Hawaii, 2019).

30. For a summary of the developments that led to the emergence of
Bitcoin, see Adam Hayes, "The Socio-technological Lives of Bitcoin,"
*Theory, Culture, & Society* 36, no. 4 (2019): 1–24, https://doi.org/10.1177
/0263276419826218.

31. Bitcoin transfers can be made free by the transactioners or the
exchanges that mediate the transactions.

32. Casey Detrio, "Smart Markets for Stablecoins," July 2015, http://cdetr
.io/smart-markets/.

33. This is also why there has been an explosion of blockchain and cryptocurrency events and internet forums around the world. For a detailed
study of forums concerning Bitcoin on Reddit and other websites, see
Shaw, "The Meanings of New Money."

34. A few of these publications use the computer screen as the page unit
and have not been converted to pdfs. In order to be able to compare
their length and page statistics, three white papers were formatted to fit
on a U.S. legal-size page.

35. I guessed or identified the authors' gender from their first names, LinkedIn
data, and photographs, but I make no assumptions regarding the gender identities these writers have. The person who chose the pseudonym
Satoshi Nakamoto to represent a male name in Japanese also claimed
once to be a man who lived in Japan, according to one of his posts that
can be accessed at https://web.archive.org/web/20120529203623/http://
p2pfoundation.ning.com/profile/SatoshiNakamoto.

36. Craig Calhoun, *Dictionary of the Social Sciences* (New York: Oxford University Press, 2002), https://doi.org/10.1093/acref/9780195123715 .001.0001.

37. The text corpus of the white papers was analyzed to determine the frequency and distribution of the 1,800 concepts from Calhoun's *Dictionary of the Social Sciences*. Core social-scientific categories were stemmed to represent their concentration; for example, *finance* and *financial* are plotted together, as are *economies* and *economy*.

38. The stems of these concepts (such as *econo-*) were plotted to check for the relative distribution of their focus on economic, social, financial, cultural, and political matters of concern.

39. An exception is the Ontology white paper, which locates its blockchain as a bridge between "the real world" and "distributed data systems."

40. For example, according to Nakamoto, "the Bitcoin system requires minimal structure to work" (Nakamoto, 2008, p. 1).

41. The technical literature concerning cryptocurrencies rightfully characterizes private blockchains as permissioned blockchains that locate authority nodes for the accounting process. For a discussion of the evolution of these permissioned chains, see Arvind Narayanan and Jeremy Clark, "Bitcoin's Academic Pedigree," *Communications of the ACM* 60, no. 12 (2017): 36–45.

42. Zook and Blankenship, "New Spaces of Disruption?."

43. Tapscott and Tapscott, *Blockchain Revolution*.

44. The calculation draws on Bitcoin exchange data available at https:// coinmarketcap.com and https://www.blockchain.com/, accessed January 22, 2019.

45. For example, www.cryptomapia.org places blockchains in twenty-five categories based on their services. Technical papers and semiacademic reports also propose taxonomies but mostly from a performance point of view; see N. S. Tinu, "A Survey of Blockchain Technology: Taxonomy, Consensus Algorithms, and Applications," *International Journal of Computer Sciences and Engineering* 6, no. 5 (2018): 691–96.

46. For an excellent discussion and illustration of this point specifically and of mining generally, see Donald MacKenzie, "Pick a Nonce and Try a Hash," *London Review of Books* 48, no. 8 (2019): 35–38.

## 3. UNDERSTANDING CRYPTOCURRENCY EXCHANGE PLATFORMS AND MARKETS

1. DuneAnalytics, 2020.

2. Gabrielle Hecht, "Rupture-Talk in the Nuclear Age: Conjugating Colonial Power in Africa," *Social Studies of Science* 32, no. 5–6 (2002): 691–727, https://doi.org/10.1177/030631270203200504.

3. Dan Tapscott and Alex Tapscott, *Blockchain Revolution: How the Technology Behind Bitcoin Is Changing Money, Business, and the World* (New York: Penguin Random House, 2016).

4. "The Guardian View on Cryptocurrencies: A Greater Fool's Gold," *The Guardian*, January 7, 2018, https://www.theguardian.com/commentisfree /2018/jan/07/the-guardian-view-on-cryptocurrencies-a-greater-fools -gold.

5. Warren Buffett, interview by Becky Quick, CNBC, May 18, 2018, https://www.cnbc.com/video/2020/02/24/watch-cnbcs-full-interview -with-berkshire-hathaway-ceo-warren-buffett.html.

6. Nigel Dodd, "The Social Life of Bitcoin," *Theory, Culture, & Society* 35, no. 3 (2018): 35–56. https://doi.org/10.1177/0263276417746464.

7. Quinn DuPont, *Cryptocurrencies and Blockchains* (Cambridge: Polity, 2019); Quinn DuPont, "Experiments in Algorithmic Governance: A History and Ethnography of 'The DAO,' a Failed Decentralized Autonomous Organization," in *Bitcoin and Beyond: Cryptocurrencies, Blockchains, and Global Governance*, ed. M. Campbell-Verduyn (London: Routledge, 2019), 157–77.

8. Lana Swartz, "Blockchain Dreams: Imagining Techno-economic Alternatives After Bitcoin," in *Another Economy Is Possible: Culture and Economy in a Time of Crisis*, ed. M. Castells (Cambridge: Polity, 2017), 82–105.

9. Taylor C. Nelms, Bill Maurer, Lana Swartz, and Scott Mainwaring, "Social Payments: Innovation, Trust, Bitcoin, and the Sharing Economy," *Theory, Culture, & Society* 35, no. 3 (2018): 13–33, https://doi.org /10.1177/0263276417746466.

10. Jillian Crandall, "Blockchains and the 'Chains of Empire': Contextualizing Blockchain, Cryptocurrency, and Neoliberalism in Puerto Rico," *Journal of the Design Studies Forum* 11, no. 3 (2019): 279–300, https:// doi.org/10.1080/17547075.2019.1673989; Erkan Saka, "Cryptocurrency

Usage in Turkey," *Anthropology News*, September 11, 2020, https://doi.org/10.14506/AN.1491; A. Thieser, "These Roses Don't Think About Each Other Either: Competition, Collaboration and Utopianism in a Blockchain Community," unpublished manuscript, 2019.

11. Wenjun Feng, Yiming Wang, and Zhengjun Zhang, "Informed Trading in the Bitcoin Market," *Finance Research Letters* 26 (2018): 63–70, https://doi.org/10.1016/j.frl.2017.11.009; Qiang Ji, Elie Bouri, Chi Keung Marco Lau, and David Roubaud, "Dynamic Connectedness and Integration in Cryptocurrency Markets," *International Review of Financial Analysis* 63 (2019): 257–72, https://doi.org/10.1016/j.irfa.2018.12.002; Nikolaos A. Kyriazis, "A Survey on Efficiency and Profitable Trading Opportunities in Cryptocurrency Markets," *Journal of Risk and Financial Management* 12, no. 2 (2019): 67, https://doi.org/10.3390/jrfm12020067; Andrew Urquhart, "The Inefficiency of Bitcoin," *Economics Letters* 148 (2016): 80–82, https://doi.org/10.1016/j.econlet.2016.09.019.

12. Shaen Corbet, Brian Lucey, Andrew Urquhart, and Larisa Yarovaya, "Cryptocurrencies as a Financial Asset: A Systematic Analysis," *International Review of Financial Analysis* 62 (2019): 182–99, https://doi.org/10.1016/j.irfa.2018.09.003; Paolo Giudici and Iman Abu-Hashish, "What Determines Bitcoin Exchange Prices? A Network VAR Approach," *Finance Research Letters* 28 (2019): 309–18, https://doi.org/10.1016/j.frl.2018.05.013; Theodore Panagiotidis, Thanasis Stengos, and Orestis Vravosinos, "On the Determinants of Bitcoin Returns: A LASSO Approach," *Finance Research Letters* 27 (2018): 235–40, https://doi.org/10.1016/j.frl.2018.03.016.

13. Refk Selmi, Walid Mensi, Shawkat Hammoudeh, and Jamal Bouoiyour, "Is Bitcoin a Hedge, a Safe Haven, or a Diversifier for Oil Price Movements? A Comparison with Gold," *Energy Economics* 74 (2018): 787–801, https://doi.org/10.1016/j.eneco.2018.07.007.

14. Paraskevi Katsiampa, "Volatility Estimation for Bitcoin: A Comparison of GARCH Models," *Economics Letters* 158 (2017): 3–6, https://doi.org/10.1016/j.econlet.2017.06.023; Paraskevi Katsiampa, Shaen Corbet, and Brian Lucey, "High Frequency Volatility Co-movements in Cryptocurrency Markets," *Journal of International Financial Markets, Institutions, and Money* 62 (2019): 35–52, https://doi.org/10.1016/j.intfin.2019.05.003.

15. Shaen Corbet, Veysel Eraslan, Brian Lucey, and Ahmet Sensoy, "The Effectiveness of Technical Trading Rules in Cryptocurrency Markets,"

*Finance Research Letters* 31 (2019): 32–37, https://doi.org/10.1016/j.frl
.2019.04.027.

16. Emre Akyildirim, Shaen Corbet, Paraskevi Katsiampa, Neil Kellard, and Ahmet Sensoy, "The Development of Bitcoin Futures: Exploring the Interactions Between Cryptocurrency Derivatives," *Finance Research Letters* 34 (2020): 101234, https://doi.org/10.1016/j.frl.2019.07.007.

17. Theophilos Papadimitriou, Periklis Gogas, and Fotios Gkatzoglou, "The Evolution of the Cryptocurrencies Market: A Complex Networks Approach," *Journal of Computational and Applied Mathematics* 376 (2020): 112831, https://doi.org/10.1016/j.cam.2020.112831.

18. Athanasios P. Fassas, Stephanos Papadamou, and Alexandros Koulis, "Price Discovery in Bitcoin Futures," *Research in International Business and Finance* 52 (2020): 101116, https://doi.org/10.1016/j.ribaf.2019 .101116.

19. Wash trading is a market manipulation practice whereby the same person, acting simultaneously as buyer and seller, transfers the ownership of an underlying asset between two accounts that they control in order to produce misleading inflation of activity in the market.

20. Blockchain Transparency Institute, 2018.

21. According to the 2020 report of BTI, "only 31 percent of the CMC top 25 is being wash-traded compared to over 90 percent just 1 year ago, a 3x improvement with their new rankings system. 8 major wash trading exchanges still found on the current CMC top 25 have found a way to beat the new ranking system by faking orderbook liquidity, using ghost trades, and purchasing web visits" (BTI, 2020, 1).

22. Jennifer Alexander and Paul Alexander, "What's a Fair Price? Price Setting and Trading Partnership in Javanese Markets," *Man* 26, no. 3 (1991): 493–512, https://doi.org/10.2307/2803879; Jane Guyer, *Marginal Gains: Monetary Transactions in Atlantic Africa* (Chicago: University of Chicago Press, 2004); Claes-Fredrik Helgesson and Fabian Muniesa, "For What It's Worth: An Introduction to Valuation Studies," *Valuation Studies* 1, no. 1 (2013): 1–10, https://doi.org/10.3384/vs.2001-5992.13111; David Stark, *The Sense of Dissonance: Accounts of Worth in Economic Life* (Princeton, NJ: Princeton University Press, 2009); Olav Velthuis, "Symbolic Meanings of Prices: Constructing the Value of Contemporary Art in Amsterdam and New York Galleries," *Theory and Society* 32, no. 2 (2003): 181–215, https://doi.org/10.1023/A:1023995520369.

23. Koray Caliskan, "Price as a Market Device: Cotton Trading in Izmir Mercantile Exchange," *Sociological Review* 55, no. 2 (2007): 241–60, https://doi.org/10.1111/j.1467-954X.2007.00738.x, and "The Meaning of Price in World Markets," *Journal of Cultural Economy* 2, no. 3 (2009): 239–68, https://doi.org/10.1080/17530350903345462; Haidy Geismar, "What's in a Price? An Ethnography of Tribal Art at Auction," *Journal of Material Culture* 6, no. 1 (2001): 25–47, https://doi.org/10.1177/135918350100600102; Vassily Pigounidès, "Predicting Prices, Persuading Users: Price Recommendations and the Rhetorical Logic of Algorithms," *Research in Economic Anthropology* 40 (2020): 71–89, https://doi.org/10.1108/S0190 -128120200000040003; Brian Uzzi and Ryon Lancaster, "Embeddedness and Price Formation in the Corporate Law Market," *American Sociological Review* 69, no. 3 (2004): 319–44, https://doi.org/10.1177 /000312240406900301.

24. Vincent Antonin Lépinay, "Decoding Finance: Articulation and Liquidity Around a Trading Room," in *Do Economists Make Markets? On the Performativity of Economics*, ed. Fabien Muniesa and Lucia Siu (Princeton, NJ: Princeton University Press, 2007), 87–127; Donald MacKenzie, *An Engine, Not a Camera: Financial Models Shape Markets* (Cambridge. MA: MIT Press, 2006).

25. Susan Leigh Star, "The Ethnography of Infrastructure," *American Behavioral Scientist* 43, no. 3 (1999): 377–91, https://doi.org/10.1177 /00027649921955326.

26. Timothy Mitchell, *Carbon Democracy: Political Power in the Age of Oil* (London: Verso, 2011).

27. Annelise Riles, "Property as Legal Knowledge: Means and Ends," *Journal of the Royal Anthropological Institute* 10, no. 4 (2004): 775–95, https://doi.org/10.1111/j.1467-9655.2004.00211.x.

28. Alexandre Mallard, "Compare, Standardize and Settle Agreement: On Some Usual Metrological Problems," *Social Studies of Science* 28, no. 4 (1998): 571–601, https://doi.org/10.1177/030631298028004003.

29. Brian Uzzi, "The Sources and Consequences of Embeddedness for the Economic Performance of Organizations: The Network Effect," *American Sociological Review* 61, no. 4 (1996): 674–98, https://doi.org /10.2307/2096399.

30. Gernot Grabher and Jonas König, "Performing Network Theory? Reflexive Relationship Management on Social Network Sites," in

*Networked Governance: New Research Perspectives*, ed. Betina Holl-stein, Wenzel Matiaske, and Schnapp Kai-Uwe (Cham. Switzerland: Springer, 2017), 121–40, https://doi.org/10.1007/978-3-319-50386-8.

31. The multiplication and intersectionality of these platform works empirically support the call for a rapprochement between platform studies and infrastructure studies. Jean-Christophe Plantin, Carl Lagoze, Paul N. Edwards, and Christian Sandvig, "Infrastructure Studies Meet Platform Studies in the Age of Google and Facebook," *New Media & Society* 20, no. 1 (2018): 293–310, https://doi.org/10.1177/1461444816661553.

32. Coinbase, 2020.

33. Steven C. Wheelwright and Kim B. Clark, "Creating Project Plans to Focus Product Development," *Harvard Business Review* 70, no. 2 (1992): 67–83, https://hbr.org/1992/03/creating-project-plans-to-focus-product-development.

34. Susan Sanderson and Mustafa Uzumeri, "Managing Product Families: The Case of the Sony Walkman," *Research Policy* 24, no. 5 (1995): 761–82, https://doi.org/10.1016/0048-7333(94)00797-B; Karl Ulrich, "The Role of Product Architecture in the Manufacturing Firm," *Research Policy* 24, no. 3 (1995): 419–40, http://dx.doi.org/10.1016/0048-7333(94)00775-3.

35. Greg Flurry and Wayne Vicknair, "The IBM Application Framework for E-Business," *IBM Systems Journal* 40, no. 1 (2001): 8–24, https://dol.org/10.1147/sj.401.0008.

36. Bernard Caillaud and Bruno Jullien, "Competing Cybermediaries," *European Economic Review* 45, no. 4–6 (2001): 797–808, https://doi.org/10.1016/S0014-2921(01)00123-4.

37. Julian Wright, "One-Sided Logic in Two-Sided Markets," *Review of Network Economies* 3, no. 1 (2003): 1, http://dx.doi.org/10.2139/ssrn.459362.

38. Jean-Charles Rochet and Jean Tirole, "Platform Competition in Two-Sided Markets," *Journal of the European Economic* Association 1, no. 4 (2003): 990–1029, https://doi.org/10.1162/154247603322493212; Jean-Charles Rochet and Jean Tirole, "Two-Sided Markets: A Progress Report," *RAND Journal of Economics* 37, no. 3 (2006): 645–67, https://doi.org/10.1111/j.1756-2171.2006.tb00036.x.

39. Rochet and Tirole, "Platform Competition in Two-Sided Markets."

40. David S. Evans and Richard Schmalensee, "The Industrial Organization of Markets with Two-Sided Platforms" (Working Paper No. 11603, National Bureau of Economic Research, Cambridge, MA, 2005).

41. Attila Ambrus and Rossella Argenziano, "Network Markets and Consumer Coordination" (Working Paper No. 1317, CESifo, Munich, 2004), https://www.cesifo.org/en/publikationen/2004/working-paper/network-markets-and-consumer-coordination.

42. Annabella Gawer, *Platforms, Markets, and Innovation* (Cheltenham, UK: Edward Elgar, 2009).

43. Lapo Filistrucchi, Damien Geradin, and Eric van Damme, "Identifying Two-Sided Markets" (Discussion Paper No. 2012-008, Tilburg Law and Economics Center, Tilburg, Netherlands, 2012), http://dx.doi.org/10.2139/ssrn.2008661.

44. OECD, 2009.

45. Koray Caliskan and Michel Callon, "Economization, Part 1: Shifting Attention from the Economy Towards Processes of Economization," *Economy and Society* 38, no. 3 (2009): 369–98, https://doi.org/10.1080/03085140903020580, and "Economization, Part 2: A Research Programme for the Study of Markets," *Economy and Society* 39, no. 1 (2010): 1–32, https://doi.org/10.1080/03085140903424519.

46. Caliskan and Callon, "Economization, Part 1."

47. Caliskan and Callon, "Economization, Part 2," 3.

48. For a concise discussion of this approach, referred to as DARN (devices, actors, representations, network), as a way to move beyond actor-network theory, see Koray Caliskan, "Data Money: The Socio-technical Infrastructure of Cryptocurrency Blockchains," *Economy and Society* 49, no. 4 (2020): 540–61, https://doi.org/10.1080/03085147.2020.1774258; and Koray Caliskan and Matt Wade, "DARN Part 1: What is Strategic Design? Social Theory and Intangible Design in Perspective," *She Ji: The Journal of Design, Economics, and Innovation* 8, no. 3 (2022): 299–318. https://doi.org/10.1016/j.sheji.2022.10.001; Koray Caliskan and Matt Wade, "*DARN Part 2: An Evidence-Based Research and Prototyping Methodology for Strategic Design," She Ji: The Journal of Design, Economics, and Innovation* 8, no. 3 (2022): 319–335. https://doi.org/10.1016/j.sheji.2022.11.002.

49. Benjamin H. Bratton, *The Stack: On Software and Sovereignty* (Cambridge, MA: MIT Press, 2016), xvii.

50. Bratton, *The Stack*, xvii.

51. Ori Schwarz, "Facebook Rules: Structures of Governance in Digital Capitalism and the Control of Generalized Social Capital," *Theory, Culture, & Society* 36, no. 4 (2019): 132, https://doi.org/10.1177/0263276419826249.

52. For raw data on all of these terms-of-use documents and the R code, see Koray Caliskan and Ilker Birbil, "White Papers of Top 100 Cryptocurrencies and Their Blockchains," Github, 2020, https://github.com/sibirbil/DataMoney.

53. Koray Caliskan and Michel Callon, "Economization, Part 2," 5.

54. For a discussion of how regional and local traders describe their marketization processes, see Koray Caliskan, *Market Threads: How Cotton Farmers and Traders Create a Global Commodity* (Princeton, NJ: Princeton University Press, 2011).

55. For derivatives and derivation, see Jane Guyer, *Marginal Gains: Monetary Transactions in Atlantic Africa* (Chicago: University of Chicago Press, 2004); and Vincent Antonin Lépinay, *Codes of Finance: Engineering Derivatives in a Global Bank* (Princeton, NJ: Princeton University Press, 2011).

56. Koray Caliskan, "The Meaning of Price in World Markets," *Journal of Cultural Economy* 2, no. 3 (2009): 239–68, https://doi.org/10.1080/17530350903345462; Caliskan, *Market Threads*.

57. The top twenty exchanges in terms of monthly trading volume as of July 7, 2020, are the following (from the largest to the smallest): Binance, Coinbase, Upbit, Bitstamp, Gate.io, Bitfinex, Liquid, Kraken, Poloniex, Bitflyer, Bithumb, Coinone, Bittrex, Gemini, Bitso, Paribu, Zaif, BTC Markets, Indodax, and ItBit. On the same date, these exchanges carried out more than 8.45 and less than 10 percent of all cryptocurrency exchange platform trading in the world. I did not record the trading volume of one exchange for that particular date and could not locate the exact volume later. Hence, I cannot calculate their exact collective trading volume and instead have estimated a reliable range.

58. Binance, "Terms of Use," 2020, https://accounts.binance.com/en/terms.

59. A third type—flash lending—is also emerging in decentralized exchanges but is still not found in centralized platforms. Users borrow an amount for a very short period of time—for instance, ten seconds—and pay it back at the end of the time interval. The transaction order is embedded in these data money forms and thus automated. The trader makes their buy and sell decisions simultaneously.

60. I excluded nonconcepts such as *third*.

61. For an excellent analysis of these materialities and their agency in socioeconomic relations, see Donald MacKenzie, *Material Markets: How Economic Agents Are Constructed* (Oxford: Oxford University Press, 2009).

62. For a discussion of data as representation and the materialities associated with these data, see Paul Dourish, The *Stuff of Bits: An Essay on the Materialities of Information* (Cambridge, MA: MIT Press, 2017).

63. For a detailed discussion of how the documentary circulation of representations precedes and makes possible the actual circulation of commodities, see Koray Caliskan, "Making a Global Commodity: The Production of Markets and Cotton in Egypt, Turkey, and the United States" (PhD diss., New York University, 2005), ch. 2.

64. Craig Calhoun, *Dictionary of the Social Sciences* (New York: Oxford University Press, 2002), https://doi.org/10.1093/acref/9780195123715.001.0001.

64. For this analysis, core social-scientific categories are stemmed to represent the terms-of-service documents' foci. For example, *finance* and *financial* were plotted together.

65. Rochet and Tirole, "Platform Competition in Two-Sided Markets."

66. Evans and Schmalensee, "The Industrial Organization of Markets with Two-Sided Platforms."

67. Bratton, *The Stack*. For a fruitful discussion of how the literature sees platforms as markets, infrastructures, and ecosystems, see Gernot Grabher and Jonas König, "Disruption, Embedded: A Polanyian Framing of the Platform Economy," *Sociologica* 14, no. 1 (2020): 95–118, https://doi.org/10.6092/issn.1971-8853/10443.

68. Dodd, "The Social Life of Bitcoin"; Bill Maurer, "Blockchains Are a Diamond's Best Friend: Zelizer for the Bitcoin Moment," in *Money Talks: Explaining How Money Really Works*, ed. Nina Bandelj, Frederick F. Wherry, and Viviana A. Zelizer (Princeton, NJ: Princeton University Press, 2017), 215–29; Parkin, 2019; Ludovico Rella, "Steps Towards an Ecology of Money Infrastructures: Materiality and Cultures of Ripple," *Journal of Cultural Economy* 13, no. 2 (2020): 236–49, https://doi.org/10.1080/17530350.2020.1711532; Lynette Shaw, "The Meanings of New Money: Social Constructions of Value in the Rise of Digital Currencies" (PhD diss., University of Washington, 2016); Lana Swartz, "Blockchain Dreams"; Matthew A. Zook and Joe Blankenship, "New Spaces of Disruption? The Failures of Bitcoin and the Rhetorical Power of Algorithmic Governance," *Geoforum* 96 (2018): 248–55.

69. Garrod, 2019; Kristopher Jones, "Toward a Political Sociology of Blockchain" (PhD diss., Queens University, 2018).

70. Rochet and Tirole, "Platform Competition in Two-Sided Markets."

71. Gawer, *Platforms, Markets, and Innovation.*

72. José van Dijck, Thomas Poell, and Martijn de Waal, *The Platform Society* (Oxford: Oxford University Press, 2018); Evans and Schmalensee, "The Industrial Organization of Markets with Two-Sided Platforms"; Peter C. Evans and Annabelle Gawer, "The Rise of the Platform Enterprise: A Global Survey," Center for Global Enterprise, 2016, https://www.thecge.net/archived-papers/the-rise-of-the-platform -enterprise-a-global-survey/.

73. Ambrus and Argenziano, "Network Markets and Consumer Coordination."

74. McKenzie Wark, *Capital Is Dead* (London: Verso, 2019).

75. (Zuboff, 2018).

76. Florian Butollo, "Digitalization and the Geographies of Production: Towards Reshoring or Global Fragmentation?," *Competition & Change* 25, no. 2 (2020), https://doi.org/10.1177/1024529420918160; Michael A. Cusumano, Annabelle Gawer, and David B. Yoffie, *The Business of Platforms: Strategy in the Age of Digital Competition, Innovation, and Power* (New York: Harper Business, 2019); Michael G. Jacobides, Carmelo Cennamo, and Annabelle Gawer, "Towards a Theory of Ecosystems," *Strategic Management Journal* 39, no. 8 (2018): 2255–76, https://doi.org/10.1002/smj.2904.

77. Rahul Kapoor, "Ecosystems: Broadening the Locus of Value Creation," *Journal of Organization Design* 7, no. 1 (2018): 12, https://doi.org/10.1186 /s41469-018-0035-4; Andrew Shipilov and Annabelle Gawer, "Integrating Research on Interorganizational Networks and Ecosystems," *Academy of Management Annals* 14, no. 1 (2020): 92–121, https://doi.org/10.5465 /annals.2018.0121.

78. Marc Andreessen, "Analyzing the Facebook Platform, Three Weeks In," *Blog Pmarca*, June 12, 2007, http://web.archive.org/web/20071021003047/ blog.pmarca.com/2007/06/analyzing_the_f.html, quoted in Ian Bogost and Nick Montfort, "Platform Studies: Frequently Questioned Answers," in *Proceedings of the Digital Arts and Culture Conference* (Irvine: University of California, Irvine, 2009), 4, https://escholarship.org/uc/item/01rok9br.

## 4. GLOBAL CRYPTOCURRENCY COMMUNITIES AS DATA MONEY MAKERS

1. Josephine Nelson, "Cryptocommunity Currencies," *Cornell Law Review* 105, no. 4 (2020): 909–58.

2. Jillian Crandall, "Blockchains and the 'Chains of Empire': Contextualizing Blockchain, Cryptocurrency, and Neoliberalism in Puerto Rico," *Journal of the Design Studies Forum* 11, no. 3 (2019): 279–300, https://doi .org/10.1080/17547075.2019.1673989; Ludovico Rella, "Steps Towards an Ecology of Money Infrastructures: Materiality and Cultures of Ripple," *Journal of Cultural Economy* 13, no. 2 (2020): 236–49, https://doi.org/10.1080 /17530350.2020.1711532; Erkan Saka, "Cryptocurrency Usage in Turkey," *Anthropology News*, September 11, 2020, https://doi.org/10.14506/AN.1491; A. Thieser, "These Roses Don't Think About Each Other Either: Competition, Collaboration, and Utopianism in a Blockchain Community" (unpublished manuscript, 2019).

3. Matthias Tarasiewicz and Andrew Newman, "Cryptocurrencies as Distributed Community Experiments," in *Handbook of Digital Currency: Bitcoin, Innovation, Financial Instruments, and Big Data*, ed. David Lee Kuo Chuen (London: Academic Press, 2015), 201–22.

4. Megan Knittel, Shelby Pitts, and Rick Wash, "'The Most Trustworthy Coin': How Ideological Tensions Drive Trust in Bitcoin," *Proceedings of the ACM on Human-Computer Interaction* 3, no. CSCW (2019): 1–23, https://doi.org/10.1145/3359138.

5. D. Arjaliès, "'At the Very Beginning, There's This Dream': The Role of Utopia in the Workings of Local and Cryptocurrencies," in *The Palgrave Handbook of Technological Finance*, ed. R. Raghavendra, W. Robert, and Z. Luigi (London: Palgrave Macmillan, 2021), 95–137; Lana Swartz, "What Was Bitcoin, What Will It Be? The Techno-Economic Imaginaries of a New Money Technology," *Cultural Studies* 32, no. 4 (2018): 623–50, https://doi.org/10.1080/09502386.2017.1416420; Lana Swartz, *New Money: How Payment Became Social Media* (New Haven, CT: Yale University Press, 2020).

6. Jonas V. Andersen and Claire Ingram Bogusz, "Patterns of Self-Organising in the Bitcoin Online Community: Code Forking as Organising in Digital Infrastructure" (paper presented at the thirty-eighth International Conference on Information Systems, Seoul, December 10–13, 2017).

7. Claire Ingra Bogusz and Marcel Morisse, "How Infrastructures Anchor Open Entrepreneurship: The Case of Bitcoin and Stigma," *Information Systems Journal* 28, no. 6 (2018): 1176–212, https://doi.org/10.1111/isj .12204.

8. Christoph F. Breidbach and Silviana Tana, "Betting on Bitcoin: How Social Collectives Shape Cryptocurrency Markets," *Journal of Business Research* 122 (2021): 311–20; Aiden Walton and Kevin Johnston, "Exploring Perceptions of Bitcoin Adoption: The South African Virtual Community Perspective," *Interdisciplinary Journal of Information, Knowledge, & Management* 13 (2018): 165–82.

9. Antoon Spithoven, "Theory and Reality of Cryptocurrency Governance," *Journal of Economic Issues* 53, no. 2 (2019): 385–93, https://doi.org/10.1080 /00213624.2019.1594518.

10. Eduardo H. Diniz, Adrian Kemmer Cernev, Denis A. Rodrigues, and Fabio Daneluzzi, "Solidarity Cryptocurrencies as Digital Community Platforms," *Information Technology for Development* 27, no. 3 (2020): 524–38, https://doi.org/10.1080/02681102.2020.1827365.

11. Jieyu Xu, Wen Bai, Miao Hu, Haibo Tian, and Di Wu, "Bitcoin Miners: Exploring a Covert Community in the Bitcoin Ecosystem," *Peer-to-Peer Networking and Applications* 14, no. 2 (2021): 644–54.

12. Quinn DuPont, *Cryptocurrencies and Blockchains* (Cambridge: Polity, 2019); Quinn DuPont, "Experiments in Algorithmic Governance: A History and Ethnography of 'The DAO,' a Failed Decentralized Autonomous Organization," in *Bitcoin and Beyond: Cryptocurrencies, Blockchains, and Global Governance*, ed. M. Campbell-Verduyn (London: Routledge, 2019), 157–77; Ludovico Rella, "Money's Infrastructures: Blockchain Technologies and the Ecologies of the Memory Bank" (PhD diss., Durham University, 2021); Swartz, *New Money*.

13. Koray Caliskan and Michel Callon, "Economization, Part 1: Shifting Attention from the Economy Towards Processes of Economization," *Economy and Society* 38, no. 3 (2009): 369–98, https://doi.org/10.1080 /03085140903020580; M. Callon, "What Does It Mean to Say That Economics Is Performative?," in *Do Economists Make Markets? On the Performativity of Economics*, ed. D. MacKenzie, F. Muniesa, and L. Siu (Princeton, NJ: Princeton University Press, 2007), 311–57; Donald MacKenzie, "The Big, Bad Wolf and the Rational Market: Portfolio Insurance, the 1987 Crash, and the Performativity of Economics," *Economy and Society* 33, no. 3 (2004): 303–34; Donald MacKenzie, "Globalization and Its Discontents," *Public Choice* 120, no. 1–2 (2004): 234–39; Simone Polillo, "Crisis, Reputation, and the Politics of Expertise:

Fictional Performativity at the Bank of Italy," *Review of Social Economy* (2020), 1–21, https://doi.org/10.1080/00346764.2020.1857822.

14. Electra Protocol is the financial and infrastructural reincarnation of Electra, proposed by the same community that had maintained Electra. This chapter observes a continuity from Electra's to Electra Protocol's community and treats them as the same community. The old Electra was left behind and now has neither a community nor monetary value.

15. These languages, in the order of most to least frequently used, are English, German, Russian, Chinese, Spanish, Dutch, Korean, Turkish, Italian, French, and Portuguese.

16. https://www.electraprotocol.com/team/.

17. I removed two outlying responses from the calculation because they estimated very active membership to be ten thousand and fifty thousand.

18. I removed twenty-one outlying responses from the calculation because they estimated moderately active membership to be more than 1 million or less than eleven.

19. I removed thirty-one outlying responses from the calculation because they estimated less active membership to be between 1 and 101 or more than 1 million.

20. Yet these very active members are also more dedicated to the project and may tend to imagine their community to be larger than it actually is.

21. *Good* is also used, although rarely, to refer to a commodity.

22. Koray Caliskan, "Data Money: The Socio-technical Infrastructure of Cryptocurrency Blockchains," *Economy and Society* 49, no. 4 (2020): 540–61, https://doi.org/10.1080/03085147.2020.1774258.

23. Callon, "What Does It Mean to Say That Economics Is Performative?"; Donald MacKenzie, "An Equation and Its Worlds: Bricolage, Exemplars, Disunity, and Performativity in Financial Economics," *Social Studies of Science* 33, no. 6 (2003): 831–68.

24. These performativities at times take the shape of fictional performativities that call for changing the way in which they see their past and future according to their interest, much like institutional actors such as the Bank of Italy do; cf. Polillo, "Crisis, Reputation, and the Politics of Expertise."

25. https://github.com/electracoin-ECA/electra-open-paper/blob/master/ElectraWhitePaper-TheOpenPaper.md.

26. For the data on which this analysis is based, see Enis Simsar and Koray Caliskan, "Twitter Interaction Data of Electra Cryptocurrency Community's Twitter Handle Followers and a Code for Follower Interaction Analysis," Github, 2021, https://github.com/enisimsar/DataMoney.

27. This illustration was prepared with the help of graphcommons.com, an open-source tool for network visualization.

28. For a detailed theoretical discussion of these dynamics, see Burak Arikan, "Analyzing Data Networks," *Medium*, April 7, 2016, https://medium.com/graph-commons/analyzing-data-networks-f4480a28fb4b.

29. https://discord.com/why-discord-is-different, accessed January 19, 2021.

30. Finn Brunton, *Digital Cash: The Unknown History of the Anarchists, Utopians, and Technologists Who Built Cryptocurrency* (Princeton, NJ: Princeton University Press, 2019); DuPont, *Cryptocurrencies and Blockchains*; DuPont, "Experiments in Algorithmic Governance"; Swartz, *New Money*.

31. See, for instance, Koray Caliskan, *Market Threads: How Cotton Farmers and Traders Create a Global Commodity* (Princeton, NJ: Princeton University Press, 2011) for a review of ethnographies of trading.

32. Caliskan and Callon, "Economization, Part 1."

## 5. THE EMERGENCE AND DEMISE OF A CRYPTOCURRENCY COMMUNITY

1. Dan Tapscott and Alex Tapscott, *Blockchain Revolution: How the Technology Behind Bitcoin Is Changing Money, Business, and the World* (New York: Penguin Random House, 2016).

2. https://electraproject.weebly.com/.

3. https://bitcointalk.org/index.php?topic=1848351.0.

4. He was using Morfuso as a pseudonym when he first joined Bitcointalk.

5. Koray Caliskan and Michel Callon, "Economization, Part 1: Shifting Attention from the Economy Towards Processes of Economization," *Economy and Society* 38, no. 3 (2009): 369–98, https://doi.org/10.1080/03085140903020580; Koray Caliskan and Michel Callon, "Economization, Part 2: A Research Programme for the Study of Markets,"

*Economy and Society* 39, no. 1 (2010): 1–32, https://doi.org/10.1080
/03085140903424519; Michel Callon, Yuval Millo, and Fabian Muniesa, *Market Devices* (Malden. MA: Blackwell, 2007); Sam Dallyn, "Cryptocurrencies as Market Singularities: The Strange Case of Bitcoin," *Journal of Cultural Economy* 10, no. 5 (2017): 462–73, https://doi.org/10.1
080/17530350.2017.1315541; Marion Fourcade and Kieran Healy, "Seeing Like a Market," *Socio-economic Review* 15, no. 1 (2016): 9–29, https://doi.org/10.1093/ser/mww033; Katy Mason, Hans Kjellberg, and Johan Hagberg, "Exploring the Performativity of Marketing: Theories, Practices, and Devices," *Journal of Marketing Management* 31. no. 1–2 (2015): 1–15.

6. Electraoi disagreed with my interpretation in the final draft of this chapter and proposed the following correction: "I was not interested in calling the shots. For me, a fork means chaos. A good fork requires no mistakes to be made in the new code and effective coordination between all exchanges and users. They all need to be notified of the update and cooperate and if they don't you can run into many potential issues."

7. He continued to communicate by direct messages with individual members of the community. His lack of public communication does not suggest that he was completely absent.

8. https://bitcointalk.org/index.php?topic=1848351.0. Accessed January 4, 2021.

9. https://bitcointalk.org/index.php?topic=1848351.940. Accessed January 4, 2021.

10. Koray Caliskan, "Data Money: The Socio-technical Infrastructure of Cryptocurrency Blockchains," *Economy and Society* 49, no. 4 (2020): 540–61, https://doi.org/10.1080/03085147.2020.1774258.

11. For pioneer studies on the nature of fieldwork among digital communities, see Tom Boellstorff, *Coming of Age in Second Life: An Anthropologist Explores the Virtually Human* (Princeton, NJ: Princeton University Press, 2008), and *Ethnography and Virtual Worlds: A Handbook of Method* (Princeton, NJ: Princeton University Press, 2012).

12. "The Trust Machine," *The Economist*, October 31, 2015, https://www.economist.com/leaders/2015/10/31/the-trust-machine.

13. Viviana A. Zelizer, *The Social Meaning of Money* (New York: Basic Books, 1994).

## 6. A NEW FRAMEWORK FOR CRYPTOCURRENCY TAXATION AND EXCHANGE PLATFORM REGULATION

1. Finn Brunton, *Digital Cash: The Unknown History of the Anarchists, Utopians, and Technologists Who Built Cryptocurrency* (Princeton, NJ: Princeton University Press, 2019); Nigel Dodd, "The Social Life of Bitcoin," *Theory, Culture, & Society* 35, no. 3 (2017): 35–56, https://doi.org /10.1177/0263276417746464; Quinn DuPont, *Cryptocurrencies and Block-chains* (Cambridge: Polity, 2019); Quinn DuPont, "Experiments in Algorithmic Governance: A History and Ethnography of 'The DAO,' a Failed Decentralized Autonomous Organization," in *Bitcoin and Beyond: Cryptocurrencies, Blockchains, and Global Governance*, ed. M. Campbell-Verduyn (London: Routledge, 2019), 157–77; Ludovico Rella, "Steps Towards an Ecology of Money Infrastructures: Materiality and Cultures of Ripple," *Journal of Cultural Economy* 13, no. 2 (2020): 236–49, https://doi.org/10.1080/17530350.2020.1711532; Lana Swartz, "What Was Bitcoin, What Will It Be? The Techno-economic Imaginaries of a New Money Technology," *Cultural Studies* 32, no. 4 (2018): 623–50, https://doi.org/10.1080/09502386.2017.1416420

2. The former SEC president Jay Clayton declared that "every ICO I've seen is a security" and ordered the SEC to go after every company that sold cryptocurrency. Nathanial Popper, "Subpoenas Signal S.E.C. Crackdown on Initial Coin Offerings," *New York Times*, February 28, 2018, https://www.nytimes.com/2018/02/28/technology/initial-coin -offerings-sec.html.

3. "Bitcoin Basics," U.S. Commodity Futures Trading Commission, https:// www.cftc.gov/sites/default/files/2019-12/oceo_bitcoinbasics0218.pdf.

4. Notice 2014-21, Internal Revenue Service, https://www.irs.gov/pub/irs -drop/n-14-21.pdf.

5. S. Alkadri, "Defining and Regulating Cryptocurrency: Fake Internet Money or Legitimate Medium of Exchange?," *Duke Law & Technology Review* 17 (2018): 71–98, https://scholarship.law.duke.edu/dltr/vol17/iss1/3.

6. IFRIC, "International Financial Reporting Interpretations Committee Report on Holdings of Cryptocurrencies," 2019, https://www.ifrs .org/content/dam/ifrs/supporting-implementation/agenda-decisions /holdings-of-cryptocurrencies-june-2019.pdf.

7. Josephine Nelson, "Cryptocommunity Currencies," *Cornell Law Review* 105, no. 4 (2020): 909–58.

8. I. Cvetkova, "Cryptocurrencies Legal Regulation," *BRICS Law Journal* 5, no. 2 (2018): 128–53.

9. E. Hewitt, "Bringing Continuity to Cryptocurrency: Commercial Law as a Guide to the Asset Categorization of Bitcoin," *Seattle University Law Review* 39 (2016): 619–49. For a more comprehensive review of how data monies are seen in other legal contexts and countries, see O. S. Bolotaeva, A. A. Stepanova, and S. S. Alekseeva, "The Legal Nature of Cryptocurrency," *IOP Conference Series: Earth and Environmental Science* 272 (2019): 032166; OECD, *Taxing Virtual Currencies: An Overview of Tax Treatments and Emerging Tax Policy Issues* (Paris: OECD, 2020); and K. Solodan, "Legal Regulation of Cryptocurrency Taxation in European Countries," *European Journal of Law and Public Administration* 6 (2019): 64–74.

10. Christoph F. Breidbach and Silviana Tana, "Betting on Bitcoin: How Social Collectives Shape Cryptocurrency Markets," *Journal of Business Research* 122 (2021): 311–20; Paraskevi Katsiampa, "Volatility Estimation for Bitcoin: A Comparison of GARCH Models," *Economics Letters* 158 (2017): 3–6, https://doi.org/10.1016/j.econlet.2017.06.023; C. Westermeier, "Money Is Data—the Platformization of Financial Transactions," *Information, Communication, & Society* 23, no. 14 (2020): 2047–63, https://doi.org/10.1080/1369118X.2020.1770833.

11. Jean-Charles Rochet and Jean Tirole, "Platform Competition in Two-Sided Markets," *Journal of the European Economic* Association 1, no. 4 (2003): 990–1029, https://doi.org/10.1162/154247603322493212, and "Two-Sided Markets: A Progress Report," *RAND Journal of Economics* 37, no. 3 (2006): 645–67, https://doi.org/10.1111/j.1756-2171.2006.tb00036.x.

12. Nigel Dodd, "The Social Life of Bitcoin," *Theory, Culture, & Society* 35, no. 3 (2018): 35–56; https://doi.org/10.1177/0263276417746464; David Golumbia, "Bitcoin as Politics: Distributed Right-Wing Extremism," in *MoneyLab Reader: An Intervention in Digital Economy*, ed. Geert Lovink, Nathaniel Tkacz, and Patricia DeVries (Amsterdam: Institute of Network Cultures, 2015), 117–31; Ludovico Rella, "Money's Infrastructures: Blockchain Technologies and the Ecologies of the Memory Bank" (PhD diss., Durham University, 2021).

13. A. Christians, "Tax Cryptographia: Exploring the Fiscal Design of Cryptocurrencies," *McGill Law Journal* 64, no. 4 (2019): 683–706.

14. For the SEC Chairman Jay Clayton's testimony, see https://www .banking.senate.gov/imo/media/doc/Clayton%20Testimony%202-6-18 .pdf. For the CFTC Chairman J. Christopher Giancarlo's testimony, see https://www.banking.senate.gov/imo/media/doc/Giancarlo%20Testimony %202-6-18b.pdf.

15. USA: Crypto Exchanges & Regulation—Top Exchanges in USA by Coincub Criteria, Coincub, https://coincub.com/country/usa/.

16. A. Bal, "Developing a Regulatory Framework for the Taxation of Virtual Currencies," *Intertax* 47, no. 2 (2019): 219–33.

17. Notice 2014-21, Internal Revenue Service.

18. Digital Assets, Internal Revenue Service, last reviewed or updated November 22, 2022, https://www.irs.gov/businesses/small-businesses -self-employed/virtual-currencies.

19. Frequently Asked Questions on Virtual Currency Transactions, last reviewed or updated December 1, 2022, https://www.irs.gov/individuals /international-taxpayers/frequently-asked-questions-on-virtual-currency -transactions.

20. Notice 2014-21, Internal Revenue Service.

21. J. E. Penner, *The Idea of Property in Law* (Oxford: Oxford University Press, 1997).

22. Penner, *The Idea of Property in Law*.

23. Nelson, "Cryptocommunity Currencies."

24. G. E. Kalbaugh, "Virtual Currency, Not a Currency?," *Journal of International Business and Law* 16, no. 1 (2016): 26–35, https://scholarly commons.law.hofstra.edu/jibl/vol16/iss1/5.

25. D. Arner, D. Auer, and J. Frost, "Stablecoins: Risks, Potential, and Regulation" (Working Paper No. 905, Bank for International Settlements, Basel, 2020).

26. T. G. Massad, *It's Time to Strengthen the Regulation of Crypto-Assets* (Washington, DC: Brookings Institution, 2019), https://www .brookings.edu/research/its-time-to-strengthen-the-regulation-of -crypto-assets/.

27. Board of Governors of the Federal Reserve System, "Federal Reserve Chair Jerome H. Powell Outlines the Federal Reserve's Response to Technological Advances Driving Rapid Change in the Global Payments

Landscape," press release, May 20, 2021, https://www.federalreserve.gov/newsevents/pressreleases/other20210520b.htm.

28. SEC v. W. J. Howey Co., 328 U.S. 293 (1946).

29. O. A. Karpenko, T. K. Blokhina, and L. V. Chebukhanova, "The Initial Coin Offering (ICO) Process: Regulation and Risks," *Journal of Risk and Financial Management* 14, no. 12 (2021): 599, https://www.mdpi.com/1911-8074/14/12/599.

30. Commodity Exchange Act, 7 U.S.C. § 1a, https://www.law.cornell.edu/uscode/text/7/1a.

31. In the Matter of Coinflip, Inc., CFTC No. 15-29 (Commodity Futures Trading Commission, 2015), https://www.cftc.gov/sites/default/files/idc/groups/public/@lrenforcementactions/documents/legalpleading/enfcoinfliprorder09172015.pdf.

32. Massad, *It's Time to Strengthen the Regulation.*

33. J. Dewey, *Blockchain and Cryptocurrency Regulation* (London: Global Legal Group, 2019).

34. https://www.dfs.ny.gov/apps_and_licensing/virtual_currency_businesses/bitlicense_faqs.

35. B. D. Feinstein and K. Werbach, "The Impact of Cryptocurrency Regulation on Trading Markets," *Journal of Financial Regulation* 7, no. 1 (2021): 48–99.

36. F. Eigelshoven, A. Ullrich, and D. Parry, "Cryptocurrency Market Manipulation: A Systematic Literature Review," in *International Conference on Information Systems 2021 Proceedings* (2021).

37. However, in competitive or fully authoritarian contexts, such a measure would increase the repressive capacity of the state and would most probably be resisted, for legitimate reasons, from actors on the ground.

## 7. WHAT IS TO BE DONE WITH CRYPTO ECONOMIES?

1. Bell Company, *Annual Report of the Directors of American Telephone and Telegraph Company to the Stockholders for the Year Ending December 31, 1908* (Boston: Geo. H. Ellis Co., 1909).

2. Jeffery Rohlfs, "A Theory of Interdependent Demand for a Communications Service," *Bell Journal of Economics* 5 (Spring 1974): 16–37.

3. See, for example, Michael L. Katz and Carl Shapiro, "Systems Competition and Network Effects," *Journal of Economic Perspectives* 8, no. 2 (Spring 1994): 93–115.

4. However, in competitive or full authoritarian contexts, such a measure would increase the repressive capacity of the state and would most probably be resisted, for legitimate reasons, by actors on the ground.

# BIBLIOGRAPHY

Aglietta, Michel. *Money: 5,000 Years of Debt and Power*. London: Verso, 2018.

Akyildirim, Emre, Shaen Corbet, Paraskevi Katsiampa, Neil Kellard, and Ahmet Sensoy. "The Development of Bitcoin Futures: Exploring the Interactions Between Cryptocurrency Derivatives." *Finance Research Letters* 34 (2020): 101234. https://doi.org/10.1016/j.frl.2019.07.007.

Alexander, Jennifer, and Paul Alexander. "What's a Fair Price? Price-Setting and Trading Partnerships in Javanese Markets." *Man* 26, no. 3 (1991): 493–512. https://doi.org/10.2307/2803879.

Alkadri, S. "Defining and Regulating Cryptocurrency: Fake Internet Money or Legitimate Medium of Exchange?" *Duke Law & Technology Review* 17 (2018): 71–98. https://scholarship.law.duke.edu/dltr/vol17/iss1/3.

Ambrus, Attila, and Rossella Argenziano. "Network Markets and Consumer Coordination." Working Paper No. 1317, DESifo, Munich, 2004. https://www.cesifo.org/en/publikationen/2004/working-paper/network-markets-and-consumer-coordination.

Anand, Nikhil. "Municipal Disconnect: On Abject Water and Its Urban Infrastructures." *Ethnography* 13, no. 4 (2012): 487–509. https://doi.org/10.1177/1466138111435743.

Andersen, Jonas V., and Claire Ingram Bogusz. "Patterns of Self-Organising in the Bitcoin Online Community: Code Forking as Organising in Digital Infrastructure." Paper presented at the thirty-eighth International Conference on Information Systems, Seoul, December 10–13, 2017.

Andreessen, Marc. "Analyzing the Facebook Platform, Three Weeks In." *Blog Pmarca*, June 12, 2007. http://web.archive.org/web/20071021003047/blog.pmarca.com/2007/06/analyzing_the_f.html.

Appel, Hannah. "Offshore Work: Oil, Modularity, and the How of Capitalism in Equatorial Guinea." *American Ethnologist* 39, no. 4 (2012): 692–709.

Arikan, Burak. "Analyzing Data Networks." *Medium*, April 7, 2016. https://medium.com/graph-commons/analyzing-data-networks-f4480a28fb4b.

Arjaliès, D. "The Role of Utopia in the Workings of Local and Cryptocurrencies." In *The Palgrave Handbook of Technological Finance*, ed. R. Raghavendra, W. Robert, and Z. Luigi, 95–137. London: Palgrave Macmillan, 2021.

Arner, D., D. Auer, and J. Frost.. "Stablecoins: Risks, Potential, and Regulation." Working Paper No. 905, Bank for International Settlements, Basel, 2020.

Bal, A. "Developing a Regulatory Framework for the Taxation of Virtual Currencies." *Intertax* 47, no. 2 (2018): 219–33.

Bandelj, Nina, Frederick F. Wherry, and Viviana A. Zelizer, eds. *Money Talks: Explaining How Money Really Works*. Princeton, NJ: Princeton University Press, 2017.

Barry, Andrew. *Material Politics: Disputes Along the Pipeline*. Chichester, West Sussex: Wiley-Blackwell, 2013.

Bear, Laura. *Lines of the Nation: Indian Railway Workers, Bureaucracy, and the Intimate Historical Self*. New York: Columbia University Press, 2007.

Bell Company. *Annual Report of the Directors of American Telephone and Telegraph Company to the Stockholders for the Year ending December 31, 1908*. Boston: Geo. H. Ellis Co., 1909.

Binance. "Terms of Use," 2020. https://accounts.binance.com/en/terms.

Birbil, S. Ilker, and Koray Caliskan. "Terms of Service Agreements of 251 Cryptocurrency Exchanges Representing 99.99 Percent of Centralized Data Money Transactions." Github, 2020. https://github.com/sibirbil/TermsofService.

Bjerg, Ole. "How Is Bitcoin Money?" *Theory, Culture, & Society* 33, no. 1 (2016): 53–72.

Boellstorff, Tom. *Coming of Age in Second Life: An Anthropologist Explores the Virtually Human*. Princeton, NJ: Princeton University Press, 2008.

Boellstorff, Tom. *Ethnography and Virtual Worlds: A Handbook of Method*. Princeton, NJ: Princeton University Press, 2012.

Bogost, Ian, and Nick Montfort. "Platform Studies: Frequently Questioned Answers." In *Proceedings of the Digital Arts and Culture Conference*. Irvine: University of California, Irvine, 2009. https://escholarship.org/uc/item/01rok9br.

Bolotaeva, O. S., A. A. Stepanova, and S. S. Alekseeva. "The Legal Nature of Cryptocurrency." *IOP Conference Series: Earth and Environmental Science* 272, no. 3 (2020): 032166.

Bratton, Benjamin H. *The Stack: On Software and Sovereignty.* Cambridge, MA: MIT Press, 2015.

*Brave the World* (blog). "We Declare Bitcoin's Independence," August 13, 2014. http://bravetheworld.com/2014/08/13/declare-bitcoins-independence/.

Breidbach, Christoph F., and Silviana Tana. "Betting on Bitcoin: How Social Collectives Shape Cryptocurrency Markets." *Journal of Business Research* 122 (2021): 311–20.

Brian, Larkin. "The Politics and Poetics of Infrastructure." *Annual Review of Anthropology* 42 (2013): 327–43.

Brunton, Finn. *Digital Cash: The Unknown History of the Anarchists, Utopians, and Technologists Who Built Cryptocurrency.* Princeton, NJ: Princeton University Press, 2019.

Buffet, Warren. "Interview with Warren Buffet." By Becky Quick. CNBC, May 18, 2018. https://www.cnbc.com/video/2020/02/24/watch-cnbcs-full-interview-with-berkshire-hathaway-ceo-warren-buffett.html.

Butollo, Florian. "Digitalization and the Geographies of Production: Towards Reshoring or Global Fragmentation?" *Competition & Change* 25, no. 2 (2020). https://doi.org/10.1177/1024529420918160.

Caillaud, Bernard, and Bruno Jullien. "Competing Cybermediaries." *European Economic Review* 45, no. 4–6 (2001): 797–808. https://doi.org/10.1016/S0014-2921(01)00123-4.

Calhoun, Craig. *Dictionary of the Social Sciences.* New York: Oxford University Press, 2002. https://doi.org/10.1093/acref/9780195123715.001.0001.

Caliskan, Koray. "Data Money: The Socio-technical Infrastructure of Cryptocurrency Blockchains." *Economy and Society* 49, no. 4 (2020): 540–61. https://doi.org/10.1080/03085147.2020.1774258.

Caliskan, Koray. "Making a Global Commodity: The Production of Markets and Cotton in Egypt, Turkey, and the United States." PhD diss., New York University, 2005.

Caliskan, Koray. *Market Threads: How Cotton Farmers and Traders Create a Global Commodity.* Princeton, NJ: Princeton University Press, 2011.

Caliskan, Koray. "The Meaning of Price in World Markets." *Journal of Cultural Economy* 2, no. 3 (2009): 239–68. https://doi.org/10.1080/17530350903345462.

Caliskan, Koray. "Platform Works as Stack Economization: Cryptocurrency Markets and Exchanges in Perspective." *Sociologica* 14, no. 3 (2021): 115–42. https://doi.org/10.6092/issn.1971-8853/11746.

Caliskan, Koray. "Price as a Market Device: Cotton Trading in Izmir Mercantile Exchange." *Sociological Review* 55, no. 2 (2007): 241–60. https://doi.org/10.1111/j.1467-954X.2007.00738.x.

Caliskan, Koray. "The Rise and Fall of Electra: A Cryptocurrency Community in Perspective." *Review of Social Economy*, 2022. https://doi.org/10.1080/00346764.2022.2039404.

Caliskan, Koray, and Ilker Birbil. Computational Text Analysis of Cryptocurrency Blockchain White Papers. 2019.

Caliskan, Koray, and Ilker Birbil. "White Papers of Top 100 Cryptocurrencies and Their Blockchains." Github, 2020. https://github.com/sibirbil/DataMoney.

Caliskan, Koray, and Michel Callon. "Economization, Part 1: Shifting Attention from the Economy Towards Processes of Economization." *Economy and Society* 38, no. 3 (2009): 369–98. https://doi.org/10.1080/03085140903020580.

Caliskan, Koray, and Michel Callon. "Economization, Part 2: A Research Programme for the Study of Markets." *Economy and Society* 39, no. 1 (2010): 1–32. https://doi.org/10.1080/03085140903424519.

Caliskan, Koray, and Matt Wade, "DARN Part 1: What is Strategic Design? Social Theory and Intangible Design in Perspective," *She Ji: The Journal of Design, Economics, and Innovation* 8, no. 3 (2022): 299–318. https://doi.org/10.1016/j.sheji.2022.10.001.

Caliskan, Koray, and Matt Wade, "*DARN Part 2: An Evidence-Based Research and Prototyping Methodology for Strategic Design," She Ji: The Journal of Design, Economics, and Innovation* 8, no. 3 (2022): 319–335. https://doi.org/10.1016/j.sheji.2022.11.002

Callon, Michel. *The Laws of the Markets*. Malden, MA: Blackwell/Sociological Review, 1998.

Callon, Michel. "What Does It Mean to Say That Economics Is Performative?" In *Do Economists Make Markets? On the Performativity of Economics*, ed. D. MacKenzie, F. Muniesa, and L. Siu, 311–57. Princeton, NJ: Princeton University Press, 2007.

Callon, Michel, Yuval Millo, and Fabian Muniesa. *Market Devices*. Malden, MA: Blackwell, 2007.

Castronova, Edward. *Wildcat Currency: How the Virtual Money Revolution Is Transforming the Economy*. New Haven, CT: Yale University Press, 2014.

Christians, A. "Tax Cryptographia: Exploring the Fiscal Design of Cryptocurrencies." *McGill Law Journal* 64, no. 4 (2019): 683–706.

Ciaian, Pavel, Miroslava Rajcaniova, and d'Artis Kancs. "The Economics of BitCoin Price Formation." *Applied Economics* 48, no. 19 (2016): 1799–815. https://doi.org/10.1080/00036846.2015.1109038.Corbet, Shaen, Veysel Eraslan, Brian Lucey, and Ahmet Sensoy. "The Effectiveness of Technical Trading Rules in Cryptocurrency Markets." *Finance Research Letters* 31 (2019): 32–37. https://doi.org/10.1016/j.frl.2019.04.027.

Corbet, Shaen, Brian Lucey, Andrew Urquhart, and Larisa Yarovaya. "Cryptocurrencies as a Financial Asset: A Systematic Analysis." *International Review of Financial Analysis* 62 (2019): 182–99. https://doi.org/10.1016/j.irfa.2018.09.003.

Couldry, Nick, and Ulises A. Mejias. "Data Colonialism: Rethinking Big Data's Relation to the Contemporary Subject." *Television & New Media* 20, no. 4 (2018): 336–49. https://doi.org/10.1177/1527476418796632.

Crandall, Jillian. "Blockchains and the 'Chains of Empire': Contextualizing Blockchain, Cryptocurrency, and Neoliberalism in Puerto Rico." *Journal of the Design Studies Forum* 11, no. 3 (2019): 279–300. https://doi.org/10.1080/17547075.2019.1673989.

Cusumano, Michael A., Annabelle Gawer, and David B. Yoffie. *The Business of Platforms: Strategy in the Age of Digital Competition, Innovation, and Power*. New York: Harper Business, 2019.

Cvetkova, I. "Cryptocurrencies Legal Regulation." *BRICS Law Journal* 5, no. 2 (2018): 128–53.

Dallyn, Sam. "Cryptocurrencies as Market Singularities: The Strange Case of Bitcoin." *Journal of Cultural Economy* 10, no. 5 (2017): 462–73. https://doi.org/10.1080/17530350.2017.1315541.

Desan, Christine. *Making Money: Coin, Currency, and the Coming of Capitalism*. Oxford: Oxford University Press, 2014.

Dewey, J. *Blockchain and Cryptocurrency Regulation*. London: Global Legal Group, 2019.

Dijck, José van, Thomas Poell, and Martijn de Waal. *The Platform Society*. Oxford: Oxford University Press, 2018.

Detrio, Casey. "Smart Markets for Stablecoins." July 2015. http://cdetr.io/smart-markets/.

Diniz, Eduardo H., Adrian Kemmer Cernev, Denis A. Rodrigues, and Fabio Daneluzzi. "Solidarity Cryptocurrencies as Digital Community Platforms." *Information Technology for Development* 27, no. 3 (2020): 524–38. https://doi .org/10.1080/02681102.2020.1827365.

Dodd, Nigel. *Money in Social Theory: Economics, Reason, and Contemporary Society.* Oxford: Polity, 1993.

Dodd, Nigel. "The Social Life of Bitcoin." *Theory, Culture, & Society* 35, no. 3 (2018): 35–56. https://doi.org/10.1177/0263276417746464.

Dodd, Nigel. *The Sociology of Money: Economics, Reason, and Contemporary Society.* New York: Continuum, 1994.

Dourish, Paul. The *Stuff of Bits: An Essay on the Materialities of Information.* Cambridge, MA: MIT Press, 2017.

DuPont, Quinn. *Cryptocurrencies and Blockchains.* Cambridge: Polity, 2019.

DuPont, Quinn. "Experiments in Algorithmic Governance: A History and Ethnography of 'The DAO,' a Failed Decentralized Autonomous Organization." In *Bitcoin and Beyond: Cryptocurrencies, Blockchains, and Global Governance,* ed. M. Campbell-Verduyn, 157–77. London: Routledge, 2019.

DuPont, Quinn. "Politics of Bitcoin: Software as Right-Wing Extremism." *Journal of Cultural Economy* 10, no. 5 (2017): 474–76. https://doi.org/10.1080 /17530350.2017.1322997.

Eigelshoven, F., A. Ullrich, and D. Parry. "Cryptocurrency Market Manipulation: A Systematic Literature Review." In *International Conference on Information Systems 2021 Proceedings.* x, 2021.

Elyachar, Julia. *Markets of Dispossession: NGOs, Economic Development, and the State in Cairo.* Durham, NC: Duke University Press, 2005.

Evans, David S., and Richard Schmalensee. "The Industrial Organization of Markets with Two-Sided Platforms." Working Paper No. 11603, National Bureau of Economic Research, Cambridge, MA 2005.

Evans, Peter C., and Annabelle Gawer. *The Rise of the Platform Enterprise: A Global Survey.* New York: Center for Global Enterprise, 2016. https:// www.thecge.net/archived-papers/the-rise-of-the-platform-enterprise -a-global-survey/.

Fassas, Athanasios P., Stephanos Papadamou, and Alexandros Koulis. "Price Discovery in Bitcoin Futures." *Research in International Business and Finance* 52 (2020): 101116. https://doi.org/10.1016/j.ribaf.2019.101116.

Feinstein, B. D., and K. Werbach. "The Impact of Cryptocurrency Regulation on Trading Markets." *Journal of Financial Regulation* 7, no. 1 (2022): 48–99.

Feng, Wenjun, Yiming Wang, and Zhengjun Zhang. "Informed Trading in the Bitcoin Market." *Finance Research Letters* 26 (2018): 63–70. https://doi .org/10.1016/j.frl.2017.11.009.

Filistrucchi, Lapo, Damien Geradin, and Eric van Damme. "Identifying Two-Sided Markets." Discussion Paper No. 2012-008, Tilburg Law and Economics Center, Tilburg, Netherlands, 2012. http://dx.doi.org/10.2139 /ssrn.2008661.

Flurry, Greg, and Wayne Vicknair. "The IBM Application Framework for E-Business." *IBM Systems Journal* 40, no. 1 (2001): 8–24. https://doi.org /10.1147/sj.401.0008.

Fourcade, Marion, and Kieran Healy. "Seeing Like a Market." *Socio-economic Review* 15, no. 1 (2016): 9–29. https://doi.org/10.1093/ser/mww033.

Foucault, Michel, and Colin Gordon. *Power/Knowledge: Selected Interviews and Other Writings, 1972–1977.* New York: Pantheon Books, 1980.

Gawer, Annabella. *Platforms, Markets, and Innovation.* Cheltenham, UK: Edward Elgar, 2009.

Geismar, Haidy. "What's in a Price? An Ethnography of Tribal Art at Auction." *Journal of Material Culture* 6, no. 1 (2001): 25–47. https://doi.org/10.1177 /13591835010060102.

Giudici, Paolo, and Iman Abu-Hashish. "What Determines Bitcoin Exchange Prices? A Network VAR Approach." *Finance Research Letters* 28 (2019): 309–18. https://doi.org/10.1016/j.frl.2018.05.013.

Golumbia, David. "Bitcoin as Politics: Distributed Right-Wing Extremism." In *MoneyLab Reader: An Intervention in Digital Economy,* ed. Geert Lovink, Nathaniel Tkacz, and Patricia DeVries, 117–31. Amsterdam: Institute of Network Cultures, 2015.

Graeber, David. *Debt: The First 5,000 Years.* Brooklyn, New York: Melville House, 2011.

Grabher, Gernot, and Jonas König. "Disruption, Embedded: A Polanyian Framing of the Platform Economy." *Sociologica* 14, no. 1 (2020): 95–118. https://doi.org/10.6092/issn.1971-8853/10443.

Grabher, Gernot, and Jonas König. "Performing Network Theory? Reflexive Relationship Management on Social Network Sites." In *Networked Governance: New Research Perspectives,* ed. Betina Hollstein, Wenzel

Matiaske, and Schnapp Kai-Uwe, 121–40. Cham, Switzerland: Springer, 2017. https://doi.org/10.1007/978-3-319-50386-8.

"The Guardian View on Cryptocurrencies: A Greater Fool's Gold." *The Guardian*, January 7, 2018. https://www.theguardian.com/commentisfree /2018/jan/07/the-guardian-view-on-cryptocurrencies-a-greater-fools -gold.

Guyer, Jane. *Marginal Gains: Monetary Transactions in Atlantic Africa*. Chicago: University of Chicago Press, 2004.

Hart, Keith. *The Memory Bank: Money in an Unequal World*. London: Profile Books, 2000.

Harvey, Penny, and Hannah Knox. *Roads: An Anthropology of Infrastructure and Expertise*. Ithaca, NY: Cornell University Press, 2015.

Hayes, Adam. "The Socio-technological Lives of Bitcoin." *Theory, Culture, & Society* 36, no. 4 (2019): 1–24. https://doi.org/10.1177/0263276419826218.

Hecht, Gabrielle. "Rupture-Talk in the Nuclear Age: Conjugating Colonial Power in Africa." *Social Studies of Science* 32, no. 5–6 (2002): 691–727. https:// doi.org/10.1177/030631270203200504.

Helgesson, Claes-Fredrik, and Fabian Muniesa. "For What It's Worth: An Introduction to Valuation Studies." *Valuation Studies* 1, no. 1 (2013): 1–10. https://doi.org/10.3384/vs.2001-5992.13111.

Hewitt, E. "Bringing Continuity to Cryptocurrency: Commercial Law as a Guide to the Asset Categorization of Bitcoin." *Seattle University Law Review* 39 (2016): 619–49.

IFRIC. "International Financial Reporting Interpretations Committee Report on Holdings of Cryptocurrencies." 2019. https://www.ifrs.org/content /dam/ifrs/supporting-implementation/agenda-decisions/holdings-of -cryptocurrencies-june-2019.pdf.

Ingra Bogusz, Claire, and Marcel Morisse. "How Infrastructures Anchor Open Entrepreneurship: The Case of Bitcoin and Stigma." *Information Systems Journal* 28, no. 6 (2018): 1176–212. https://doi.org/10.1111/isj.12204.

Islam, Najmul, Matti Mäntymäki, and Marja Turunen. "Understanding the Role of Actor Heterogeneity in Blockchain Splits: An Actor-Network Perspective to Bitcoin Forks." Paper presented at the fifty-second Hawaii International Conference on System Sciences, Wailea, HI, 2019.

Jacobides, Michael G., Carmelo Cennamo, and Annabelle Gawer. "Towards a Theory of Ecosystems." *Strategic Management Journal* 39, no. 8 (2018): 2255–76. https://doi.org/10.1002/smj.2904.

Jang, Huisi, and Jaewook Lee. "An Empirical Study on Modeling and Prediction of BitCoin Prices with Bayesian Neural Networks Based on Blockchain Information." *IEEE Access* 6 (2018): 5427–37.

Jensen, Casper Bruun. "Power, Technology and Social Studies of Health Care: An Infrastructural Inversion." *Health Care Analysis* 16, no. 4 (2017): 355–74.

Ji, Qiang, Elie Bouri, Chi Keung Marco Lau, and David Roubaud. "Dynamic Connectedness and Integration in Cryptocurrency Markets." *International Review of Financial Analysis* 63 (2019): 257–72. https://doi.org/10.1016/j.irfa.2018.12.002.

Jones, Kristopher. "Toward a Political Sociology of Blockchain." PhD diss., Queens University, 2018.

Kalbaugh, G. E. "Virtual Currency, Not a Currency?" *Journal of International Business and Law* 16, no. 1, (2016): 26–35. https://scholarlycommons.law.hofstra.edu/jibl/vol16/iss1/5.

Kapoor, Rahul. "Ecosystems: Broadening the Locus of Value Creation." *Journal of Organization Design* 7, no. 1 (2018): 12. https://doi.org/10.1186/s41469-018-0035-4.

Karlstrøm, Henrik. "Do Libertarians Dream of Electric Coins? The Material Embeddedness of Bitcoin." *Journal of Social Theory* 15, no. 1 (2014): 23–36. https://doi.org/10.1080/1600910X.2013.870083.

Karpenko, O. A., T. K. Blokhina, and L. V. Chebukhanova. "The Initial Coin Offering (ICO) Process: Regulation and Risks." *Journal of Risk and Financial Management* 14, no. 12 (2021): 599. https://www.mdpi.com/1911-8074/14/12/599.

Katsiampa, Paraskevi. "Volatility Estimation for Bitcoin: A Comparison of GARCH Models." *Economics Letters* 158 (2017): 3–6. https://doi.org/10.1016/j.econlet.2017.06.023.

Katsiampa, Paraskevi, Shaen Corbet, and Brian Lucey. "High Frequency Volatility Co-movements in Cryptocurrency Markets." *Journal of International Financial Markets, Institutions, and Money* 62 (2019): 35–52. https://doi.org/10.1016/j.intfin.2019.05.003.

Katz, Michael L., and Carl Shapiro. "Systems Competition and Network Effects." *Journal of Economic Perspectives* 8, no. 2 (Spring 1994): 93–115.

Knittel, Megan, Shelby Pitts, and Rick Wash. "'The Most Trustworthy Coin': How Ideological Tensions Drive Trust in Bitcoin." *Proceedings of the ACM on Human-Computer Interaction* 3, no. CSCW (2019): 1–23. https://doi.org/10.1145/3359138.

Kyriazis, Nikolaos A. "A Survey on Efficiency and Profitable Trading Opportunities in Cryptocurrency Markets." *Journal of Risk and Financial Management* 12, no. 2 (2019): 67. https://doi.org/10.3390/jrfm12020067.

Larkin, Brian. "The Politics and Poetics of Infrastructure." *Annual Review of Anthropology* 42 (2013): 327–43. https://doi.org/10.1146/annurev-anthro-092412-155522.

Latour, Bruno. *Reassembling the Social: An Introduction to Actor-Network-Theory.* Oxford: Oxford University Press, 2005.

Latour, Bruno. *Science in Action: How to Follow Scientists and Engineers Through Society.* Cambridge, MA: Harvard University Press, 1987.

Lépinay, Vincent Antonin. *Codes of Finance: Engineering Derivatives in a Global Bank.* Princeton, NJ: Princeton University Press, 2011.

Lépinay, Vincent Antonin. "Decoding Finance: Articulation and Liquidity Around a Trading Room." In *Do Economists Make Markets? On the Performativity of Economics,* ed. Fabien Muniesa and Lucia Siu, 87–127. Princeton, NJ: Princeton University Press, 2007.

MacKenzie, Donald. "The Big, Bad Wolf and the Rational Market: Portfolio Insurance, the 1987 Crash, and the Performativity of Economics." *Economy and Society* 33, no. 3 (2004): 303–34.

MacKenzie, Donald. *An Engine, Not a Camera: Financial Models Shape Markets.* Cambridge, MA: MIT Press, 2006.

MacKenzie, Donald. "An Equation and Its Worlds: Bricolage, Exemplars, Disunity, and Performativity in Financial Economics." *Social Studies of Science* 33, no. 6 (2003): 831–68.

MacKenzie, Donald. "Globalization and Its Discontents." *Public Choice* 120, no. 1–2 (2004): 234–39.

MacKenzie, Donald. *Material Markets: How Economic Agents Are Constructed.* Oxford: Oxford University Press, 2009.

MacKenzie, Donald. "Pick a Nonce and Try a Hash." *London Review of Books* 48, no. 8 (2019): 35–38.Mallard, Alexandre. "Compare, Standardize, and Settle Agreement: On Some Usual Metrological Problems." *Social Studies of Science* 28, no. 4 (1998): 571–601. https://doi.org/10.1177/030631298028004003.

Mason, Katy, Hans Kjellberg, and Johan Hagberg. "Exploring the Performativity of Marketing: Theories, Practices, and Devices." *Journal of Marketing Management* 31, no. 1–2 (2015): 1–15.

Massad, T. G. *It's Time to Strengthen the Regulation of Crypto-Assets*. Washington, DC: Brookings Institution. 2019. https://www.brookings.edu/research/its -time-to-strengthen-the-regulation-of-crypto-assets/.

Maurer, Bill. "The Anthropology of Money." *Annual Review of Anthropology* 35 (2006): 15–36.

Maurer, Bill. "Blockchains Are a Diamond's Best Friend: Zelizer for the Bitcoin Moment." In *Money Talks: Explaining How Money Really Works*, ed. Nina Bandelj, Frederick F. Wherry, and Viviana A. Zelizer, 215–29. Princeton, NJ: Princeton University Press, 2017.

Mitchell, Timothy. *Carbon Democracy: Political Power in the Age of Oil*. London: Verso, 2011.

Mitchell, Timothy. *Rule of Experts: Egypt, Techno-politics, Modernity*. Berkeley: University of California Press, 2002.

Morita, Atsuro. "Multispecies Infrastructure: Infrastructural Inversion and Involutionary Entanglements in the Chao Phraya Delta, Thailand." *Ethnos* 82, no. 4 (2017): 738–57. https://doi.org/10.1080/00141844.2015.1119175.

Muniesa, Fabian. "Market Technologies and the Pragmatics of Prices." *Economy and Society* 36, no. 3 (2007): 377–95.

Narayanan, Arvind, and Jeremy Clark. "Bitcoin's Academic Pedigree." *Communications of the ACM* 60, no. 12 (2017): 36–45.

Nelms, Taylor C., Bill Maurer, Lana Swartz, and Scott Mainwaring. "Social Payments: Innovation, Trust, Bitcoin, and the Sharing Economy." *Theory, Culture, & Society* 35, no. 3 (2018): 13–33. https://doi.org/10.1177 /0263276417746466.

Nelson, Josephine. "Cryptocommunity Currencies." *Cornell Law Review* 105, no. 4 (2020): 909–58.

Noam, Eli. "The Macro-Economics of Crypto-Currencies: Balancing Entrepreneurialism and Monetary Policy." Entrepreneurship & Policy Initiative Working Paper Series, Columbia University School of International and Public Affairs, New York, n.d. Accessed November 28, 2021. https://sipa.columbia.edu/sites/default/files/25222_SIPA-White-Paper -MacroEconomics-web.pdf.

OECD. *Taxing Virtual Currencies: An Overview of Tax Treatments and Emerging Tax Policy Issues*. Paris: OECD, 2020.

Panagiotidis, Theodore, Thanasis Stengos, and Orestis Vravosinos. "On the Determinants of Bitcoin Returns: A LASSO Approach." *Finance Research Letters* 27 (2018): 235–40. https://doi.org/10.1016/j.frl.2018.03.016.

Papadimitriou, Theophilos, Periklis Gogas, and Fotios Gkatzoglou. "The Evolution of the Cryptocurrencies Market: A Complex Networks Approach." *Journal of Computational and Applied Mathematics* 376 (2020): 112831. https://doi.org/10.1016/j.cam.2020.112831.

Penner, J. E. *The Idea of Property in Law*. Oxford: Oxford University Press, 1997.

Perkins, David W. "Cryptocurrency: The Economics of Money and Selected Policy Issues." Report No. R45427, Congressional Research Service, Washington, DC, 2020. https://crsreports.congress.gov.

Pigounidès, Vassily. "Predicting Prices, Persuading Users: Price Recommendations and the Rhetorical Logic of Algorithms." *Research in Economic Anthropology* 40 (2020): 71–89. https://doi.org/10.1108/S019012812020000 00040003.

Plantin, Jean-Christophe, Carl Lagoze, Paul N. Edwards, and Christian Sandvig. "Infrastructure Studies Meet Platform Studies in the Age of Google and Facebook." *New Media & Society* 20, no. 1 (2018): 293–310. https://doi.org/10.1177/1461444816661553.

Polillo, Simone. "Crisis, Reputation, and the Politics of Expertise: Fictional Performativity at the Bank of Italy." *Review of Social Economy* (2020), 1–21. https://doi.org/10.1080/00346764.2020.1857822.

Prasad, Eswar S. *The Future of Money: How the Digital Revolution Is Transforming Currencies and Finance*. Cambridge, MA: Belknap Press of Harvard University Press, 2021.

Rella, Ludovico. "Money's Infrastructures: Blockchain Technologies and the Ecologies of the Memory Bank." PhD diss., Durham University, 2021.

Rella, Ludovico. "Steps Towards an Ecology of Money Infrastructures: Materiality and Cultures of Ripple." *Journal of Cultural Economy* 13, no. 2 (2020): 236–49. https://doi.org/10.1080/17530350.2020.1711532.

Riles, Annelise. "Property as Legal Knowledge: Means and Ends." *Journal of the Royal Anthropological Institute* 10, no. 4 (2004): 775–95. https://doi.org/10.1111/j.1467-9655.2004.00211.x.

Rochet, Jean-Charles, and Jean Tirole. "Platform Competition in Two-Sided Markets." *Journal of the European Economic Association* 1, no. 4 (2003): 990–1029. https://doi.org/10.1162/154247603322493212.

Rochet, Jean-Charles, and Jean Tirole. "Two-Sided Markets: A Progress Report." *RAND Journal of Economics* 37, no. 3 (2006): 645–67. https://doi.org/10.1111/j.1756-2171.2006.tb00036.x.

Rohlfs, Jeffery. "A Theory of Interdependent Demand for a Communications Service." *Bell Journal of Economics* 5 (Spring 1974): 16–37.

Roitman, Janet. *Fiscal Disobedience: An Anthropology of Economic Regulation in Central Africa*. Princeton, NJ: Princeton University Press, 2005.

Saka, Erkan. "Cryptocurrency Usage in Turkey." *Anthropology News*, September 11, 2020. https://doi.org/10.14506/AN.1491.

Sanderson, Susan, and Mustafa Uzumeri. "Managing Product Families: The Case of the Sony Walkman." *Research Policy* 24, no. 5 (1995): 761–82. https://doi.org/10.1016/0048-7333(94)00797-B.

Schwarz, Ori. "Facebook Rules: Structures of Governance in Digital Capitalism and the Control of Generalized Social Capital." *Theory, Culture, & Society* 36, no. 4 (2019): 117–41. https://doi.org/10.1177/0263276419826249.

Selmi, Refk, Walid Mensi, Shawkat Hammoudeh, and Jamal Bouoiyour. "Is Bitcoin a Hedge, a Safe Haven, or a Diversifier for Oil Price Movements? A Comparison with Gold." *Energy Economics* 74 (2018): 787–801. https://doi.org/10.1016/j.eneco.2018.07.007.

Shaw, Lynette. "The Meanings of New Money: Social Constructions of Value in the Rise of Digital Currencies." PhD diss., University of Washington, 2016.

Shipilov, Andrew, and Annabelle Gawer. "Integrating Research on Interorganizational Networks and Ecosystems." *Academy of Management Annals* 14, no. 1 (2020): 92–121. https://doi.org/10.5465/annals.2018.0121.

Simsar, Enis, and Koray Caliskan. "Twitter Interaction Data of Electra Cryptocurrency Community's Twitter Handle Followers and a Code for Follower Interaction Analysis." Github, 2021. https://github.com/enisimsar/DataMoney.

Slater, Don, and Fran Tonkis. *Market Society: Markets and Modern Social Theory*. Cambridge: Polity, 2001.

Solodan, K. "Legal Regulation of Cryptocurrency Taxation in European Countries." *European Journal of Law and Public Administration* 6 (2019): 64–74.

Spithoven, Antoon. "Theory and Reality of Cryptocurrency Governance." *Journal of Economic Issues* 53, no. 2 (2019): 385–93. https://doi.org/10.1080/00213624.2019.1594518.

Star, Susan Leigh. "The Ethnography of Infrastructure." *American Behavioral Scientist* 43, no. 3 (1999): 377–91. https://doi.org/10.1177/00027649921955326.

Stark, David. *The Sense of Dissonance: Accounts of Worth in Economic Life*. Princeton, NJ: Princeton University Press, 2009.

Swartz, Lana. "Blockchain Dreams: Imagining Techno-economic Alternatives After Bitcoin." In *Another Economy Is Possible: Culture and Economy
in a Time of Crisis*, ed. M. Castells, 82–105. Cambridge: Polity, 2017.

Swartz, Lana. *New Money: How Payment Became Social Media*. New Haven,
CT: Yale University Press, 2020.

Swartz, Lana. "What Was Bitcoin, What Will It Be? The Techno-economic
Imaginaries of a New Money Technology." *Cultural Studies* 32, no. 4
(2018): 623–50. https://doi.org/10.1080/09502386.2017.1416420.

Tapscott, Dan, and Alex Tapscott. *Blockchain Revolution: How the Technology Behind Bitcoin Is Changing Money, Business, and the World*. New York:
Penguin Random House, 2016.

Tarasiewicz, Matthias, and Andrew Newman. "Cryptocurrencies as Distributed Community Experiments." In *Handbook of Digital Currency: Bitcoin,
Innovation, Financial Instruments, and Big Data*, ed. David Lee Kuo Chuen,
201–22. London: Academic Press, 2015.

Thieser, A. "These Roses Don't Think About Each Other Either Competition, Collaboration, and Utopianism in a Blockchain Community."
Unpublished manuscript, 2019.

Tinu, N. S. "A Survey of Blockchain Technology: Taxonomy, Consensus
Algorithms, and Applications." *International Journal of Computer Sciences
and Engineering* 6, no. 5 (2018): 691–96.

Tonkiss, Fran. (2004). "Analysing Text and Speech: Content and Discourse
Analysis." In *Researching Society and Culture*, ed. C. Seale, 367–82. London:
SAGE.

"The Trust Machine." *The Economist*, October 31, 2015. https://www.economist
.com/leaders/2015/10/31/the-trust-machine.

Ulrich, Karl. "The Role of Product Architecture in the Manufacturing
Firm." *Research Policy* 24, no. 3 (1995): 419–40. http://dx.doi.org/10.1016
/0048-7333(94)00775-3.

Urquhart, Andrew. "The Inefficiency of Bitcoin." *Economics Letters* 148 (2016):
80–82. https://doi.org/10.1016/j.econlet.2016.09.019.

Uzzi, Brian. "The Sources and Consequences of Embeddedness for the
Economic Performance of Organizations: The Network Effect." *American
Sociological Review* 61, no. 4 (1996): 674–98. https://doi.org/10.2307/2096399.

Uzzi, Brian, and Ryon Lancaster. "Embeddedness and Price Formation in the
Corporate Law Market." *American Sociological Review* 69, no. 3 (2004):
319–44. https://doi.org/10.1177/000312240406900301.

Velthuis, Olav. "Symbolic Meanings of Prices: Constructing the Value of Contemporary Art in Amsterdam and New York Galleries." *Theory and Society* 32, no. 2 (2003): 181–215. https://doi.org/10.1023/A:1023995520369.

Walton, Aiden, and Kevin Johnston. "Exploring Perceptions of Bitcoin Adoption: The South African Virtual Community Perspective." *Interdisciplinary Journal of Information, Knowledge, & Management* 13 (2018).

Wark, McKenzie. *Capital Is Dead.* London: Verso, 2019.

Welbers, Kasper, Wouter Van Atteveldtb, and Kenneth Benoit. "Text Analysis in R." *Communication Methods and Measures* 11, no. 4 (2017): 245–65. https://doi.org/10.1080/19312458.2017.1387238.

Wenjun J. Feng, Yiming Y. Wang, and Zhengjun Z. Zhang. "Informed Trading in the Bitcoin Market." *Finance Research Letters* 26 (2018): 63–70. https://doi.org/10.1016/j.frl.2017.11.009.

Westermeier, C. "Money Is Data—the Platformization of Financial Transactions." *Information, Communication, & Society* 23, no. 14 (2020): 2047–63. https://doi.org/10.1080/1369118X.2020.1770833.

Wheelwright, Steven C., and Kim B. Clark. "Creating Project Plans to Focus Product Development." *Harvard Business Review* 70, no. 2 (1992): 67–83. https://hbr.org/1992/03/creating-project-plans-to-focus-product-development.

Wright, Julian. "One-Sided Logic in Two-Sided Markets." *Review of Network Economies* 3, no. 1 (2003). http://dx.doi.org/10.2139/ssrn.459362.

World Bank. National Accounts Data, 2020. https://data.worldbank.org/indicator/NY.GDP.MKTP.CD?year_high_desc=false.

Xu, Jieyu, Wen Bai, Miao Hu, Haibo Tian, and Di Wu. "Bitcoin Miners: Exploring a Covert Community in the Bitcoin Ecosystem." *Peer-to-Peer Networking and Applications* 14, no. 2 (2021): 644–54.

Zelizer, Viviana A. "The Social Meaning of Money: 'Special Monies.'" *American Journal of Sociology* 95, no. 2 (1989): 342–77.

Zelizer, Viviana A. *The Social Meaning of Money.* New York: Basic Books, 1994.

Zimmer, Zac. "Bitcoin and Potosi Silver Historical Perspectives on Cryptocurrency." *Technology and Culture* 58, no. 2 (2017): 307–34.

Zook, Matthew A., and Joe Blankenship. "New Spaces of Disruption? The Failures of Bitcoin and the Rhetorical Power of Algorithmic Governance." *Geoforum* 96 (2018): 248–55.

# INDEX

Printed and bound by CPI Group (UK) Ltd, Croydon, CR0 4YY

25/01/2024

08227313-0001